SOONER SPIRIT

SOONER SPIRIT

The Rise of the Most Fanatical Fandom in College Sports

Eddie Malone

UNIVERSITY OF OKLAHOMA PRESS : NORMAN

This book is published thanks in part to the generous assistance of the Wallace C. Thompson Endowment Fund, University of Oklahoma Foundation.

1 2 3 4 5 6 7 8 9 10

Library of Congress Cataloging-in-Publication Data

Names: Malone, Eddie, 1974– author

Title: Sooner spirit : the rise of the most fanatical fandom in college sports / Eddie Malone.

Description: Norman : University of Oklahoma Press, [2026] | Includes bibliographical references and index. | Summary: "An ethnography and study of sports culture and fandom at the University of Oklahoma" — Provided by publisher.

Identifiers: LCCN 2025045838 | ISBN 9780806197043 hardcover

Subjects: LCSH: University of Oklahoma—Sports | Sports spectators—Oklahoma | Sports—Social aspects—Oklahoma | College sports—Oklahoma

Classification: LCC GV691.U577 M35 2026

LC record available at https://lccn.loc.gov/2025045838

The paper in this book meets the guidelines for permanence and durability of the Committee on Production Guidelines for Book Longevity of the Council on Library Resources, Inc. ∞

The manufacturer's authorized representative in the EU for product safety is Mare Nostrum Group B.V., Mauritskade 21D, 1091 GC Amsterdam, The Netherlands, email: gpsr@mare-nostrum.co.uk.

For Jenn, who said yes to every adventure

The Sooner Spirit grew into full bloom when Oklahoma defeated Missouri on the gridiron. It gave birth to such demonstrations as Snake Dances, Shirt-tail Parades, Bonfires and Pep Meetings galore.

—*The Sooner Yearbook*, 1915

Have your feet ever stuck to the floor from spilled pop? Ever been kicked in the back or shoved around? How about having stinking cigar smoke blown in your face?

Ever thought you were at a rodeo when you walked into a stadium and choked on all the dust flying around from the herds of people crowding in? Had that sick feeling from the stench of buttered popcorn?

Were you ever offended by the foul language you heard? Felt like you were going nuts from the screaming and crying kids?

Did you think you were going to sweat to death from the sweltering heat? Or freeze to death from the wind and rain? Or suffocate from the stuffy gymnasium atmosphere?

If you've suffered from any of these symptoms, your condition is critical: You're a Sooner fan.

—Michelle Williams, *The Sooner Yearbook*, 1981

CONTENTS

PROLOGUE

IN EARLY OCTOBER 1954, Larry LeVieux was a senior at the University of Oklahoma. With his graduation a few months away, and the Sooner football team set to play the Texas Longhorns that weekend—as they had for nearly every year since 1900—he had the feeling that he'd seen it all before. The quiet on campus midweek was familiar. The game was close but somehow still distant, and students seemed more concerned about Monday's academic commitments—a quiz or paper due—than the contest on Saturday.

That all changed on Friday. For decades already, Sooners had been calling the day before the big game "Migration Day": thousands would travel south to Dallas from various parts of Oklahoma to support Big Red. Campus was buzzing Friday morning; LeVieux saw cars painted with "Beat Texas," with red and white streamers flying in the wind. By ten o'clock, the exodus south had backed up US 77.

Two hundred miles later, LeVieux was firmly in enemy territory, though it was also true that Dallas felt like a neutral site thanks to the abundance of Sooner fans. The sheer size of the crowds was disconcerting. In an article he wrote for *Sooner Magazine*, published a month after the rivalry game, LeVieux compared his fellow fans to a swarm of ants: "They were everywhere; in the streets, in hotels, restaurants, night clubs and private homes. As a senior I had seen the football festival several times. There was no change from the previous years except that the crowd was bigger, the noise louder, the confusion greater."

A street ran in front of the two hotels where the teams were staying—the Baker and Adolphus—and it was a thoroughfare of student display: hundreds of cars full of either Sooner or Longhorn fans sped past, with the young people inside "screaming like banshees." Competing pep rallies materialized. In front of the Adolphus, red and white banners and badges appeared throughout the crowd; the Sooner cheerleaders directed the rooting. Nearby, at the Baker, the Longhorns made their own racket. To be fair, students from both schools "yelled their young lungs out." The crowds eventually dispersed to sample the city's food and entertainment. Whenever a group of Sooner fans met a group of Longhorn fans, the competition began anew. A "Beat OU" chant was countered with a chorus of "We're number one, hey!" The Sooners were currently the top-ranked football team in the country.

The partying continued into the night. "Boomer Sooner," played by a local band, could be heard in the nightclubs. At such an hour, none of the student revelers were thinking of Monday morning or academic consequences.

Downtown looked abandoned on Saturday morning. Dallas police could take a breath. Fans started to filter onto the streets by midmorning, and LeVieux could sense a change in atmosphere. The cocksure attitude, adopted by many the night before, had been replaced by doubt and uncertainty. OU–Texas, regardless of the teams' rankings, was usually a close game. Willpower seemed to determine the outcome as much as each team's talents. Who wanted it more this year?

By noon, the hordes of fans had descended on Fair Park and the State Fair of Texas. Soon to be at war, these fans slowly trekked, shoulder to shoulder, to their seats in the Cotton Bowl. There was no taunting; it was a peaceful, temporary coexistence. If you caught someone's eye from the other team, you gave them a nod and got one in return.

Inside the stadium, the crowd grew to a record-breaking 76,204. It was October and technically fall, but the sun and heat, with temperatures in the nineties, made it feel like summer. The Cotton Bowl was a sauna.

The game was competitive, the fans hysterical. The Sooners were in the midst of a golden era thanks to the leadership of head coach Charles Burnham "Bud" Wilkinson, a Minnesotan who had come to Norman as an assistant coach after serving in the navy in World War II. He was only thirty-one years old when he took over as head coach. From 1948 to 1950, his Sooners won thirty-one straight games. In his fourth season, the Sooners were crowned the 1950 national champions. Their period of gridiron supremacy reached its zenith with a forty-seven-game winning streak that ran from 1953 to 1957 and brought two more national titles to Norman. No college football team since has managed to win that many games in a row.

Donald Fixico, an OU alumnus and history professor at Arizona State University, first encountered a Wilkinson team as an eight- or nine-year-old, watching on a black-and-white TV in the family home. The players on both teams wore white helmets, which made it hard to distinguish between them. Eventually, he figured out that one team was Oklahoma and the other Oklahoma State; his first-ever game was a Bedlam matchup.

"For some unknown reason, I wanted OU to win and I had no idea Bud Wilkinson was a legendary coach," Fixico told me. "I loved baseball growing up. But I liked watching how the Sooners played tough football."

His affinity for the football team led him, in the 1970s, to the University of Oklahoma where he earned three degrees and watched, with delight, as Barry Switzer's teams won national titles in 1974 and 1975.

Back in 1954, the rivalry game with Texas was still in the balance—the score 14–7 in favor of the Sooners with thirty seconds left in the fourth quarter—when "rabid" Oklahoma students prematurely rushed the field and pulled down the goalposts at one end. In the stands, LeVieux wondered what the referees would do for the extra point, if the Longhorn offense scored in the dying seconds.

But the Longhorns failed and the game ended. The victorious Sooners marched on. The noise and tension of the previous three hours suddenly relented, and the fans slowly left their seats and wound their way through the innards of the Cotton Bowl until they spilled onto the fairgrounds. Once again, crimson mixed with burnt orange. There appeared to be no hard feelings. Sooner fans were magnanimous. Ribbing of the beaten foe was light and rare.

By Sunday evening, LeVieux and his classmates were back in Norman, tired but buzzing from the excitement of the weekend. Dread crept in as Monday's classes approached: a dose of reality. A group of students descended on the university president's house, located on Boyd Street and across from campus, to try and pressure him to cancel Monday's classes. After the defeat of the Longhorns, they argued, the celebrations should be carried forward. George Lynn Cross, OU's seventh president, dutifully came to the door, stood on his porch, and listened to the students. Though a huge football fan himself (he would later write a book about Coach Wilkinson and those championship years in the 1950s), he could not be swayed. Perhaps facetiously, he threatened to cancel other holidays. In his article, LeVieux describes the mood: "Resigned to their fate, the disappointed students returned to their residences."

The following week saw a return to normalcy as students prepared for midterm exams and tackled assignments. But the memory of Dallas was still there, along with a wistful pledge to do it all over again. "Wait till next year," they said.

■ ■ ■

In October 2023, I made my own pilgrimage to Dallas for the annual Red River Rivalry: the 119th time that Oklahoma and Texas would play each other in football. My goal was professional. I was writing a book on Sooner fandom. The plan was to spend the year tailgating and going to games, in a variety of Sooner sports, and then write about it. Certain questions would guide me: What was it like to be a devoted Sooner fan? What did fandom mean? I was not Sooner born. In fact, as a kid growing up in North Texas, I cheered for the Texas Longhorns. But instead of heading to Austin for college I stayed local and matriculated to Texas Christian University where I rejected sports and assumed the pose of a would-be writer. My estrangement didn't last long. By my mid-twenties, I was working as a sports journalist, and I would continue to write about sports—mostly on a freelance basis—for the next twenty years.

A job offer from the University of Oklahoma brought me to Norman in 2015. My rented house was a mile from campus, and on Saturdays in the fall I heard a roar from the stadium whenever the Sooners scored a touchdown. I was a slow convert and watched Oklahoma on TV with a dispassionate eye. Baker Mayfield's heroics turned me into a believer. However, I stayed away from Oklahoma Memorial Stadium, preferring to watch from the comforts of home. My first in-person game involved a New Year's trip to Pasadena where the Sooners were playing the Georgia Bulldogs in the Rose Bowl, a berth in the 2018 national title game on the line. It proved a nerve-shattering experience as Mayfield and his team fell short in overtime. The next season, I attended my first home game, a blowout win against Baylor.

By early October 2023 ahead of OU–Texas, I'd tailgated before all three home games and watched the team prevail against mediocre opposition beneath a boiling sun in Memorial Stadium. My girlfriend Jenn and I had traveled to Tulsa for an away game, another comfortable victory.

Then came the Red River rivalry. The Longhorns promised to be a problem that year. This was the best Texas team since 2006 when the program won its last national championship. They were ranked number two in the country and had beaten mighty Alabama convincingly in Tuscaloosa. Moreover, they had trounced OU 49–0 the year before, arguably the worst beating in series history (though the Sooners handed the Longhorns a 65–13 loss in 2003).

I was pessimistic. Like more than a few fans, I saw Brent Venables's team as a work in progress while the Longhorns looked fully formed.

Jenn and I drove down on Migration Day. By late afternoon, the lobby in our downtown Dallas hotel was full of fans for the game, most of them wearing burnt orange. I didn't feel besieged, but that would change. After checking in, we took the elevator to our room, relaxed for a bit, and then got dressed for dinner. I put on a crimson Sooners football shirt. Our plan was to start with a drink in the lobby bar. Downstairs, as we walked from the elevators down a corridor, I felt it for the first time: visible as a

Sooner fan. Earlier, without wearing Sooner red, I'd been anonymous. Now people would know *who I was*, and suddenly I felt on edge.

The bar was full of Longhorn fans. It felt like people were looking at us. I ordered drinks and brought them back to a table a few yards away from the entertainment: a young cowboy singing country covers.

From there, we left the hotel and walked to an Irish pub for dinner. On the patio was a group of festive Texas fans—ten to twelve of them—and we walked past on our way inside. We ate indoors, and I glanced at the party from time to time, as if to make sure they kept their distance.

We paid our bill and left the restaurant through a side door, but that didn't stop what happened next. As we walked away, the Texas fans started chanting, "OU sucks! OU sucks!" Clearly, they'd seen us and were just waiting for their moment.

Jenn and I laughed. From a certain angle, it was ridiculous. We'd inspired a group of strangers to yell at us, all because of an item of clothing. A minute later, once we cleared the scene, I told her with bravado that it had taken every ounce of self-control to not turn around and give them the middle finger (or a horns down).

I got my revenge (sort of) the next morning. Dressed in Sooner colors, we left our room for the game and waited at the bank of elevators. The doors opened to reveal a space filled with Texas fans. "Hell no," I said. "Texas fans." Then I stepped to the side to wait for the next elevator. Jenn started laughing. Indeed, it was a funny moment, in retrospect, but at the time I meant every word. I didn't want to be near them.

At the fairgrounds, comingling with Texas fans was inevitable. We got absorbed into a great mass of people moving toward the entrance of the Cotton Bowl. I was surprised not to hear calls of "Boomer!" and "Sooner!" Likewise, none of the UT fans were chanting whatever it was they chanted: the words to "The Eyes of Texas"? "Hook 'em Horns"? The crowd was focused, its only mission to get up the stairs and through the entrance.

We sat on the south side of the stadium with the other Sooner fans. In the distance sat the enemy, wearing a different color. I could see the Longhorn band, tucked behind a burnt orange end zone; their white cowboy hats were specks in my vision.

It was a beautiful fall day, mild and sunny, though the temperature, in the low seventies, would prove deceptive. For the four hours we sat in the same spot, I didn't sweat profusely but I would burn, particularly on my left side. I was wearing a sleeveless T-shirt, and a tan line on my shoulder, neck, and back would linger for the next month.

What happened next proved that the universe was against me. Two Longhorn fans—a forty-something woman in a Texas ball cap and her friend or partner—were already sitting in front of us when right before kickoff two teenage boys, clad in all black, took the seats to my left. They looked like goth kids, minus the ostentatious hair: in other words, the furthest thing from stereotypical football fans. And yet one carried a burnt orange rally towel. Texas fans were all around us.

What were they doing in *our* section? Didn't they know that they were supposed to sit on the north side? Where were their *parents?* Of course, as I found out early, they were not going to just sit there quietly. They were kids among adults, Texas fans surrounded by Oklahoma fans, but the atmosphere failed to intimidate them. To be fair, one was quiet. The other kid, who sat next to me and wore glasses and had braces on his teeth, more than made up for his friend. Loudly, he cheered his team. Every single play he shouted encouragement or poured scorn on the Sooners. Profanity streamed from his mouth. Throughout the game I looked toward the heavens, the Dallas sky an immaculate blue, as if to plead with God: *Please don't let me get into a fight with this teenager. Please don't let me go to jail.*

I lost my cool during a tight first quarter that ended 7–7. I talked trash to the boys. "What're ya'll doing here? You're supposed to sit over there," I said, pointing to the other side of the Cotton Bowl.

My neighbor, the mouthy one, passed the buck. "He got the tickets," he said, turning toward his buddy. The poor kid, the culprit, looked sheepish, and for a second I felt bad. But as the game resumed the feeling didn't last. My neighbor went back to his antics, for which, later on, I would give him credit. He was passionate and not afraid to show it, even while surrounded by Sooners.

As I thought it would, the Red River rivalry proved illuminating. The game was thrilling, and it ended well for the Sooners: revenge for the previous year's thrashing. What's more, the whole experience provided more data for the book. Since the summer I'd been casting the net wide with my research. I studied the groups I considered foundational to OU fandom: the football team, the RUF/NEKS, and the Pride of Oklahoma. I read about the early days of the university: how the institution came to be. I interviewed Native American fans of Big Red. With Jenn, I watched the home games of the women's soccer team at John Crain Field. I tailgated with the superfan Mr. OU on a sweltering Saturday before the football team played Iowa State.

It was a challenge to make sense of such a wide variety of information. Some of the data was sensory and experiential. At the other end of the research spectrum, I was reading old student newspapers that tracked the origins of the football team and thus the origins of campus fandom. In a November 1897 issue of *The University Umpire*, OU's first student newspaper, a long discourse on literary societies could be found next to a section labeled "Athletic Notes." Underneath the latter appeared a statement full of the swagger and boldness that would characterize Sooner football for the next century and beyond: "Harry Ford, the manager of the foot-ball team, would be glad to receive a challenge from some big eleven who think themselves the center of gravitation."

I delighted in reading about campus mischief and the ebullience of youth. The early students at OU, though they came from hardscrabble backgrounds, were, in a sense, no different from the students I taught today. I saw my own experience at OU–Texas echoed in the experience of Larry LeVieux: the OU senior who documented his Dallas adventures in *Sooner Magazine* in 1954. On certain days, sitting in my office and reading digitized copies of *The Oklahoma Daily* from a hundred years ago, it felt like I was communing with the dead.

A breakthrough came at the annual homecoming parade, in mid-October, when suddenly all my research came into focus. (I chronicle this breakthrough in the epilogue.) What I witnessed at the pep rally—the music of the Pride of Oklahoma, the routines of the cheerleaders and Pom Squad, and a competition between the sororities and fraternities—made me feel as if I'd been transported. Time collapsed, and the past and present were somehow happening simultaneously.

In this book, before I get to the homecoming parade, I immerse the reader in the culture and history of Sooner sports. I share what I've learned about the people who came before us: the athletes, coaches, spirit groups, fans, and superfans. There are chapters on groups who have worked across the decades to feel included in Sooner Nation: women, Native Americans, and African Americans. For women, access to spirit groups, the band, and sports happened piecemeal. Native Americans joined the student body within the first decade of the university's launch; early on, they found ways to participate in campus life, but opportunities for representation and inclusion were few and far between. African Americans were barred from enrolling at OU until 1948 when a federal court overturned the status quo. As with women and Native Americans, it's been a long journey to involvement and acceptance for African Americans. While researching the book, I saw a gradual expansion of the "big top" tent inside which Sooner fans enjoy a sense of belonging. This tent is certainly larger and more accommodating than ever before. However, members of the aforementioned groups would argue that there's still much work to be done.

Also in the book, with an eye on fandom in the present, I sit in the stands at the newly christened Love's Field and watch Patty Gasso's juggernaut of a softball team. I'm there for OU football's inaugural season in the Southeastern Conference.

I use many sources to tell the story of Sooner fandom, relying especially on the student newspaper *The Oklahoma Daily* and the university publication *Sooner Magazine*. Most of the issues that I use as source material were published many decades ago. In a way, this book is a salute to those student and alumni writers that provided the university with both a voice and identity. As I tell the story of fandom on campus, I quote sometimes from *The Oklahoma Daily* or *Sooner Magazine* without attribution. My reason has to do with the overall momentum of the storytelling. The reader should assume that any quote that appears without attribution comes from one or the other source.

Each Sooner sport creates its own ecosystem of fans, with unique practices and traditions. OU men's and women's basketball have Top Daug: a canine mascot born in the 1980s and known for energizing the crowds at Lloyd Noble Center. Volleyball has the Frankenfields, Dena and Howard: The couple has attended almost every home match since 1985, unnerving the opposition with their raucous support of the Sooners. An encyclopedic book about Sooner fandom would cover every sport along with every fan base, celebrating the charged environment at venues like McCasland Field House where student-athletes from volleyball and wrestling ply their trade.

In a similar vein, an encyclopedic book would pay tribute to every OU spirit group, like the cheerleaders and Pom Squad, that has contributed to the game day atmosphere in Norman across the decades.

It's easy to see the value of such a book, but I chose not to take the encyclopedic approach. On the sports front, softball, football, and soccer feature in these pages. The success and popularity of the softball team in recent years, along with the possibility of a fourth straight national championship, made the team a must-see attraction. Football, of course, was still king on campus. Any study of fandom at the University of Oklahoma would have to reckon with the ways in which football, from the late nineteenth century to the present day, drove campus life and shaped Sooner identity. To complement softball and football, both powerhouse sports, I thought it would be instructive to follow the OU soccer team. From the fan's perspective, what was it like to root for a "minor" sport at the University of Oklahoma? What's more, the women's soccer team's captain was a former student of mine. I was curious. She'd been exceptional in the classroom; what was she like on the soccer field?

On the spirit front, I focus on the RUF/NEKS, the Sooner Schooner, and the Pride of Oklahoma. Little Red, the controversial mascot who danced at Owen Field for more than a decade, stars in the chapter on the Native American experience at OU. The respective histories of these purveyors of spirit captured my imagination and inspired my pen, so to speak. What's more, I knew that there was only so much space in the book; I couldn't write about everybody. Difficult decisions about whom to include were made.

Despite the exclusion of some sports and spirit groups that many Sooners hold close to the heart, readers of this book should find much about Sooner history and fandom that is pleasing, recognizable, and even extraordinary. Essentially, it's a book that joins the past and present at the University of Oklahoma. In it, I hope that Sooners find their own reflection.

Part I

ROOTS

▪ 1 ▪

THE FEVER LAYS HOLD

THE FIRST STUDENT to enroll at the University of Oklahoma was a fourteen-year-old boy named Marion Donehew. In 1945, a photograph of the boy, wearing the black suit he wore on the day of his enrollment, was sent to OU's Alumni Office by Donehew's teenage daughter Lorene. In the grainy black and white photograph, the boy has the bearing of a man, his hand propped awkwardly on the edge of a desk, his pursed lips suggesting that he's never once cracked a smile. Similarly grave, his dark eyes are set deeply in his face. The suit, in tone, matches his bearing, but on closer inspection it's ill-fitting, baggy through the leg and arm. The fit reminds you that this is a boy, not a man.

Donehew's background speaks to his grim expression as well as to the general conditions of southwestern life in the late nineteenth century. He was supposed to matriculate to Baylor University, near to which he lived with his parents, but self-described "health conditions" along the Brazos River forced the family to move from Texas to Oklahoma in March of 1892. On the way, they were snowbound in Ardmore because of a historic blizzard. Eventually, following in the footsteps of settlers from the Land Run of 1889, the Donehew family staked a claim in Indian Territory, just east of present-day Oklahoma City. But they didn't last long in this location as Donehew's parents, mindful of their son's prospects, heard about the opening of a university nearby. They moved to Norman in July.

In a letter to *Sooner Magazine* in 1945, Donehew wrote about his close and early bond with the university. It's a familiar story, told by others who joined the incipient project in Norman as either faculty or student.

> My father and I hauled some of the material and brick used in the construction of the first University building. We formed an early friendship with Dr. David R. Boyd, and the rest of the faculty, and when the opening day came, my mother and I were there promptly, and I took my examination for entrance. She and I did not know that I was the first to enrol [*sic*] until I passed and received the congratulations of the entire faculty for the honor of being the first student to enrol in the University of Oklahoma.

The student body in fall 1892, the first academic semester at the new university, numbered fifty-seven. Since the first university building was still under construction, classes were held in a rented building on Main Street. The students were taught by four faculty members, including President Boyd, who understood the challenge at hand: their charges a unique demographic composed of the sons and daughters of farmers. Most of them had little to no formal education since high schools in Indian Territory had yet to be established. As a result, according to OU professor emeritus David Levy, whose two books on the university constitute an "official" history, the faculty was compelled to start a "Preparatory Department" to teach the basics of mathematics, science, English, and Latin. These courses were designed to prepare students for college-level work. Nearly all of OU's early students were assigned to this department.

In September 1893, the university's new home was ready to hold classes. From the outside, University Building was an ornate, three-story structure made of red brick that looked out of place on the wide-open prairie. One early faculty member described it as "ugly." On the inside, however, it was functional and spacious, to say the least, eventually hosting classrooms, offices, laboratories, a gymnasium, and an auditorium that doubled as a chapel. Ten years into its use, the multipurpose building fell victim to fire and was destroyed just as a second building, to be called University Hall, was nearing completion. Sadly, some four years later, this second administration building suffered the same fate, burning down in December 1907. Despite these setbacks, the university was growing. There were new buildings (Science Hall in 1904 and a library funded by and named after Andrew Carnegie in 1905) and new offerings in a variety of subject areas including fine arts, engineering, and social sciences. The faculty was growing in number too. The young people who came to Norman to study were excited about their university. But as with the generations of students who would follow in their footsteps, there was also plenty of anxiety about the future.

Adelaide Loomis Parker, class of 1906, was one such student. Her time at the university was not carefree. Writing in *Sooner Magazine* in 1929, Parker pointed out that she and her classmates suffered the same "pervading problem": "how in God's name to make a living." In chapel every morning, they were reminded of the sacrifices their parents made that enabled them to study. It was a sobering message they heard at home too, "from the little frame houses that braced themselves in such shallow toe-holds against the prairie winds."

Parker took English classes with Professor Vernon Louis Parrington, who had graduated from Harvard before establishing the English department at OU (he also became the university's first real football coach, on which I'll soon elaborate). According to Parker, students could relax once they entered Parrington's quiet classroom and "for an hour at least we lived in a different world." This world consisted of Shakespeare, Milton, and the other giants of English literature. Parrington's "smooth and quiet" voice gave them an appreciation for words; his argument that language should not be "abused" stayed with them. In her "Appreciation" of Parrington following his death, published in the July 1929 issue of *Sooner Magazine*, Parker stressed that she and her classmates had been blessed with professors who not only educated them but taught them about life: "In those days we were not so many but that sooner or later we all sat under the highest and the best. But somehow in Professor Parrington's room we forgot the dry sun and the never-ending wind, and the painful and pressing problem of how to make a living, and, while we were there, we lived."

The sentiment here is lofty and idealistic, and it was broadly held, even in the early days of the university. Students at the University of Oklahoma viewed their modest campus as an oasis of culture in a town and territory they characterized as anti-intellectual. The writers of the first student newspaper, the *University Umpire*, suggested as much in an issue from November 1898: "The University stands for something in Oklahoma. Here if anywhere within our borders, are the means of attaining culture. Whatever is highest and best in life, here is freely recognized and gladly followed."

High-mindedness, a student trait that cuts across the generations, was thankfully not the only force driving the student body. Like all young people, OU attendees liked their fun and each other. There were dances and socials to attend. Clubs for oratory and debate were formed. A student pep band, created to support the football team, was established in 1904. Athletics were stressed, with a baseball team taking the diamond in 1898. The first basketball team appeared in 1907. The football team's first season, in 1895, consisted of a single game: a 34–0 shellacking (or it could have been 64–0; the score is disputed) at the hands of a ragtag bunch from Oklahoma City. Greek life came to campus in 1905. With these offerings, the university aimed to forge students of sophistication and substance.

No doubt they aspired toward the loftier things, but anarchy and rebellion lived inside them as well. Class fights were an annual occurrence until 1913, when the administration banned them, and consisted of one class battling another class in a rough and tumble game of capture the flag. In September 1912, the *Umpire* reported in detail about the recent tussle between the freshmen and sophomores. In the minutes before dawn broke, after being outside in the cold all night, seventy-five freshmen lined up on campus across from fifty sophomores, both sides "armed with ropes, chains and bailing." With a yell, they rushed at each other and "fought like trojans." The goal was to subdue and tie up members of the other side, and forty-five minutes later the superior numbers of the freshmen won out. All fifty sophomores had their hands tied behind their back, and Charles Curry Bell, brawny basketball player and leader of the sophomores, verbally conceded the "fight."

This fighting spirit would find new expression a few years later when the United States entered World War I in 1917. Though the devastating war in Europe had been going on for three years, it hardly registered with OU students, according to historian David Levy, until America joined the fray. Instead of the war, OU's student body had been preoccupied with student life: "the big game, the big dance, the big parties of fraternities and sororities, the latest campus gossip." President Woodrow Wilson's declaration of war on April 6 changed the atmosphere instantly. Headlines like "SPIRIT OF WAR INVADES SOONERLAND" appeared in *The Oklahoma Daily*. OU's male students gathered for an emergency meeting where consensus was quickly reached. With OU president Stratton Brooks's blessing, the Student Volunteer Regiment was born, a motivated group of would-be soldiers who drilled together for several hours a week, with little equipment or guidance. The self-styled regiment disbanded a month later, but by the fall the State Board of Regents for Education had mandated military training for all male OU students. This would remain a requirement until 1965. In all, 2,300 students, alumni, and faculty served in the military during the Great War, a testament to the patriotism that existed on campus. OU's female population was similarly motivated to serve; hundreds volunteered for Red Cross duty. Only a generation later, war would again shatter the calm in Norman, leading to an exodus of male Sooners eager to strike at Germany and Japan.

A student organization, founded allegedly in 1906, called the Deep Dark Mystery Club (DDMC) added to the wild and stormy tenor of the age. The group was the topic of an *Umpire* article from October 1911: "The D.D.M.C. is a secret organization and nothing is known of its workings or membership beyond the fact that it is composed of University students." Pranks were a specialty. Members buried the commemorative class of 1906 stone, heavy and substantial, that sat in front of the administration building, splashed paint on sidewalks and campus buildings, and painted "D.D.M.C. '14" on the smokestack of the heating plant. In June 1912, the group stole a cannon from the Norman city park and chained it to a tree near campus; the group's letters were painted on the barrel along with a message of support for OU president Brooks: "To back up the new president."

DDMC evolved to include in its mission more serious matters, such as the safeguarding of the university's integrity and reputation. A headline from *The Oklahoma Daily* in February 1919 read "D.D.M.C. TO GO AFTER CHEATERS" and told of a warning, printed on cards, that had been found in fraternity and student boarding houses. The cards were allegedly placed there by the secret society in response to "the report that 'cribbing' in examinations and quizzes is getting to be of such proportions that faculty members are advocating that the honor system be taken out of the hands of the student council."

Despite this honorable pivot, things didn't end well for the DDMC. In the 1920s, the group turned into the morality police. Dressed in black and wearing masks, its members patrolled campus at night looking to break up card games and prevent liaisons between the sexes. In one case, documented in Levy's official history of OU, members of DDMC kidnapped and harangued a professor "suspected of pestering female students." The response from all quarters—the university, the Norman community, the newspapers—was condemnatory. The group was banned. This, however, failed to extinguish the DDMC, which continued its questionable work until an ugly episode in 1932 proved the final straw. *Time* magazine jumped on the lurid story in its January 1933 issue. A month prior, "six burly students in black robes with black hoods bearing the letters D.D.M.C." had snatched an eighteen-year-old sophomore from his bed in the middle of the night and taken him to an off-campus field where they "lashed Student Stephens ten times across the back with a three-quarter-inch rope. Then they gave him an overcoat, a pair of boots, told him to walk home." Allegedly, the student's crime was writing about fraternity hazing in the campus newspaper. An investigation, led by OU president William Bennett Bizzell, unmasked the culprits: "four footballers, the basketball captain, last year's swimming captain, the top-ranking tennis player, a poloist, a boxer and a track man." The Board of Regents promptly expelled the students, who then turned to Oklahoma governor William H. "Alfalfa Bill" Murray for help. The eccentric and puritanical governor had long been an enemy of OU, and according to *Time* magazine he saw college athletics and Greek life—staples at the university—as "tomfoolery and idleness." Surprisingly, he ordered the students' reinstatement. The only condition, which they accepted, was that they disband the DDMC.

On campus, a tug of war existed within the hearts of the university's young men who sought an outlet for their aggression while pursuing an education. Professor Parrington, the aforementioned founder of the English department, understood these twin urges and embodied both the tough and the civilized. He began coaching the football team in 1897. Though from Kansas and only twenty-six, he looked every bit the eastern aesthete, clothed in a coat and tie with beard and spectacles. His deadly serious expression in photographs tells you everything about his approach to life. At Harvard, he had developed a passion for both literature and football. He brought eastern tactics as well as an emphasis on discipline and fitness to the OU team. Parrington also brought an "Eastern atmosphere" to games, according to Harold Keith, who worked as OU's sports publicity director for thirty-nine years. Keith wrote in *Sooner Magazine* in July 1945 about the "accoutrements" Parrington introduced to OU, which included "organized cheering" and a formal dance for the visiting team after the game.

Clyde Bogle played for Parrington. He said of himself that he had an "average mind" and "sturdy body," and he loved to box and wrestle. He worked his way through school by going into the dairy business. He owned three cows and a one-horse buggy that he would drive around Norman to deliver milk to customers. After his morning work, he'd ride to campus on horseback for his classes with football practice afterward. Then he'd "gallop" back home "to work far into the night."

The game was ever evolving. Though stakeholders, mostly from the eastern colleges, had assembled in Springfield, Massachusetts, in 1876 to create a set of unified rules, football in the late nineteenth century looked different from the modern game. Bogle's description of the sport, in its primitive form, appeared in a 1965 issue of *Sooner Magazine*:

> The strategy in those days was not to open up a hole in front of a man with the ball, but to get behind him with a "thousand pounds of force" charging toward the opponent. With four or five guys pushing

> him, that man with the ball had better not fall down, because he'd sure get tromped on. We didn't have any huddle; instead, after each play, the offensive team would get up and start another one. The idea was to line up and get the ball out of there so as to wear down the defense as soon as possible.

Like much of America in the late nineteenth century, the campus in Norman quickly became fanatical about football. Four hundred "rooters" showed up to Parrington's first game in charge against a team from Oklahoma City on Thanksgiving Day 1897. The field was carved out of the prairie northwest of the university's first building, with a fence around it. From the spectator side of things, there were touches of the refined: men's and women's quartets, drawn from the student body, sang from an improvised stage at halftime. Other than that, the rowdy atmosphere created by the fans in attendance was one we've come to expect from football crowds. In Keith's account of the game, spectators (including President Boyd and other faculty) jumped the fence, which had been erected as a barrier, and rushed the field. They were so loud and close to the players that OU's signal-caller couldn't be heard by his teammates. In addition to his other duties, Parrington wrote colorful and detailed reports of the games, with the occasional exaggerated flourish, and in *The Umpire* he described the president of the university as barely capable of containing his emotions: "President Boyd kept saying: 'Come, boys, we must get back, give them room,' and then he would take a step or two forward [and] brandish his hard-shell in the most reckless fashion." The faculty, in fact, seemed like the group most taken by the atmosphere. In Parrington's words,

> Prof. DeBarr was equally careless of best clothes and kept edging forward with Mr. Jas [with] D. Maguire trying to outdo him in amount of noise made. He had just come from Prof. Elder's dinner table, [and] when he got up from the table—according to reliable authority—he was so full of turkey and cranberries he couldn't talk above a whisper. It is surprising how quickly he recovered the use of his tongue once the game began. Prof. Buchanan would hug Prof. Paxton and then they would both open their mouths and yell.

The university team comfortably beat Oklahoma City 16–0 on the day. The last sentence of Parrington's report is a wry departure. Instead of sounding like the enthusiastic chronicler, he finally writes like the detached professor, removed from the scenes of football-induced euphoria: "Curious, isn't it, how the fever lays hold of some."

Students, too, caught the fever. In November 1906, they marched alongside members of the pep band onto Boyd Field to cheer on the football team in its last scrimmage before the weekend's game. Boyd Field, established in 1905 and named for the university's first president, was sited just west of present-day McCasland Field House. The next morning, at chapel, football was still on everyone's mind; players were carried in on the shoulders of students and placed on an "improvised platform," according to an account in *The Umpire.* A pep rally took place with "live college songs" followed by an "extempore program" involving faculty members, students, and players. What happened next was wonderfully commensurate with the image of collegiate life as full of impromptu spirit. The players exited the chapel as they had entered—on the shoulders of classmates—and together they made a tour of both campus and town: "The bunch then fell in and proceeded from building to building and from room to room breaking up all of the morning classes. Then the march was continued down town where a number of prominent business men were induced to make short football talks."

For the first decade of its existence, the football team went by different nicknames: the Varsity, the Rough Riders, or the Boomers. The latter referenced the mostly white settlers who took advantage of several "land runs," starting in 1889, which provided them with access to "Unassigned Lands" in Indian Territory: present-day Oklahoma to which the Five Tribes (the Choctaw, Creek, Seminole, Cherokee, and Chickasaw) were compelled to relocate from the southeastern United States between 1830 and 1850. This forced march of refugees became known infamously as the Trail of Tears.

For the land run settlers, speed was of the essence; it was first come, first serve: stake your claim before someone else does. It was literally a race, and as with any race there was an official start time to ensure fairness.

Per human nature, some sought an advantage and crossed over early, earning the contempt of those who played by the rules. According to the Oklahoma Historical Society, a couple of derogatory names emerged to describe these people. They were called "moonshiners" for sneaking into Indian Territory "by the light of the moon" or "Sooners" because of a "sooner clause," addressing early entry, in the Indian Appropriation Act of March 2, 1889. In any case, wrote historian Angie Debo in her 1949 book *Oklahoma: Foot-Loose and Fancy-Free*, no one wished to be associated with these law-breaking Sooners: "It was a fighting word at first. No honest homesteader or city builder would be classed with those who got an unfair start and tried to hold it, when challenged, by perjury." For two decades, the term was considered a slur; then, rambunctious students at the University of Oklahoma got ahold of it. As young people are wont to do, they rejected the older generation's conception of a Sooner and around 1908 repurposed the name for their beloved football team. By the 1920s, the name had stuck.

■ ■ ■

Just as the game was played differently in the late nineteenth and early twentieth centuries, football was also conceptualized differently by the sport's caretakers. Today, we think of football as the epitome of sports entertainment; its players are celebrities. Back then, however, the college presidents and professors who institutionalized football thought of the game in idealistic terms. Historian Brian Ingrassia writes about the evolution of the game in his book *The Rise of Gridiron University: Higher Education's Uneasy Alliance with Big-Time Football.* The physicality of the Civil War had taught the nation's leaders a lesson; it wasn't enough for our young collegiate men, the leaders of the future, to sit in libraries and study. Manliness involved physical fitness in addition to intellectual and commercial know-how. After the Civil War, athletics joined the college curriculum as a tool "to train young men's bodies, minds, and morals for modern life." There was considerable anxiety about a new market economy that in its dedication to the dollar seemed to encourage a brand of nihilism. According to Ingrassia, "colleges thus had to find the right mix of utility and morality." The masculinity that emerged was multidimensional. A man must possess physical and mental strength. He had to be moral and self-disciplined and understand how to work within a team. Competition was stressed but within a framework of gentlemanly behavior. His natural aggression was to be harnessed and directed in an appropriate manner. As football began to draw spectators, educators were eager to control what happened on the field and in the stands. They continued to stress the pedagogical aspect of athletics: sport as a tool to improve the character of both player and spectator.

Fielding Yost, the pioneering football coach at the University of Michigan, gave voice to this position in his 1905 book *Football for Player and Spectator.* Described by one newspaper in 1901 as magnetic and among the "best natured on earth," Yost was highly competitive and doggedly temperate. When he arrived at Ann Arbor, age thirty, he was so eager to start work as the new football coach that he ran from the train station to campus, suitcase in hand. Invited by an alumnus to a saloon following practice one afternoon, Yost told the man, "I have never taken a drink in my life—in fact, I cannot even imagine what it would taste like." Yost believed in a chain reaction of influence involving football, players, and fans. Football helped unleash the "sentiment and spirit" that "lie dormant" in men. This philosophy, presented in his 1905 book, saw football as a vehicle for acquiring the masculine attributes of "self-reliance, moral courage, 'sand' determination, energy, discipline, judgment, self-restraint and enthusiastic interest." Seeing these qualities exhibited on the playing field, students would thus be inspired to apply these qualities to their own endeavors "for the glory of the college and the physical welfare of the owner." Yost was keenly aware of the growing popularity of football, which was already drawing hundreds of thousands of fans annually to games. The fan base had grown beyond the student body to include people from "all walks of life" who appreciated the game "solely as a spectacle and an exhibition of concerted pluck and action." "There is no crowd so cosmopolitan," he wrote in his book, "as that at a football game."

Popularity attracts critics. They decried the game's brutality, especially after the 1905 season when across the nation incidents on the football field caused the deaths of several players: fifteen in high school and three in college. Along with the deaths that happened every year, the injuries suffered, both minor and catastrophic, caused such a moral panic that President Teddy Roosevelt got involved. Roosevelt wasn't a disinterested party: his son was on Harvard's freshman football team. He even referenced the violence in football in his 1905 Harvard commencement address: "Brutality in playing a game should awaken the heartiest and most plainly shown contempt for the player guilty of it." The answer wasn't abolition, though some advocated for this; reform was the better option. As reported in *Smithsonian* magazine, the representatives of sixty-two colleges convened in December 1905 with a goal of making the sport safer: "They made a number of changes, including banning the 'flying wedge,' a mass formation that often caused serious injury, created the neutral zone between offense and defense and required teams to move 10 yards, not 5, in three downs." The most consequential change, in the long term, had little do with safety: the college administrators made the forward pass a legal play.

Apart from the sport's safety, critics believed that football was starting to overshadow the mission of the university, which was to educate young people and generate knowledge. Additionally, some argued that the game was corrupting; one of its wicked effects was a burgeoning illegal gambling trade.

According to Ingrassia, educators wanted to have it both ways. They saw their institutions as removed from the marketplace: sites of knowledge-creation in an era of scientific boom. But they also recognized the utilitarian aspects of having football on campus. The profits, ever-expanding, helped to fund the institution, and, moreover, football acted as a public relations tool—outreach to the working classes—bringing name recognition and renown.

The building of large, concrete stadiums, especially after World War I, and the formation of athletic departments signaled the permanence of sports on campus. College football, the erstwhile project of utopian educators, had broken free like the monster in *Frankenstein*. Abounding with flaws and splendors, it belonged to all Americans now.

■ ■ ■

The pairing of masculinity and football happened in Norman too. Under a headline that read "Why O.U. Should Be Proud," an article from *The Umpire* in May 1912 sang the praises of the football team, which had gone 8–0 the previous season, defeating "the great state universities of Kansas, Texas, and Missouri" along the way: "In recognition of this fact, and of the sportsmanship and manliness of Coach Bennie Owen and the Sooner players, many more large universities than could be accommodated have asked for games with the Sooners for next season."

What Yost was to Michigan as a coach, Owen became to Oklahoma. Owen, in fact, played quarterback for Yost at Kansas in 1899: the heralded team went 10–0. Six years later, Owen was hired to coach at OU, where he met adversity from the very start. Because of the financial paucity of the athletic association, according to Harold Keith (OU's long-running PR man), Owen's salary only covered three months of the fall; he made ends meet by managing a restaurant. In addition, the talent pool to draw from in Oklahoma Territory was small because of the lack of high schools. Players of experience, stature, and skill were hard to come by. In 1907, personal tragedy afflicted Owen when he lost his right arm in a hunting accident.

Owen, a "builder and a dreamer," turned the Sooner football team into a juggernaut despite these challenges. His tenure of twenty-two seasons, from 1905 to 1926, yielded a record of 122–54–16, with four undefeated seasons and three conference championships. He guided the school to its first win over Texas in his first season. Charles H. Newell, a student reporter, witnessed Owen's coaching from up close and wrote that despite never using profanity or abusing players for "boneheaded" decisions on the field he was still able to make his players "feel their failures and learn valuable lessons." Owen's favorite refrain was rather dark. He would say "murder, murder, murder" after a missed tackle in practice or a broken play. Like Yost, his mentor, Owen was a teetotaler, but he wasn't a judge or scold. After a Thanksgiving win on the road, happy students invited the coach to the neighborhood saloon in Santa Fe. Owen's response was diplomatic, but he made sure to stress one of the tenets of his philosophy, that character was king: "Boys I feel just great the way I am about the victory this afternoon. . . . I don't blame you for feeling as you do. If you must celebrate try to remember that your conduct tonight will reflect on your school just as the team's conduct reflected on it this afternoon."

Owen innovated on the field. He emphasized speed and was among the first to make prodigious use of the forward pass. By 1914, his Sooner team was passing more than it was running the ball. But it was his general approach to both football and life that made the greatest impact on his players and the university. OU president George Lynn Cross said of Owen in 1949 that "thousands of boys who played football under him today are still living by his philosophy that clean speech and clean living are essential to winning, that it is important not only to take victory modestly but to accept defeat gracefully."

When Owen took the mantle, the Sooners played their home games on Boyd Field; a grandstand accommodated five hundred spectators, and the field was encircled by a thick hedge. As Owen's teams attracted more fans to games, there rose a clamor for a stadium. Other colleges were building their own, and the need in Norman was clear. After Boyd Field hosted its largest crowd ever in November 1921, an OU defeat of the Kansas Jayhawks, the first paragraph of *The Oklahoma Weekly*'s report articulated the obvious: "The attendance was estimated at 11,000 and was cited by many as proof of Soonerland's need for an athletic stadium." Indeed, the call for action could be found in a variety of contexts, some quite funny. A sardonic advertisement placed by a local tailor's shop in *The Oklahoma Daily*, from late 1921, illustrates this perfectly: "DOES O.U. NEED A STADIUM. *Do baggy trousers need pressing?*"

A "Stadium for Oklahoma" committee was set up, headed by the Alumni Association, whose aim was to raise the $500,000 required for the construction of an athletic complex, which would include a stadium (with a football field and a track for athletics inside), tennis courts, a baseball diamond, and practice fields for football and baseball. Exhortations to join the fundraising drive appeared at the tail end of the spring 1922 semester in *The Oklahoma Daily*; each member of the student body, whose number had grown to twenty-seven hundred, was asked to pledge one hundred dollars to the cause. If every student donated this amount, it would pay for one-fourth of the stadium. Myrtle Lenau, from Norman, was the first student to make good on her pledge. She wrote a check for five dollars, with further installments to come.

By the end of spring's "stadium week" drive, students had pledged $10,000. In the fall, the drive continued. Student committees, led by male spirit groups the Ruf Neks and Jazz Hounds, were formed to drum up support for the stadium. A sense of competition was in the air as other colleges were also collecting money for stadiums. OU's student newspapers regularly reported on the progress made at the University of Kansas and the University of Indiana.

In February 1923, the bleachers were moved from Boyd Field to Owen Field, site of the new stadium, which had been named after the football coach. In the same month, a fire destroyed the campus YMCA building; in the aftermath, the stadium committee proposed to widen the project to include a student union building to house the YMCA and student organizations. In a unanimous vote, the student body approved the addition. The budget went from $500,000 to $1 million.

OU's students brought creative energy to the hustle. To raise money for the stadium–union fund, they held recitals and set up fraternity basketball leagues. They put on dramatic plays, and almost every weekend there was a student dance, with music from the likes of the Sooner Serenaders. *The Oklahoma Daily* urged students, on trips home, to take the campaign with them: "The opportunity that every student will have to assist in putting over the proposition lies in the good-will to be created in the various towns over the state. When you go home, tell your friends, and business men [*sic*] of the town how much Oklahoma needs a student union building."

In fall 1923, the first football game was played at Owen Field, a 62–7 blowout of Washington (from Missouri, not Washington state); additionally, the fundraising drive went nationwide. Despite the clear enthusiasm, it was a slow race, not a sprint, to raise the necessary funds, and some complained that Norman, as a town, was lax in its efforts. By February 1925, just over $400,000 had been pledged, and a sense of urgency was in the air, with the football season a few months away. Stadium planners hoped to have permanent seating installed on the west side of Owen Field by the first home game, in October, but a financial threshold of $500,000 had to be met. A final fundraising push was initiated, with April 15 as the deadline for the start of construction.

They didn't quite make it, though by April 18 the requisite half a million dollars had been pledged. Two weeks later, on May 2, thousands were on hand for the groundbreaking ceremony, which took place ahead of a track and field meet for high school athletes. As reported in *The Oklahoma Daily*, the pep band and the ROTC band performed songs before James S. Buchanan, OU's fourth president, made a short speech and then "turned the first spade of earth." He handed over the shovel to four others: Bennie Owen, football coach and athletic director; Eddie Brockman, captain of the football team; William J. Holloway, lieutenant governor of Oklahoma; and Frank Buttram, oilman and OU alumnus as well as national chairman of the stadium–union fund drive. Buttram's remarks at the ceremony harkened back to OU's past:

> Thirty-three years ago this spot where we stand was virgin prairie over which the trail of progress wound its way. Oklahoma's pioneers, with far-seeing vision, established this university, which now our Alma Mater, is a source of pride and strength for this great state. I firmly believe that this moment represents a definite turn in the road toward the ultimate goal of the biggest and best university in the southwest.

Based on these words, you'd be forgiven for thinking the destiny of the university was linked with the destiny of its sports teams, football most of all. Few Oklahomans, at the time, would have had qualms with anyone making this connection.

Five months after the ceremony, in late October, workers were scrambling to finish the project ahead of the first home game against Drake University. Inspired by the stadium at the University of Minnesota—lauded as the best in the country—the west stand at Owen Field was four hundred feet long, with sixty-two rows of seating, and built with red tile, brick, and concrete. Against Drake, on the first-ever "Dad's Day" at OU, the conditions were fine for football. According to *The Daily Oklahoman*, there was no sun to interfere with the players' eyesight and no wind to disturb the flight of the ball. The field, though subjected to recent rains and harboring a few "soft and slippery spots," was in good shape. The air was "cold enough to put the players on edge [but] not sharp enough to discomfort the spectators." Even so, the attendance was "disappointingly small." Though the student body had filled the bleachers on the east side of Owen Field, the newly constructed west stand of Memorial Stadium—so named to honor the three faculty members and twenty-one OU students killed in World War I—held only four thousand fans, a fourth of its capacity. On the bright side, the Sooners defeated Drake 7–0: revenge for a lopsided loss to the Iowans the year before. It wasn't a picture-perfect start to a new era, but there was plenty to be optimistic about. The university was growing—the Oklahoma Memorial Union and Bizzell Memorial Library would be built in 1928 and 1929, respectively—and thanks to the leadership of Vernon Parrington and Bennie Owen the football team had a winning tradition and regional reputation. However, difficult times lay ahead for both the university and the Sooner football team. In 1926, Owen's retirement from coaching initiated a period of relative stagnation for Sooner football. The Great Depression and a historic drought would bring economic devastation to the state, and OU would not escape unscathed. Another world war would strip the university of male students as many went overseas to serve.

The post-football lives of Parrington and Owen, who guided the Oklahoma program in those early years, were strikingly different. After giving up the reins of the football team in 1900, Parrington stayed another eight years at the university. Portrayed as decadent (Parrington's smoking perturbed the townsfolk), he was fired for essentially political reasons, along with President Boyd and other faculty deemed unfit by the state governor. Parrington taught at the University of Washington in Seattle for the rest of his career and won the Pulitzer Prize for History in 1928 for his three books covering the American literary tradition: *Main Currents in American Thought.* Parrington died suddenly in 1929 while visiting England with his wife. He was fifty-seven years old. Today, Parrington Oval, on the north side of OU's campus, is named after him.

After football, Owen continued to serve as director of athletics until 1934. In 1949, he was honored with OU's Distinguished Service Award, and two years later he was inducted into the National College Football Hall of Fame. In November 1955, five hundred friends and former players gathered in the Union Ballroom for a banquet to honor the man. *Sooner Magazine* described the evening. At the age of eighty, Owen smiled and removed his glasses to wipe tears from his eyes as "Bennie's boys," gray-haired men now, told stories about their coach. Owen was presented with a citation of appreciation, marking his fiftieth year at OU, as well as a gift from his former lettermen: a new set of luggage. When Owen took the stage to speak, he wondered aloud if any of his female athletes—for a time, he coached women's basketball—were in the audience. One person stood up; Elizabeth Eagleton Courtright, class of 1914, had traveled from Ann Arbor, Michigan, to see him.

Earlier in the week, in an interview published in *The Oklahoma Daily*, a student reporter had marveled at Owen's age. To the young reporter, the former coach looked no older than "50 or 55 at the most." While admitting that he was "bothered" somewhat by Owen's missing right arm, the reporter got past this to guide a conversation about the modern and bygone eras of football. Owen pointed out that his players were smaller and perhaps more "brainy" than modern players. On his undefeated team of 1911, no player weighed more than 150 pounds, and four of them earned Phi Beta Kappa honors for academics. At the conclusion of the interview, the reporter said to the coach, on the eve of his banquet, "I'm proud for you Mr. Owen." The last two lines in his article continue to have the ring of truth: "I might be wrong about Bennie Owen's age. . . . But there's one thing I'm pretty sure of, he will live forever at the University of Oklahoma."

Owen died in 1970 at the age of ninety-four. Owen Field is one of many monikers still used for the football stadium. A statue of the coach can be found in the courtyard next to the stadium's south end.

▪ 2 ▪

FANS

History and Taxonomy

IT DIDN'T TAKE LONG for Sooner identity to become entangled with the football team. A student or supporter of the university was necessarily a rooter for the Varsity men. A poem in *The Oklahoma Daily* from 1923, after a lopsided 62–7 win against Washington, tells of the synergy between team and fans.

It was all the pep and cheering
And the songs and all the noise
Made by loyal O.U. rooters
That inspired the football boys.
It was the Ruf Neks, Band and Freshmen

And the plunging squad of men
That made touchdown after touchdown
In that great one-sided win.

Rooting for the team was not just important, it was expected. Freshmen were educated on this aspect of student life early on. An October 1923 article in *The Oklahoma Daily* ordered freshmen to show up to Owen Field promptly at one-thirty on Saturday and to wear "red or red and white sweaters." These "yearlings" were instructed to sit in a particular section in the stands. At halftime of the football game, they would play a pivotal role in entertaining the fans: "All frosh, vigilance men included, must participate in the snake dance between halves. [We extend] An invitation to freshman girls to participate. Girls are requested to dress in red and white." After the game, the young men's responsibilities included remaining in the stands while the band played "Boomer Sooner" and then going onto the field "to carry off all members of both football teams who are in uniform."

Further down in the article the reader learns that the so-called vigilance men were in possession of paddles for which there was a regulation size: "Vigilants must not use any paddle that is longer, broader, or thicker than ordinary barrel stave. If caught using one, they must pay penalty."

Archival photographs from the 1920s reveal that a snake dance resembled the conga line dance of today, with a student's hands on the hips or shoulders of the person in front of him or her. This all sounds rather benign, though when coupled with peer group vigilantes armed with paddles the picture admittedly turns ominous. Things looked exponentially grimmer for the freshmen thanks to another article on the same page whose headline read "'Bull Pen' New Device Used to Torture Frosh." This article revealed that in addition to participating in the snake dance, freshmen were to be the test subjects of a new invention created by the vigilantes who, in this context, sound like a cross between the villains in a Kafka story and agents of the Gestapo: "After running the gauntlet the freshmen will be escorted into the mysterious 'bull pen': a new device carefully constructed for torturing erring freshmen in the presence of a crowd of roaring football fans who 'holler' for blood and demand their money's worth."

The student newspaper was full of short directives for freshmen, with the promise that vigilantes were watching their every move to ensure correct behavior. Self-policing and collective responsibility were commonplace. In September 1924, a freshman parade got out of hand, and damage was done to local businesses. A new movie screen at the University Theater on Main Street was torn, and a bookstore was looted of books, fountain pens, and pennants. *The Oklahoma Daily* reported that the total damage amounted to nearly three hundred dollars. At the behest of the freshman class president, vigilantes gathered at every campus entrance to "tag" all freshmen. The tag meant that the male student, regardless of his involvement in September, was expected to contribute seventy cents to a fund that would be distributed to the merchants affected.

An article from *The Oklahoma Daily* in mid-October 1924 speaks, without ambiguity or shame, to the purpose of vigilante paddles. Freshmen who failed to attend a Friday pep rally had gotten the attention of the "frosh police squad," who responded by raiding fraternity and boarding houses looking for the absentees. In downtown Norman, they discovered around twenty-five freshmen, some with dates, at the movies. The twenty-five were made to run an improvised "gauntlet" down Main Street. One freshman, sitting "placidly" in the Sooner Theatre, tried to convince his interrogator that he'd been at the pep rally. The vigilante who tapped him on the shoulder asked about the rally's speakers:

> "That bird Kimbell, did he have anything to say?"
>
> "Kimbell, yeah, he's captain of the vigs. I should say he did talk . . . say that Kimbell sure poured it on us."
>
> "Guess you better come with me, buddy, my name's Kimbell. I wasn't even at the meeting."

The unlucky freshman, in the words of the *Daily*'s writer, became another one that "bit the dust." All told, seventy-five freshmen were paddled in Friday's "raid," and at the game the next day such was the condition of their backsides that the "yearlings were separated from bleacher seats by cushions."

■ ■ ■

An October 1941 *Sooner Magazine* article described the art of watching a football game, ironically devising systems of fan classification. The first "system" included fans who were rather boring. There was a lack of investment as they casually, from their seat in the stands, took in the action on the field and the behavior of their neighbors. Later, in very civilized fashion, they would head home and listen to an analysis of the game on the radio or read an account in Sunday's newspaper.

At the other end of the spectrum were the football experts belonging to the "Don't Look Now" System. While most fans fixated on the ball carrier, this breed of fan insisted that the intricacies of football could only be found in the trenches with the linemen. "It's the big tough linemen who take a terrific beating and really do the work," they said. "Forget about those flashy halfbacks and focus on the line."

The fan in the next system over also stood atop the mountain, breathing rarefied air. In addition to a feeling of superiority, this fan exhibited at least two other emotions: scorn and resentment. The moniker assigned to this group—the Sour Grapes or Whadda I Care System of Football Watching—described a philosophy centered on geography. These disgruntled fans were ambivalent about their seats, as if the arrangement was out of their control, a punishment bestowed by the football gods. After bemoaning that others had employed machination to secure their seats, these fans, from their perch at the goal line, insisted that the best vantage point was their own; seats at the fifty-yard line were overrated. "I wouldn't have one if you would give it to me," one of these fans was quoted as saying. "Nothing important happens in mid-field, just a lot of punting. The real scoring plays and the fast action happen down close to the goal line. That's where I like to sit." The quoted fan then gazed into his lap to read a magazine as the Sooners and the day's opponent were currently occupied at the other end of Owen Field.

The "Feminine or What Happened Then" System would later be debunked in Betty Friedan's 1963 book *The Feminine Mystique*, which kicked off second-wave feminism and defended female fans of the gridiron. According to this system, Sooner fans of the fairer sex were expected to obsessively track the ball and rely on the guidance of the stadium announcer. One such stakeholder described her approach while twirling her hair and smacking on chewing gum: "I just kind of watch the two teams and try to find where the ball is. Then I quick look down the field to see if somebody is going to catch a pass and then I look back and probably the play is all over and so I listen to the public address system to tell whether to cheer or not."

"The More the Merrier" System involved a group of friends, one of whom had purchased a block of tickets to ensure that everyone sat together. In addition to guaranteeing that one had an audience for their predictions and lamentations during the game, such a strategy provided a sense of security in case opposing fans were seated nearby.

The "Take Turns" System was a cousin to the "Don't Look Now" System in that both featured self-nominated football experts. The former entailed the allocation of one's attention, as if watching the game were a rigorous, scientific endeavor. In the first quarter, one watched only the ends: in the second quarter the center, tackles, and guards. After halftime, one watched the backfield. The fourth quarter was inarguably the most important for this group, with its highbrow tastes and appreciation for beauty, as its members spent the last fifteen minutes of the game focusing solely "on the blonde in the second row ahead."

It was noticed by the armchair sociologists at *Sooner Magazine* in 1941 that some fans preferred seats at the top of Memorial Stadium, the better to catch patterns of play: "It gives you a birdseye [*sic*] view, but what do birds know about football?"

Other fans liked to sit in front, just yards away from the sideline, so that they could "study the elegant English spoken by a wiry halfback who has just been kneed by a 220-pound tackle." This group was known to comprise politicians or those with political aspirations; standing up from their seats, they became visible to their constituents. Each of these fans' attendance amounted to a political advertisement: I, a man of the people, like football too. Vote for me.

Which seats were better? Aisle or inside? Fans from 1941 were split. Some preferred the aisle where you didn't have to worry about "tripping over feet, pop bottles and overcoats." Others, with strong bladders, liked the middle seats, the better to take up residence, like firmly rooted plants.

What did the "modern football watcher" of 1941 look like out in the wild? They came to campus as well-equipped for a "polar expedition with Admiral Byrd"—the famous American explorer of Antarctica—as for a football game. Among their possessions were a "program, pennant, souvenir football on a cane, arm band colors, chrysanthemum, seat cushion, raincoat, blanket, thermos jar of hot coffee, a hot dog with mustard, and a portable radio."

Some, of course, preferred to avoid the crowds. *Sooner Magazine* acknowledged them too, with a subtle nod of admiration. This fan was happy at home with a glass of booze, which lent this group its name: the "Scotch" System. A member of this group sat in an armchair next to the radio, comfortably listening to the play-by-play, and sometimes he had company, a buddy likewise enamored with Sooner football but from a respectable distance. When this latter scenario happened, it was called a "Double Scotch."

■ ■ ■

Professors called it the "stormiest day in OU history": Monday, November 22, 1938. During an eighteen-hour stretch, student mobs charged into classrooms, harassed professors, and danced wildly on Campus Corner to the chagrin of university officials. What sparked the mayhem? Two days before, Oklahoma defeated Iowa State to win the Big Six Conference and earn a trip to the Orange Bowl in Miami. The game, to be played in the new year, would represent a first for the Sooners; the football team had never appeared in a bowl game before.

The shenanigans of that day—recorded in both *The Oklahoma Daily* and *Sooner Magazine*—deserve a chronological account. On Saturday, the game was played in Ames, Iowa, and won. On Sunday night, three thousand raucous students assembled on Campus Corner tossing firecrackers and shouting, "We want a holiday!" They marched en masse to the president's house to ask for a day off to celebrate the football team's victory. For years now, OU students had done this: visit the president's doorstep after a notable Sooner win and plead for a "holiday." President Bizzell met them dressed as if it were morning instead of evening, in a dark suit and winter coat with a hat on his head. Likewise, many students were dressed in suit and tie. Photographs exist of this showdown between the president and his young charges. In one, a student with a flashlight leads Bizzell, sixty-two years old, onto the lawn of the president's house to address the crowd. Bizzell looks somber, hands in coat pockets, while the student looks directly at the camera, with an expression that can only be described as gleeful. In another photograph, the crowd has lifted Bizzell and a student onto their collective shoulders, as if it were the president himself who delivered the victory on Saturday. They're asking him to be a hero: grant us freedom from the classroom tomorrow. Bizzell looks unmoved, a stoic grandfather, and so he was. He turned down their request. The next day, he was missing from campus, on university business, as all hell broke loose.

Disappointed but not defeated, the crowd left the president's house for the nearby home of Tom Stidham, the Sooners' triumphant football coach, who was in bed when students arrived. Nevertheless, Stidham came to the door to give them a brief but rousing talk.

Cold night winds dispersed the crowd. Students were back on campus Monday morning, though class attendance was the last thing on their minds. Instead, they stood at the entrances of classroom buildings "to convince their fellows that a holiday was needed." Things progressed rapidly to intervention, with "mobs of students" entering classrooms already in session, creating a ruckus as they pleaded with professors to cancel the lesson for the day. Most acquiesced and by ten o'clock almost every classroom on campus was empty. Later that morning, more than three thousand students gathered at the Field House for a spur-of-the-moment pep rally with Coach Stidham and the football team. Stidham told the lively crowd, "We're just as happy as you are. I know we'll have a better inspired team Saturday after this demonstration."

A few hours later, Coach Stidham, aware that students were rampaging around campus, confronted a rowdy group outside the administration building. "You kids, whoop and holler all you want to, but don't go in the building and destroy property," he said. "You are all good kids and I want to see you have fun, but remember don't destroy property."

Afternoon classes were targeted by students with roughly the same amount of success. Resistance was found at only one place: the law school. In the morning and afternoon, head-to-head battles transpired between obstinate professors and bold students. The way the story is drawn, in *The Oklahoma Daily* the day after it happened, puts one in mind of slapstick comedy. Julien C. Monnet, "venerable" dean of the law school—the building that once housed the law school, on Parrington Oval, is now called Monnet Hall—was teaching his contracts class when students barged inside. Professor Monnet had locked the door, but determined students "unscrewed the hinges and stomped over the door." Once they invaded his class, one intrepid student stepped toward Monnet and then pinched and patted the man's cheek, as if he were dealing with a child instead of a university dean. "Deanie, be a good boy and let them out," the student said.

Things were just as bad, if not worse, for law professor John B. Cheadle. He was writing on the blackboard when students descended on his taxation class. One grabbed an eraser and wiped clean the blackboard; the class's assignment had been written there. When Cheadle, sitting in his chair, refused to let out class, students pulled the chair out from under him; the man crumpled to the floor. His verbal reply, under the circumstances, was composed: "The law school is glad to see an intensive school spirit. The law school is interested in the university but the effect of mob movements here is to set blocs of the legislature against the school."

Like his colleague in the law school, "white-haired" Victor H. Kulp was concerned about public reaction to the day's festivities when two hundred students stormed his two o'clock class. In addition to demanding a holiday, students shot off firecrackers in the corner of the room. Kulp yelled above the noise, "The taxpayers won't like this!"

Unbelievably, the madness spread to schoolchildren. When the elementary school located on the Norman campus excused its young pupils for the day, the children headed for the "law barn" where they loitered on the steps of the building. Fed up with the law professors' intransigence, they shouted, "Down with the law school! Down with the law school!"

Proving themselves precocious in the realm of trash talk, the children targeted law students as they entered or left the building. The little gremlins, jumping up and down, must have seemed a hallucination to the law students who were then subjected to chanting that predicted their academic demise. "You'll be no good lawyers!" the children shouted. "You won't make lawyers!"

The afternoon was fading as hundreds of students left the oval, aiming for Campus Corner. Along the way, they stopped at the intersection of Asp and Boyd, blocking traffic, with mischief on their minds. Couples danced the jitterbug in the middle of the street, forcing drivers to wait. Some were amused by the spectacle. A handful leaned on their horns.

The student-enforced holiday reached its final phase in the shops and restaurants on Campus Corner. At the Campus Drug, students danced on tables. Most other establishments saw dancing and general frivolity. President Bizzell, back in town, attempted a call to order, entering Rickner's Student Shop and demanding students return home. Once he left, students dragged a jukebox outside from the Town Tavern, so that its songs echoed down Asp. As the November evening turned cold, students coupled off for swing dancing in the street.

Eventually, as with any party, the revelers lost their enthusiasm. They left Campus Corner alone or with friends. They walked with crossed arms or huddled against one another, trying to stay warm.

The next morning, campus routines were back. The quiet and order must have made everyone—students and faculty alike—feel that the chaos of Monday had been a dream. Had it really happened? Everyone looked forward now to Thanksgiving, in two days' time. Beyond that, there was another football game at the weekend, the annual tilt with in-state rival Oklahoma A&M.

Less than a year later (and far away geographically), in September 1939, Hitler invaded Poland to start the Second World War. As with the First World War, OU was slow to react. With just the faintest awareness of what had happened to their predecessors in 1917, students cared more about football and "holidays" than the chaos in Europe. Once again, it took American involvement to wake up the campus. Two days after the attack on Pearl Harbor in December 1941, *The Oklahoma Daily* described on its front page the student reaction. As with World War I, patriotic Sooners (joined by their concerned mothers) were spoiling for a fight: "All day long, students and mothers of students formed a continuous stream of visitors at the office of James Coe Van de Carr, commandant of the Naval

Reserve Officers Training Corps. Students sought information about how to enlist in the navy or the reserves. Mothers wanted to know how their sons would be 'treated in the navy.'" Something similar happened—a "flood of queries"—at the ROTC office for the Air Corps and Army.

During the war, enrollment at OU would drop precipitously. The campus, nevertheless, made vast contributions to the war effort. Two naval bases, established north and south of the university, would train thousands of pilots and support personnel. OU's ROTC programs would commission 4,200 officers during the war. By late 1942, 3,000 alumni had joined the armed forces. Three Sooners would be awarded the Congressional Medal of Honor for bravery.

One imagines that many of the young Sooners who in November 1938 "turned the entire campus into a huge holiday arena for 18 hours" eventually joined the armed forces to fight German and Japanese fascism. No matter where they served in the war or in what capacity—as a sailor on a naval ship in the Pacific or an infantryman in an army platoon in Europe—they must have looked back on their college years in Norman with fondness and likely a sense of disbelief. Had it really happened? If only they could go back in time to study sessions in Bizzell library or football games at Memorial Stadium or Saturday nights on Campus Corner, but the circumstances of world history had swallowed them whole. Nothing would ever be the same.

▪ 3 ▪

BIRTH OF THE SUPERFAN

THERE WAS NO single big bang moment of "superfandom" at OU. It did not suddenly emerge, fully formed. Rather, superfandom was more the product of an organic process, evolving across the decades until an individual emerged to kick off the tradition. This individual's dedication to the Sooner football team was only matched by his dedication to a signature style. Singularity is a word that describes him, though it can't be the best one. It's better to say that there will never be anyone like Morris Tenenbaum, Big Red's first superfan.

At the height of his pomp and celebrity in the 1960s, Tenenbaum could be found in places he'd made his own for decades. He had no official university title, but everyone knew of him and his duties. He was the football team's security guard, gatekeeper, and in-house comedian. He handed out chewing gum, and banter, to the players as they walked onto the practice field. He was also an armchair philosopher who wrote and published a book of observations about OU's college men. He was fond of issuing aphorisms and witticisms, in his Polish-accented English, that perplexed and delighted his audience. (Tenenbaum emigrated to the United States as a boy.) *The Oklahoma Daily* and *Sooner Magazine* quoted him frequently. About the Sooner football players he said, "It's not football that hurts these boys. It's college girls. They dream about them all night." He had this to say about Earth and its inhabitants: "This planet's not moving—only the people on it." The man, forever a bachelor, produced another verbal gem, cynical to the core, about marriage: "I like the single life—don't believe in producing slaves in this generation."

Tenenbaum kept undesirables off the practice field and out of the locker room and offered strict guidelines to those granted access. He was well into his sixties, and well-versed in his role, when in October 1966, according to a profile in *The Oklahoma Daily*, he cautioned a visiting pro football scout. "Coach Mackenzie doesn't like people walkin' on the field," he said. When the "tall, husky scout" did not heed his words, Tenenbaum called after him: "You are a stranger here, but a welcome stranger."

During games, Tenenbaum sat on a bench on the Sooner sideline. Alternatively, he used a rolled-up tarp behind the team bench, sitting on top with "his feet sticking out in front of him." After the game, he would guard the dressing room at Oklahoma Memorial Stadium, ensuring that no one entered unless they got the go-ahead from the Sooner head coach. (Across his tenure, which spanned six decades, Tenenbaum saw twelve head coaches at the helm, starting with Bennie Owen in the 1920s and ending with Barry Switzer in the 1970s.) Reportedly, he once kept out a gridiron legend. Red Grange, the All-American halfback and national champion from the University of Illinois, starred for the Chicago Bears in the NFL in the 1920s and '30s. But "the Galloping Ghost's" reputation did him no favors when he tried to visit the Sooner locker room. Tenenbaum denied him entry.

If Tenenbaum's personality was larger than life, his dress sense was somehow even larger. *Sooner Magazine* in 1966 tactfully described the man's style as "distinctive." The son of a tailor, Tenenbaum sold second-hand clothes that he often purchased from broke college students. First, he had a shop on Main Street. Then he operated out of his house on Classen Boulevard. He used his tailor skills to fashion outfits that made him resemble a colorful hobo from another dimension. One of his favorite outfits involved the pairing of a red tie with a vest repurposed from a woman's skirt. Using his Singer sewing machine, he'd stitched onto the back of the vest: "U.S., Morris Tenenbaum, Norman, Oklahoma, OU." On cloudy days that promised rain, he protected his head by combining a chef's cap with a felt hat. The former was pulled over the brim of the latter. For some reason, certainly tied to the man's screwball sense of humor, the words "Chicken Inspector" were stitched in red on the front of this hybrid hat. This wasn't even the strangest of his crafted hats. There was another made from a car's hubcap. A lot of the time, a cigar or cigarette would be clenched between Tenenbaum's teeth. He walked with a customized cane that further demonstrated the miracle of his imagination. The top of the cane featured a pair of deer antlers, fused there by Tenenbaum. Between the antlers he'd glued a large silver coin featuring the likeness of the last crown prince of the German Empire, Wilhelm. (His affinity for the crown prince went unexplained in the articles I read. As a young man, he joined the US Army to fight the Germans in World War I. Knowledge of his war service only intensifies the mystery: Why feature your former enemy on your cane?) Campaign buttons of American politicians adorned the cane, the most treasured of which was one for John F. Kennedy, a man Tenenbaum greatly admired.

Tenenbaum has one of those expansive biographies that speak to America's melting pot history and its promise that happiness can be won with industry and smarts. Born at the very end of the nineteenth century, Tenenbaum emigrated to America in 1913, landing in Oklahoma City. His personal effects were meager; he came to this country with "a Bible and an American penny," according to a story in *The Oklahoma Daily*. Some reports put him in Norman in 1915. Others say he moved to Norman in 1923. In any case, he was working as a tailor and clothes seller from the beginning, apart from his stint in the army. He saw opportunity on the campus of the University of Oklahoma, which was back then a small community of often cash-deficient students. Tenenbaum stepped in to fill a need, visiting the fraternity and sorority houses, offering cash for clothes. One alumnus told *Sooner Magazine* that Tenenbaum, on these business trips, was a sight to see: "He'd have three or four hats stacked high on his head and a bundle of old clothes on his arms. Just ask him how many student trips to Dallas he's financed. He could charm the trousers off some guy who needed money for the trip." He would mend or alter the clothes then put them on sale in his shop on Main Street or sell them to buyers in Oklahoma City. If students didn't have clothes to sell but still needed money, Tenenbaum offered interest-free loans.

Early on, he was an asset to the football team. An "Around the Campus" column in *The Oklahoma Daily* in April 1939 saluted Tenenbaum for coming to the rescue of "Indian" Jack Jacobs, star of the Sooner football team as well as a member of the Muscogee Nation. After leaving OU, Jacobs enjoyed a stellar career in the pros, playing in the NFL and the Canadian league. Jacobs was in a bind after losing his combat boots ahead of an annual inspection of his ROTC unit. Luckily, Tenenbaum was on hand to help. Though it was a challenge "finding a pair of boots big enough for the Indian lad," Tenenbaum came through.

Later that year, before the Missouri game, Tenenbaum proved useful again. After hearing that Tiger "spies" might be afoot, Tenenbaum patrolled the practice field, riding his bicycle around and making "himself look 'executive' by wearing an American Legion badge." His report to Coach Tom Stidham included the fact that he'd told two suspicious guys to "scram." Three cars, with out-of-state license plates, also attracted Tenenbaum's attention; they went into his report.

Like all outsized characters, Tenenbaum attracted a variety of reactions. He was helpful and dependable. Due to his eccentricities, he was also easy to mock, either in the pages of the student newspaper or, it's likely, in conversations on campus. A letter sent to Cathey Edwards, a filmmaker who worked on a posthumous documentary of Tenenbaum, attests to the tailor's checkered reputation. The letter writer recalled an incident before World War II when members of a fraternity, who believed that Tenenbaum had broken into their house to steal their clothes, posted a sign outside which read, "No Jews."

Whatever Tenenbaum's reputation, time and consistency turned him into an institution at OU. In 1954, he was granted membership to the prestigious Varsity O Club. At one of the club's banquets, Coach Wilkinson recognized Tenenbaum's contributions to the team, prompting the tailor to stand and walk to the head table where he turned to face the audience.

He prefaced his remarks with an apology; he lacked the eloquence of Wilkinson and President Cross. A formal education had never been in the cards for him. "But I want to give this to the 'O' Club," he said. He pulled out of his pocket a check for five hundred dollars—the equivalent of more than five thousand dollars today—and handed it over. Then he returned to his seat.

In the sixties, Tenenbaum welcomed an assortment of writers to his two-story stucco home at the northwest corner of Brooks and Classen (the house, painted a sage green, still stands today), where he'd lived for decades, and they described a living space commensurate with the tailor's creative talents. Pictures of Tenenbaum with Sooner legends and even an American president (Harry Truman once visited Norman for a football game) hung on the walls. On one wall, in a picture frame, was a piece of fabric with "OU" spelled out in buttons. His curtains were a marvel: colorful and constructed from women's skirts and dresses. A large quilt, multicolored, covered his bedroom wall. "Each square of that quilt I made with a different tie. I've made twelve of them, but no more. It hurts my eyes to sew much," he told *Sooner Magazine*. By then, he was sixty-nine years old.

Tenenbaum would live for another eleven years. After his death in July 1977, he was featured in an advertisement in *The Oklahoma Daily* one last time: an announcement for an estate sale at his home on Classen. From the afterlife, Tenenbaum continued to sell his wares. The crowd that showed up was a mixture of friends—there to pay respects—and the curious. A newspaper described the estate sale as a "cultural event." Visitors found household items alongside his inspired creations. The hat made from a hubcap was available. Embroidered jerseys, shorts, vests, and quilts were for sale, along with his white 1966 Ford Falcon: "Morris" was painted in red down the side of the car.

Thereafter, a remarkable epilogue to Tenenbaum's long and rich life unfolded. The man, in death, was discovered as a "folk artist." Collectors interested in outsider art found treasures in his appliquéd clothing and patchwork quilts. They labeled as "environmental folk art" a collage of license plates and a brick tree planter decorated with railroad spikes found in his backyard. Two years after his death, in 1979, a gallery in New York City was the first to exhibit his work. Shows in Oklahoma City followed in 1981. Tenenbaum's antler cane and hubcap hat enjoyed a second life as art objects.

Some argued that the man's life itself was a work of art. More than one person, in tribute, said that Tenenbaum taught them the meaning of freedom. Randy Newman, the executor of his estate, told *The Oklahoma Daily* that Tenenbaum was "first and foremost for liberty, justice and freedom . . . he was an American." A former Sooner football player turned dentist put Tenenbaum in a similar light. In the 1980s, he wrote to Edwards, the documentary filmmaker, about Tenenbaum: "Morris represented to me what life is all about: the freedom to be different, to follow your whims and to say what's on your mind."

A poem accompanied Tenenbaum's obituary in *The Oklahoma Daily.* Fittingly, the poem centers around one of his winter coats, which had somehow passed into the hands of the unnamed writer.

> I am wearing Morris's coat—softer than it looks.
> Decorations on the inside—Big Red, out of sight.
> Athletic shirts and shorts—turned into folk art.
> Worthy of an Indian—in a jungle village.
> Worthy of a wandering Jew—who found his promised land.
> Heroes in their warmup clothes—here, on windy plains,
> I am wearing Morris's coat—next winter when it snows.

▪ ▪ ▪

The seeds of Cecil Samara's superfandom were planted in childhood. Many American boys are taken to their first football game by a father or grandfather. Samara lost his own father, a Lebanese immigrant who came to the United States in the late nineteenth century, to the flu pandemic of 1918 that killed 675,000 Americans. Samara was two years old at the time of his father's death. When the boy, at age seven, got interested in Sooner football, he relied on himself to travel to games. He hitchhiked from his family's rat-infested shack in Oklahoma City to Boyd Field in Norman to watch Bennie Owen's Sooners. Taking advantage of his small size, Samara slipped through the gates at Boyd Field and moved as close to the Sooner coach on the sideline as possible. "I was the biggest pest he knew," Samara said decades later in an interview with the Oklahoma Historical Society.

In the beginning, these regular trips to Norman were exclusively for football. But after a while, in his teenage years, he started visiting Bizzell library. Despite dropping out of school after the third grade to work, he had an appetite for learning. OU students would give him pencil and paper so that he could conduct his own studies. They made room for him in the classroom too; regularly, Samara sat in on OU classes. The professors allowed him to stay. "I wouldn't trade that education I got for anything in the world," Samara said.

Thanks to these formative experiences, Samara developed twin loyalties that would last a lifetime. He was devoted to both Sooner football and the OU student body.

To say that life early on was a struggle would be to put it mildly. Before his untimely death, Samara's father was a peddler who used a horse and buggy to drive around the city selling shoes, dresses, tablecloths, scarves, and other household items. Samara's mother plucked chickens at a processing factory. They lived in an Oklahoma City slum in a flimsy shack with pine floors whose rent was eleven dollars a month. There was no indoor toilet, much less running water. As a boy, Samara went around barefoot in overalls. His trade, after leaving school, was selling newspapers for two cents a copy at the corner of Grand and Harvey downtown. His clientele included businessmen and doctors who sometimes might not pay him for three to four weeks.

Life went on like this until he was seventeen. In the midst of the Great Depression, he started his own business, the first of many, selling ice cream that he toted around in a large bucket to different stores and office buildings downtown. His customers were often the same people who bought newspapers from him. Samara married young, and he and his wife, Lucille, were so poor that they couldn't afford to turn on the lights; they spent the first three weeks at their new home with neither gas nor electricity.

By 1941, things were looking up for the Samaras. They had started a family and Samara got a job at the new federally funded air depot in Oklahoma City (eventually called Tinker Air Force Base). He worked as a concrete testing engineer, but in line with his wheeler-dealer personality he worked two other jobs as well: as a bellhop at the Belmont Hotel and counter help at a soda shop. His entrepreneurial spirit led to the formation of a new business—Cecil's Personal Service—which tackled a range of tasks for customers. His employees could grab your groceries or mow your lawn. Adding to their business endeavors, the husband and wife became realtors and restauranteurs. Then, in the late fifties, they started Big Red Flag Service, which sold flags of all kinds.

There was nothing I found while researching that documented Samara's transformation into the "World's Biggest OU Fan." Nothing that would create in the mind a movie montage in which he, the superhero, acquires his powers and designs a costume. What the record shows, in a visual sense, is Samara in all his superfan glory—a red cowboy hat lettered with a white interlocking OU, red eyeglasses, a red sports coat with a white shirt or a red and white striped shirt underneath, a red tie with OU in white letters or an OU football helmet at the bottom, and white pants. In the 1960s, a famed bootmaker in Fort Worth customized a pair of OU boots for him. Samara carried a red and white bullhorn, which he used to amplify his message: OU football was the best in the nation. Routinely, he stood alongside the Ruf Neks on Owen Field during games; he was made an honorary Ruf Nek in 1955. In October 1972, before the Red River Rivalry, a Dallas TV reporter teased him on camera: "Big Red, are you gonna try to help the noise pollution this year and kind of hold it down a little bit?" Samara, like someone skilled in media relations, ignored the question to stay on message: "I can tell you this and I want you to remember how I'm saying it," he said. "We're going to beat Texas by *at least* five touchdowns. We're the nation's number one football team. We're going to the Orange Bowl!" (Samara was close in his prediction: The Sooners won 27–0.)

Eddie Hartwick, a Ruf Nek in the eighties, could testify to both the volume and frequency of Samara's cheering. Hartwick told *The Oklahoman*, "I think I definitely suffered hearing loss from his bullhorn. . . . He had that bullhorn going all the time." Samara was such a fanatic about the university that he could try people's patience. In 1989, a nostalgic student on the verge of graduation wrote in *The Oklahoma Daily* about certain indelible experiences; ironically, he counted Samara among the things he would never forget: "There was always Cecil Samara irritating the hell out of you with 'We're number one!' or 'Orange Bowl!' over and over again." After Samara's death in 1994, a friend told the student newspaper that you couldn't sit down with Samara for a beer without the man talking about his beloved university: "He was so wrapped up in OU. . . . It finally started to get on your nerves eventually."

If the above doesn't convince you of Samara's commitment, the following should. When the time came to replace his God-given teeth with dentures, the man paid for two different sets. One was customized with the letters "O" and "U" on the two front teeth. The other set spelled out "BIG RED." He wore them until 1986 when the attention he got, in public, finally convinced him to stop. "I couldn't eat," he said. "Everyone wanted to look at my teeth."

All these things made Samara known, but his trademark was the "Big Red Rocket": a 1923 Ford Model T that he salvaged and rebuilt. The car was a tangible manifestation of his love for the university. The Model T was small and antique, and somehow looked both robust and fragile. The top half was painted white with the bottom half Sooner red. OU, in white, was on both the driver's side and passenger side doors. White stenciling on the front fender read, "BIG RED ROCKET." The top rear of the car featured more stenciling, in red, for three different messages: "YEA . . . BIG RED"; "BOOMER SOONER"; and (after the Wilkinson era) "NATIONAL RECORD 47 WINS IN A ROW." A wreath of artificial oranges was affixed to the Model T's grill, representing the promised land for Oklahoma football. An invite to the Orange Bowl, at the end of the season, meant that you had placed yourself in a position to win the national championship. In 1968, Samara's Model T became the first car in Oklahoma to feature a personalized license plate: "BIG RED." Modern amenities were added: air-conditioning, a TV set, and a cassette tape player. Twin loudspeakers were attached to either side of the windshield frame and blasted out "Boomer Sooner" and other

Oklahoma chants and songs. Samara liked sounds; the car had a ding-dong bell, a telephone bell, and a wolf whistle. There was an old-fashioned horn that made a sound like: "AH-OOH-GA!" Samara hauled behind the Rocket a small camper trailer—painted red and white and filled with tools—in case of breakdown on the road.

Despite its nickname, the car wasn't fast; its top speed was thirty-five miles per hour. Neither was the car easy to drive; Samara's daughter Sissy Tubb said it steered like a boat, and she whispered a prayer every time she put a foot on the brakes. All of this must have factored into Samara's modest vision for the Big Red Rocket, which made its first visit to a home football game in 1950. Driving from Oklahoma City to Norman was challenge enough, but two years later the Ruf Neks and cheerleaders persuaded Samara, initially reluctant, to drive to Dallas for OU–Texas. The long trip was also a defiant response to a recent magazine article that alleged that OU's dominant football team was funded illegally by the state's richest men. On that first trip, Samara and his brother drove slowly to Dallas with an impish sign on the Rocket: "Sponsored by Oklahoma's 700 millionaires."

So began a tradition that would continue across four decades and forty games total. Samara would leave home on Tuesday of game week; it took three days to get to Dallas. Special signs were draped over the car: "BURY TEXAS" and "BULL TO BURGER in 4 Quarters." Once Samara crossed the state line, Texans took care of him. In fact, he always got a police escort to the team hotel whenever he reached the Dallas city limits. But that didn't mean the citizens of the Lone Star State lacked a sense of humor. In 1954, Samara was passing through a small Texas town when the flashing lights of a highway patrol car told him to pull over. The state trooper asked Samara to step out of the vehicle before telling him that he was under arrest. Handcuffs were slapped on the man's wrists. Bewildered, Samara found himself riding in the back of a patrol car, but instead of jail the trooper drove him to a local restaurant where the owner served him a huge steak. It was a planned stunt. "We just wanted to show you we still do things in a big way down here in Texas," the trooper said.

Longhorn pranksters, understanding what Samara meant to the OU fan base, made him a target for symbolic action. Samara once said of

Longhorn fans—the "enemy of the south"—that they hated "the sight of me and the 'Big Red Rocket' because we show the spirit behind the OU football team." In 1958, feeling mischievous after a narrow 15–14 victory, Texas fans approached the Big Red Rocket holding a can of burnt orange paint. Samara's police escort stated the obvious: "Big Red, they're going to paint your car. Do you want us to take you on the police route?" Samara had taken the defeat hard; he was crying as the Texas fans got closer. "No, they've been good sports," he told the police officer. "Let 'em paint it."

Most of the car was orange as Samara drove home on Sunday. What happened next was a remarkable show of Sooner solidarity. A group from the OU Alumni Association met him once he'd crossed back into Oklahoma, and together they went to a paint and body shop in Ardmore. The group paid to have the "Big Red Rocket" restored.

Texas fans took things too far in 1967 when Samara returned from Dallas in an unhappy mood—again, Oklahoma was on the losing end of a close game—only to discover something that made his mood worse. Longhorn fans had branded his front lawn with "T-E-X-A-S." No one had ever targeted his house before. Samara was not amused. "This is pretty dirty," he said in *The Oklahoma Daily.*

The successful journey to Dallas inspired other trips. Samara was soon driving the Rocket to road games in the Big 8 conference: Nebraska, Iowa State, Colorado, Kansas, Kansas State, and Missouri. At every stop he met with civic clubs and organizations, which hosted him for dinners and asked him to speak. Samara was an ambassador for both OU and the state of Oklahoma, extolling the virtues of each. About his home state he would talk of its agriculture, lakes, and race horsing industry. Peanuts were a favorite topic. (I can hear Samara's gravelly, sincere voice as he tells civic leaders from various towns that Oklahoma ranked eighth in the country in peanut production.)

High-profile games held farther afield acted as a siren song to Samara. He piloted the Rocket to games at Notre Dame, Chicago, and Pittsburgh.

But it was his regular trips to the Orange Bowl in Miami that boggle the mind. Typically, he would leave Oklahoma City three weeks before the bowl game was played in the new year. He first made the 1,600-mile trip in 1954, with stops in several cities and towns along the way: Texarkana, Texas; Vicksburg and Meridian, Mississippi; Bainbridge, Georgia; Ocala and Moore Haven, Florida. The driving time amounted to 77.5 hours. As he trundled along, nowhere near the speed limit, with "Boomer Sooner" on repeat, one wonders if Samara, riding all alone, must have dwelt, at times, on the edge of sanity.

The service aspect of superfandom resonated with Samara. He had a standing offer to OU students, whom he called "the greatest people in the world." They were welcome to visit his home, where he had a souvenir room devoted to OU and the football team, any time they wanted. When Jim Mackenzie, the OU football coach for a single season in 1966, died suddenly from a heart attack (tragically, he was only thirty-seven years old), Samara played a role in the grieving process. Driven to a memorial service in downtown Oklahoma City, the Rocket was decorated with wreaths and black ribbons. The car's American flag, hanging from a pole on the Model T's rear, was lowered to half-mast. Mourners gathered around the Rocket as a chaplain celebrated the life of the late coach.

By the early seventies, the Rocket had racked up more than two hundred thousand miles in its travels. Similarly, Samara's body had endured a lot. He was fifty-six years old in February 1973 when he suffered a serious back injury that forced a period of convalescence. When *The Oklahoma Daily* sent a reporter to check on him, Samara said it would make his recovery swifter to hear from as many OU students as possible. At the suggestion that he might miss some Sooner football games in the fall, the man scoffed: "Come hell or high water, I'll be at the games next year. I'll go to the games if they have to drag me."

Middle age literally knocked him down again in October that year when he fell in the aisle of an airplane. Samara was on his way to visit a daughter living in Hawaii. This sequence of ill health kept him from driving the Rocket to Dallas for OU–Texas. He sat in the passenger seat, navigating, while someone else piloted the Model T.

The seventies were a difficult decade for the Samaras. At the end of it, in February 1979, a fire severely damaged the family home; the OU room, containing more than thirty years of OU memorabilia, was a total loss.

The room had been painted red and white, with three bulletin boards full of photographs of OU players dating back to 1948. There were shelves of OU mementoes, a comprehensive collection of OU football programs, and an autographed game ball from 1956 when the football team went undefeated and won a second consecutive national championship. A tape player in the room played "Boomer Sooner" and OU pep yells. "I could care less about the furniture in the house, it can be replaced," Samara told *The Oklahoma Daily.* "But it's all the things I received in my travels to all the OU games all over the country that can never be replaced. . . . I wake up some nights and just cry, I can't believe that it's all gone."

The Samaras were living in a motel with their house under repair when an astonishing thing happened, which eventually brought Cecil out of his depression. Sports fans from across the country began to call him and write letters. They offered sympathy, help, and even money. Then came the items to help rebuild his OU room. Fans, even from "hostile territory" like Nebraska and Texas, sent him plaques and helmets. "When you have friends like that it means more than all the money in the world," Samara said.

The eighties and early nineties found Samara older but still engaged as an OU superfan. His death, at the age of seventy-seven, was front-page news in *The Oklahoma Daily* in June 1994. The man had very specific instructions regarding his funeral, though he and his family amended them later. He wanted a red and white casket, draped with the American flag, the state of Oklahoma flag, and the OU flag. He wanted an atmosphere akin to that of an OU pep rally, with "Boomer Sooner" playing. Instead of having both arms at his side, in the coffin, he wanted his right elbow bent, with all his fingers curled except for his index finger: We're number one.

What actually transpired was more subdued. The mood wasn't festive. "America" was played instead of the "Star-Spangled Banner" along with the Christian hymn "When the Roll's Called Up Yonder, I'm Going to be There." Samara wore his red jacket with an OU tie and OU belt buckle. His red cowboy hat rested beside him in the coffin, which was not painted red and white. However, the three flags he wanted were there. His right arm stayed by his side. "Boomer Sooner" was played as the family left the church.

He left behind a big family: three daughters, two sons, seven grandchildren, and one great grandchild. Lucille, his wife of forty-eight years, preceded him in death in 1990.

He was remembered in the newspaper as an honorary member of the Fraternal Order of Police, Lambda Chi fraternity, and the OU Ruf Neks. Charity work was important to him, and for many years he raised money for Oklahoma's Children's Memorial Hospital.

His obituary in *The Oklahoman* read: "It can truly be said of Cecil that he was Sooner born, was Sooner bred, and now he is peacefully Sooner dead."

But the story doesn't end there. Despite its age and the challenge of maintaining it, the Big Red Rocket lived on. In the years after Samara's death, his daughter Sissy allowed the Rocket to be towed on a flatbed trailer to Dallas for OU–Texas, the Model T decorated with a wreath, flags, and ribbons with slogans like "Beat Texas" and "Bevo to Burger." She told *The Oklahoma Daily*, "The reason I'm doing it is that I know I'll have to face him again some day . . . I'd be in a heck of a lot of trouble if I didn't do it. It has to go to the game."

The Rocket continued to make appearances at home games too, driven and cared for by the Ruf Neks. Those Ruf Neks selected to watch over the car were called "Cecil Keepers."

Wear and tear eventually caught up with the Rocket. There wasn't money to repair it, and after 2010 the car was placed in storage at the university. There was talk of refurbishment, and in 2021 an Oklahoma City attorney, Gary James, spearheaded the cause. James was a varsity letterman for the Sooners in the early eighties and told *The Oklahoman*, "While I was growing up, Cecil Samara and the Big Red Rocket were synonymous with Oklahoma football. . . . When I played football at OU, Cecil was a big part of us. He stood behind the bench and drove us nuts with that megahorn of his."

Several parties were on board with resurrecting the Rocket: the Samara family, OU officials, and the athletic department. James was hoping to raise $200,000 for a new undercarriage and new engine for the car. Discussions took place about an endowment, which would pay for its future maintenance. A timeline was mentioned in *The Oklahoman* article; James hoped to unveil the renovated Rocket for the 2022 season.

But the 2022 and 2023 football seasons came and went with no sign of Samara's iconic Model T.

■ ■ ■

I go back and forth on what I think of superfans like Morris Tenenbaum and Cecil "Big Red" Samara. Though impressed by their commitment, I can't imagine putting myself out there like that. Being that visible. Subject to critics who shake their heads: "That person is acting like a fool." There's an ambivalence that people exhibit toward the superfan; I saw it in the research. Superfans are extremists, and people tend to be wary of extremists. On the one hand, they can charm and inspire. On the other, they can annoy the hell out of you. They can seem crazy, and we tend to avoid crazy, as if it's an infection that we can catch.

Seen from another perspective, more positive, OU's tradition of superfandom illustrates a miracle of integration; it says something profound about the culture at the University of Oklahoma. No one would ever accuse the duo I've described here as coming from privilege. They weren't winners in life's lottery. Tenenbaum was a Jewish immigrant from Europe. Samara grew up poor in the slums of Oklahoma City. At a crude level, you could classify these men as loners, oddballs, misfits, or hustlers. Nevertheless, Sooner Nation took them in as family. The men found a home in Norman. They felt connected to something larger than themselves. They lived and died as Sooners, having contributed in their own unique ways.

Older fans might remember Tenenbaum and Samara, but largely these two men have passed from the Sooner imagination. In the end, superfans lack the staying power of athletes and coaches. Accordingly, it's not likely that a superfan will ever get a statue on campus. All the same, people like Tenenbaum and Samara will always be around, singing the praises of OU and its teams, because of a trait that endures in humanity: eccentricity. Eccentrics take their fandom to an extreme; they can't help themselves. It's like they are guided and compelled by some invisible force. In recent years, a number of OU superfans have picked up where Tenenbaum and

Samara left off. Cameras put them on TV during games and on the video boards at Memorial Stadium. They're active on social media. Fans stand in line to get pictures with them. I got to know one of these characters, Mr. OU, and saw him in action on game day. His story appears in part 2 of this book.

Part II

■ ■ ■

GAME DAY

▪ 4 ▪

SERIOUS LEISURE, PART I

ON THE FIRST GAME DAY of the 2023 season, Jenn and I leave the house early to tailgate before the 11 A.M. kickoff. The Sooners' opponent is the Arkansas State Red Wolves (today, they will be more sacrificial lamb than wolf). We live a mile from campus, and so we're happy to walk the distance. We've applied our sunscreen and lip balm—it's expected to be a scorcher today, in the mid-nineties—but right now it's a pleasant seventy-five degrees.

It takes us ten minutes to reach the intersection of Classen and Boyd. Diagonally to our left is the Mont, a Norman staple where locals sit on the patio sipping on Sooner Swirls (a frozen margarita blended with sangria). Just beyond the Mont are train tracks that run north–south. As we approach, we pick up the pace; no one likes getting stuck behind a train.

The homemade signs (thirty bucks to park) multiply along Boyd, and the tailgates start to appear: pop-up canopy tents that form a line as we walk down the sidewalk. Tables, folding chairs, and TVs are set up beneath the tents; people are standing or sitting, and though it's barely past eight in the morning many have already cracked open a beer.

Past Jenkins, the Norman police have shut down Boyd. Orange and white traffic barricades and a large yellow bus from Norman Public

Schools, stretched across Boyd, keep traffic away, so fans can walk freely between campus and Campus Corner. I spot "the Beast" and point before saying to Jenn, "There it is. There's Mike."

The Beast is a cream-colored school bus owned by Mike Vickrey. For home football games, it's been parked on the sidewalk in front of Campus Corner Market for the past five years. Vickrey calls it "eye candy." The vehicle is around thirty feet long, and for half of that length it's a standard, albeit shortened, school bus. The curbside door has been removed; a floor to ceiling space allows for entry. Above the windows on one side and stretching along the roof are the words "OKLAHOMA SOONERS" in crimson paint. Between the words is the Beast's logo. Have you seen the infamous image of Bigfoot supposedly trudging through a forest? It's taken from film footage shot by Roger Patterson and Robert Gimlin in 1967 in northern California: proof that Bigfoot exists. Vickrey's logo is a replica of this image: In black silhouette, the Beast strides forward, swinging its thick arms. Its calves are enormous. On its chest, in white, are the letters OU, linked diagonally.

Where the bus ends, the fun begins. Essentially, the bus was chopped off during its conversion, and an adult "play area" extends down the other half of the vehicle. Crimson guardrails mark the perimeter, and the floor is covered in green artificial grass. Park-style benches, painted in crimson and cream, give tailgaters a place to sit and rest their beverages. There's room for maybe eight on the benches, though no one is sitting now. That will come later.

Vickrey's back is turned to us. He's talking to someone. I tap him on the shoulder, and he turns around. "Hey!" he says. We shake hands.

Vickrey, fifty-nine, is thick and sturdy, sort of like the Beast. He's five-foot-ten and bald with a salt-and-pepper goatee. Camouflage sunglasses (black, white, and gray) cover his eyes. He's wearing jeans and a white T-shirt; over the heart is the Beast logo superimposed on the state of Oklahoma. Similar T-shirts are for sale; a couple of them hang from the guardrails for passersby to see.

Vickrey grew up in Norman a Sooners fan. He matriculated to OU in 1983, signed up for chemical engineering, and joined a fraternity, Delta

Chi. He excelled at the extracurriculars, so to speak, while learning that chemical engineering was no joke. He switched majors to architecture, which was difficult too, and ultimately dropped out of school. He joined the army where he spent the next thirty-one years, with tours in Afghanistan and Iraq during the war on terror. He retired a lieutenant colonel in 2018.

He's been married to his wife, Shannon, for thirty years and they have three sons.

Though he dropped out, Vickrey wasn't done as a student at OU. He went back and graduated with a liberal arts degree.

A couple of anecdotes say a lot about his personality and values. More than once, he's followed a would-be thief out of Home Depot (as a general contractor by trade, he visits the Depot often), taking part in the apprehension of said thief. Secondly, after an OU football game, he tried to break up a bar fight between fraternity guys—he was "helping out the bar staff"—and became a pugilist himself, suffering scrapes and bruises.

Vickrey isn't afraid to get involved when the circumstances call for it.

The Beast's history is as winding as Vickrey's. Originally, the bus transported students in the Moore Public Schools system. More than twenty years ago, it was decommissioned and purchased by a "guy" who "chopped off" the back of the bus, according to Vickrey. But then it sat, unused until 2018 when he bought it and began his rebuild. He put in a new engine and refurbished the whole thing.

The Beast made its debut in 2019, parking in front of King Kopy on Boyd. Then Vickrey sought a better spot. He knew the owners of Campus Corner Market, and they worked out a deal. He pays two hundred dollars per home game to park in front of the market/gas station. The market gets the Beast: a curiosity to fans who stop, chat, and take photos before heading to the market for booze and snacks.

"How can we help with setting up?" I ask.

"We'll put the cover on in just a second," Vickrey says. "You can help with that."

To protect tailgaters on the Beast from the sun, Vickrey has engineered slots along the guard railing that allow for the insertion of a canopy tent. For now, he hands out four L-shaped brackets to a few people, including

Jenn and me, to fasten the tent to the Beast. Jenn and I go to our spot and secure our bracket with two bolts; I manually turn the nuts until everything is tight.

We walk back around to the left side of the bus to appreciate the decor. Beneath the windows, along a side panel, Vickrey has created a wall of Sooner accomplishments. In crimson stenciled lettering are the names of the seven Heisman Trophy winners from OU: Billy Vessels (1952), Steve Owens (1969), Billy Sims (1978), Jason White (2003), Sam Bradford (2008), Baker Mayfield (2017), and Kyler Murray (2018). Next to this are the seven "OU NATIONAL CHAMPIONSHIPS," with the year each was won and the name of the respective coach. Bud Wilkinson and Barry Switzer have three titles apiece; Bob Stoops has one. To the right of this are the Big 12 conference titles won by the football program. The years are listed. I count them; OU has won the Big 12 fourteen times.

"I'm going to put the softball and gymnastics championships up too," Vickrey says.

There's more on the side of the bus. In a nod to the "horns down" sign used by Sooner fans to indicate their strong dislike for the Texas Longhorns, Vickrey has fixed to the Beast an upside-down sticker of Oklahoma State's mascot Pistol Pete. Placed in such a position, Pete looks especially disgruntled. Additionally, toward the dog-nose front of the bus are decals featuring the logo, including OU's, of half of the fourteen teams in the Big 12: OSU, Texas Tech, Kansas State, Kansas, and Baylor. Like Pistol Pete, Texas's logo, the head of a longhorn steer, is turned upside down in a gesture of disrespect.

I wonder about the missing decals of the other seven schools, but before I can ask, one of Vickrey's friends, a fraternity brother, returns from a trip to the bathroom. As a team of five, we set up the canopy tent. After pulling the tent open, Vickrey tells us to each grab a metal leg, which we extend before walking the tent toward the Beast. Jenn climbs up the portable stairs, leading her tent leg to its respective bracket. I'm vertically challenged and hand my leg over the railing to Erika who's sitting on a bench aboard the Beast. Nathan, the fraternity brother, is tall enough to lift and slide his leg into the bracket. Pins secure the legs to their slots on the guardrail. The party den of the Beast is now protected from the sun.

I climb aboard and introduce myself to Nathan McKibbon. Erika is his wife. Nathan, thirty-six, is bearded with black hair that curves down and past his ears. He's wearing a crimson, short-sleeved, button-up shirt with the OU logo on the left breast. Erika is a brunette and not wearing school colors. Such things, on game day, one notices.

It turns out that Erika did not attend OU; she's an alum of the University of Denver. The couple lives in Denver, Colorado, where just ten weeks ago Erika gave birth to their first child, a daughter named Emily Grace.

Unlike his wife, Nathan is Sooner born and bred. He grew up in nearby Moore; several family members went to OU: his father, brother, aunt, and uncle. After graduating from OU in 2009, he studied law at Oklahoma City University. He's an attorney now; Erika's a vice-president at a software company. They come to Norman for as many football games as possible each season.

Erika passes over her iPhone so I can see a picture of their daughter. Emily Grace is wearing an OU outfit of crimson and cream and looks happy to be a Sooner.

Nathan says that they brought her home from the hospital in an OU onesie; it's apparently a tradition in their family. Nathan wore a similar onesie on his own trip from the hospital in 1987. I ask if Emily Grace will go to college here in Norman. There's no hesitation on Nathan's part; of course she will. If there's a commandment in their household it might be: Thou shalt attend OU.

Emily Grace is with Grandma this weekend. Nathan tried to convince his mother to put on the game today in the background, so Emily Grace could follow along, to no avail. Nathan shakes his head and jokingly says he was "kind of pissed at mom for that."

"What do you love about being a fan of the Sooners?" I ask.

"The biggest thing is tradition," Nathan says. "Even in Colorado, I'll wear an OU shirt . . . I get goosebumps thinking about it."

He shows me his arm.

"At the grocery store someone will say 'Boomer,' and it makes you feel good. It's nostalgia. Even if you see a UT fan, you feel like you have something in common. We're all connected by colors and school. It's like seeing an American flag. You don't know someone but you're automatically connected."

■ ■ ■

Game days at the University of Oklahoma, in the first half of the twentieth century, looked very different from today. In 1939, alcohol was not a welcome part of the experience, despite the end of Prohibition six years earlier. *The Oklahoma Daily* warned football fans about the new drunk tank created inside of Memorial Stadium. In an article ironically titled "You May Drink Soda Pop Saturday," readers learn that they will be monitored closely by Norman police inside the stadium—more than one officer for every thousand fans. If a fan is judged to be "inebriated beyond self control" that person will be summarily marched to "a detention room beneath the wing of the stadium in which he was found." Once the offending fan is deemed sober, he can leave. OU president William Bennett Bizzell, a popcorn and soda enthusiast, sounded every bit the stern patriarch when he told the student newspaper, "I have been very much gratified with the fine conduct of those who have attended our football events in recent years. . . . There was very little drinking at any of our games last fall and I anticipate that the same situation will prevail this year."

As someone who understands both the human affinity for alcohol and the human capacity for deception, I wonder if I can trust Bizzell's assertion that Sooner football games were free of drinking.

In the early days of Bennie Owen's coaching tenure, Sooner fans made their presence felt in an unusual way. On a glacial afternoon in November 1908, Texas was in Norman (it would be the last time the Red River Rivalry was played in Oklahoma), and nightfall was threatening to suspend a game dominated by Owen's men. To ensure the game's completion, fans hurried back to their cars and positioned them around Boyd Field, so that their headlights illuminated the action. After the final whistle, which confirmed the Sooners' 50–0 victory, the student body gathered at the library and then, despite the cold, snake-danced down University Boulevard to Main Street where everyone celebrated around a huge bonfire.

It's normal for fashionistas to dress up on game days in the twenty-first century, but in 1941 male and female students alike were chided in *The Oklahoma Daily* for such attempts at "sartorial elegance." Student government consisted of a committee of Undergraduate Life, out of which formed a subcommittee of radicals unhappy that students were "dolling up" for football games. "It's got so the crowd of people going out to the stadium on Saturdays looks like a parade staged by Esquire, or Madmoiselle [*sic*]," said one disgruntled member of this rebel subcommittee, which voted close to unanimously on a resolution declaring that only "sports clothes should be worn for sports events." Students will be more likely to "join in the pep" if they are comfortably dressed, they argued. A football game, they claimed, is the wrong venue for a fashion show. The lone dissenter on the subcommittee, which admitted that it was powerless to enforce its preferences, couldn't get past the fashion crime such a resolution would force people to commit. She told *The Oklahoma Daily* that "a mum [decorative chrysanthemum] won't look very well on a sports sweater."

Food is an essential part of game day. In 1961, an ad in *The Oklahoma Daily* invited fans to the student union dining hall: "ON GAME DAY DINE LEISURELY AT THE OKLAHOMA MEMORIAL UNION." In 1956, alumni were invited to a buffet luncheon to be held in the Union ballroom before every home game of the season. Six hundred alumni were expected for the opener versus North Carolina. From 1931 to 1988, the Town Tavern at the corner of Boyd and Asp (Louie's Grill and Bar is the current tenant) operated as a greasy spoon attractive to Sooner fans. In his book *An Autumn Remembered* about the undefeated Sooner team of 1956, Gary T. King calls the Town Tavern a Norman landmark whose specialties included "chicken-fried steak, onion burgers, and pan-fried steaks, along with frosty schooners of beer." The decor was memorable; every Sooner football score from 1947 to the present day was painted on the wall in "bold lettering" and "visible from any table." Outside the Tavern before kickoff, ticket scalpers loitered, calling out to potential customers.

Traffic and parking have long proved a headache for the thousands of fans pouring into Norman on game day. In September 1950, local officials devised a traffic plan—outlined in *The Oklahoma Daily* down to the finest detail, including officer names and the streets patrolled—in which Norman police handled the flow of traffic into the city, with campus police taking over once commuters reached campus-adjacent streets. Police officials urged locals to walk to the game: "You might get a little tired when you get there but at least you will still have four good fenders left on your car when you get home."

Dads' Day started as an OU tradition in 1925. Visiting fathers in October 1961 were provided an itinerary that reads like the very definition of "tame." I present it here verbatim:

> 8 A.M.–noon. Registration in organized houses and at Holmberg hall.
> 9:15–10 A.M. Film on 1960 OU–Missouri football game at Holmberg hall.
> 10–11:30 A.M. Business meeting of Dads' Day association at Holmberg hall. Presentation of awards to outstanding senior man and woman and to outstanding senior (man or woman) in each college.
> 12:45–1:45 P.M. Shadowbox fashion club open house in Home Economics lounge.
> 2 P.M. OU–Kansas football at Owen stadium.
> 8 P.M. Engineers variety show at Holmberg hall.

With all due respect to engineers, the imagination struggles to conceive of the entertainments that might be devised by those in the trade. Would such a variety show appeal to dads of the era? Or was it more likely that they wandered across Boyd, to the Town Tavern, for a cold beer instead?

Speaking of Dads' Day, a message of appreciation was aimed at the fathers inside of Memorial Stadium in October 1955. Members of the Pep Council, embedded in the stands, spelled out "Hi Dads" using stunt cards at halftime. They also spelled out "CU" to honor the visiting Colorado Buffalos and "OU" in two different ways: "first in red on a white background and then reversed to appear in white on a red background."

Twenty years later, the card section was still around but barely operational due mostly to the conscious rebellion of the student body. Young Sooners at the last home game of the 1974 season earned the ire of *The Oklahoma Daily* when they tossed their cards like frisbees around the stands. A young boy was injured by one of the flying cards, which were made of heavy cardboard; the boy went home with a four-inch cut below the eye. "Why must O.U. students annually repeat foolish, reckless habits?" asked the editor of the student newspaper. Such were the problems—misbehavior and lack of coordination—that the card section was eliminated for the 1976 season only for it to return, with the same woeful result, the following year. The myriad problems included "absenteeism, students not sitting in the proper places, extra students trying to 'squeeze in' and with students not in unison displaying the stunts."

When the Sooners left Norman to play, fans who did not travel with the team found a way to follow the game. Before radio, in 1912, hundreds of Sooner fans would gather outside of Barbour's Drug Store on Main Street to hear a play-by-play report. Western Union supplied the action, via telegraph, which was then relayed to the crowd by a man holding a megaphone. *The Norman Transcript* hosted its own events in 1933, aided similarly by Western Union's technology. A full-page ad, with drawings of football players in action poses, appeared in a November issue of *The Oklahoma Daily*. The headline read: "*Students! Townspeople! Sooner Fans Hear the* O.U.-MISSOURI FOOTBALL GAME Play-by-Play Over Leased Western Union Wire From the Field at Columbia."

The "Football Party" in front of the newspaper's building was sponsored by local businesses and featured "sports chats" with a sportswriter as well as "musical entertainment."

▪ ▪ ▪

We bid adieu to Vickrey and the Beast before crossing over Boyd to campus where we walk between Carson Engineering Center and Devon Energy Hall. It's gotten hotter, and I've started to sweat. We walk past Gallogly Hall and take a left on Felgar Street then a right on Jenkins where the party atmosphere blooms in front of us. To our left, the canopy tents proliferate. Tailgaters have out their tables of food and drink; a TV shows the panel of pundits from ESPN's *College GameDay*. An inflatable Sooner, decked out in a football uniform, stands guard at the edge of the grass, a look of intensity on his face. To our left, Brooks Street runs into Jenkins. I look down Brooks, closed to traffic, and see cornhole boards, with OU logos on them, ready for play.

The stream of people flows toward the stadium. The first statue I see is of three African American players, standing side by side and looking stoic, helmets held at their side. The players are the Selmon brothers from

Eufaula, Oklahoma (Lee Roy, Lucious, and Dewey), who all played on the defensive line for Barry Switzer in the 1970s. OU won two national championships as they terrorized opposing offenses. All three players earned All-American status and moved onto pro football.

Past the Selmon brothers, the Party at the Palace is taking place on the lawn outside the northeast corner of the stadium. There's a bounce house for kids striped red, yellow, green, and blue. A giant inflatable sneaker, maroon and white, plays host to a couple of basketball hoops. A miniature Owen Field with yellow field goal posts and the OU logo, painted in maroon, allows kids to impersonate their gridiron heroes.

We keep walking. Heisman Park begins: OU's seven Heisman winners in a line along the sidewalk, immortalized in bronze, heroic in their respective poses. Running back Billy Sims evades a tackle with the football tucked safely against his body. A composed Sam Bradford gazes into the distance, about to throw a dime to his wide receiver downfield.

Between the Heisman statues of Steve Owens and Billy Vessels, in a roped-off area on the grass, a dozen members of the Pride of Oklahoma perform on xylophones, the mallets producing a crisp, tranquil sound.

The stadium is on our right. It goes by many names: Owen Field, Oklahoma Memorial Stadium (after OU students and faculty who died in World War I), the Palace on the Prairie, Gaylord Family—Oklahoma Memorial Stadium (the Gaylords, a prominent Oklahoma City family, have contributed tens of millions to the university). Since 1923, the stadium has been continuously updated and expanded. The original stands, on the west side of the field, held sixteen thousand. Now the stadium holds more than eighty thousand. The playing surface was changed from grass to astroturf in 1970, with a return to natural grass in 1994.

One of the updates, as part of an extensive renovation project in 2001, gave Owen Field a facelift, bringing the campus's signature red brick to the stadium façade. As I look to my right at the east side of the stadium, I see four columns of red brick and limestone. Between the inner columns are four stories of dark windows. The whole edifice looks geometric, solid.

Gate eleven has a short line, and we make it through security quickly and scan our tickets in a machine as event staff stand nearby. Then we're inside and on the concourse amid the throng of fans. Vendors like Rib Crib and Taco Mayo have lines. Eventually we find the sign for section thirty-four and the ramp that leads to stadium seating. We join the patient line of fans climbing toward the section entrance.

I don't know if the stadium was designed with this corny metaphor in mind, but it feels like we're being led to the light. It's the incline of the ramp and the sunlight pouring through the mouth of the section entrance. What's more, there's a payoff. The section entrance is like a portal; the sight, once you're through, is awe-inspiring: a vast sea of people in crimson and white and a rich field of manicured grass. Jenn is a sculptor and graduate student in art at OU. This is her first college football game. Later, she'll tell me that the whole spectacle reminded her of the Roman Colosseum.

By the time we get to our seats it's already 7–0 in OU's favor. Arkansas State is on offense, a third down, and fans all around us have lifted an arm, their hands undulating in a gesture—the thumb and index fingers in an "O" and the other three fingers extended—while they utter "Ohhhhhhh . . ." It's designed to distract and intimidate the opposing offense on this third and vital down.

Arkansas State's offense fails to convert. Their punter jogs onto the field. His punt is a good one and forces Gavin Freeman, our sophomore wide receiver, to back up behind the twenty-yard line to catch it, but in a flash he's found a seam down the middle of the field and side-stepped a diving tackler. Freeman sprints, looking for blocks and space through which to run. He finds it down the Sooner sideline. No one in a white jersey can catch him; he waltzes into the end zone accompanied by a teammate. Other teammates join the celebration. Fans are on their feet jumping up and down; high-fives circulate among our neighbors. Fireworks shoot into the sky over the south end zone: twin ribbons of white that turn crimson at the tip, with a booming gunshot to go along; the RUF/NEKS have made themselves heard. After the extra point is kicked successfully, the Sooner Schooner—the iconic Conestoga wagon pulled by the ponies "Boomer" and "Sooner" and driven by a RUF/NEK and Lil' Sis—races onto the grass to complete an arc on the north side of the field. Behind the Schooner, running as fast as he can, is a RUF/NEK carrying an enormous American flag. He pauses in front of the west stand and uses all his strength to wave the flag from side to side. Then he follows the wagon, which has already disappeared down a tunnel.

By the middle of the second quarter, the score is 42–0. The ponies powering the Schooner probably have tired legs by now. Jenn directs my attention to the north end video board where a giant photo of my former student is on display. Cailey England, captain of the women's soccer team, graced my classroom this past spring. We've been going to her games this season. On the video board, England, a redhead, is smiling, with her arms crossed against her Oklahoma jersey. The advertisement tells fans about the soccer team's next home game on September 7 against Murray State. Jenn and I will be there. I've noticed the efforts made by OU Athletics to draw fans to the less popular sports on campus. On game days, signs are put up near Campus Corner for soccer and volleyball. The video boards at Memorial Stadium play clips from other sports to entice fans.

The heat today has been as smothering as the Sooner defense, the sun bathing everyone in the stadium. At halftime, Jenn and I leave our seats to get water and a few moments of shade. The concourse is full of people. We hit the bathroom first. Upon leaving the men's, I watch a college-age guy with his arm around the shoulder of a gray-haired man, helping the latter walk. The man looks like he's succumbed to the heat.

Jenn and I buy a bottle of water and hang out in the concourse. We people-watch. Cowboy boots are ubiquitously worn by the ladies. The men are in ball caps and shorts. The older you are the more likely your shirt is tucked into your shorts.

There's been a half-time exodus. The stadium is no longer full. The mood in the third quarter is light, with the Red Wolves posing zero threat. In fact, long ago we began to feel pity for them. In the second quarter, a fan was positively zen after a facemask penalty on our defense. "Oh yeah, we'll give 'em that," he said. "Poor guy."

We're not there to see the final two touchdowns; Jenn and I leave after the third quarter, seeking shade, food, and refreshment.

The day ends at our friends' house. Steve and Shalaine, who were at the game as well, have invited us over to lounge by the pool. It's past four o'clock when we turn onto their street, southwest of campus, and the first thing we notice is the Beast. Vickrey's bus is parked in front of their house. Vickrey and Shalaine are related through marriage.

We find Steve on his living room couch watching college football.

"Mike's out there swimming in his underwear," Steve says.

Jenn and I laugh.

"Why didn't you let him borrow some trunks?" I ask.

Steve looks at me like I'm crazy. "I'm not letting him wear my trunks."

In the backyard, Vickrey is topless and wearing his camo sunglasses, his burly stomach half-submerged in the shallow end of the pool. A koozie keeps his can of beer cold.

"This one here was sleeping when I came over," Vickrey says, pointing at Shalaine who, in her bathing suit, is sitting in a chair at the edge of the pool. "They said come over and swim, and when I do she's sleeping."

"I was taking a nap," Shalaine says. "I was tired."

Then she adds, in an unfazed tone, "Mike's swimming in his underwear."

"We heard," Jenn says.

We spend the next couple hours talking and drinking. Jenn and I are sitting in plastic chairs a few feet off the lip of the pool when Vickrey gets out of the water and quickly cinches a beach towel around his waist. He walks around the curve of the pool and stands in front of us. He starts talking about the Beast; so far, he's spent seventy thousand dollars on the bus.

"It's my way of socializing," he says. "It's how I get to connect with people."

Then he walks away, down the side of the pool. Draped in a brightly colored towel, which reminds me of a sarong, he's a tan and brawny dude, just shy of sixty years old, but looks oddly chic.

▪ 5 ▪

SERIOUS LEISURE, PART II

A STUDENT COLUMN from *The Oklahoma Daily* in September 1992 speaks to traits, regarding the modern tailgate experience, that we recognize today. With the University of Southern California's football team visiting Norman for a nationally televised clash with an "absurd" early kickoff at 11 A.M., the writer Jeremy Plonk tells his readers to embrace the suck. It's not like we haven't been in this position before. In fact, the previous Saturday Plonk himself woke up early for the home opener with Arkansas State, which the Sooners won 61–0. On that morning, the writer watched the "parade of OU fans down Lincoln Avenue . . . as [he] enjoyed a hearty breakfast (You know, cold pizza and beer)." He didn't offer a prediction for the game against the Trojans—for the record, the Sooners lost 20–10—but he did anticipate that Sooner fans would excel as tailgaters: They would party all night Friday and wake up early "to do more partying Saturday before 9 A.M. than most people will do all day." He also suspected that O'Connell's, the popular bar and grill that moved from where Headington Hall is now located to Campus Corner in 2008, would be "rocking this week as the sun comes up and the roosters warm up their vocal chords [*sic*]."

Where did tailgating come from? Some scholars see its origins in the public feasts and entertainments of the Greeks and Romans. On the American front, many claim that the first tailgate was held at the initial clash of the Civil War, the First Battle of Bull Run, where the expectation, among Union sympathizers, was a quick rout of the rebels. Civilians from Washington, mostly men and including US senators and reporters, made the seven-hour trip on horse or by carriage to Centreville, Virginia, a few miles north of the battle in Manassas, some carrying food. Once they arrived, the majority couldn't be described as observers of the fighting. From their vantage point, they saw very little; instead, they dined and waited for news.

Princeton and Rutgers played the first college football game in 1869, with a hundred spectators gathered around the field to watch. Earlier, Princeton students had traveled by train with the football team, according to Princeton football's website. The Rutgers team met the visitors at New Brunswick station, and while the players went off to set the rules of the game, the student supporters "strolled around town and lunched."

The term "tailgate" was likely coined around the same time as Princeton versus Rutgers, with the Oxford English Dictionary citing an article from the *Oregon State Journal* in 1868: "The whole charge . . . [passed] through the tailgate of the wagon." Loran Smith, an athletics historian at the University of Georgia, argues that the modern conception of tailgating likely began in the 1920s with the convergence of several factors. For a couple decades, college football had been growing exponentially as a spectator sport. What's more, mass production of the Ford Model T began in 1913; Ford pickup trucks became widely available in 1925. Fans started traveling to games. After parking their vehicle, they dropped the tailgate and laid down an array of food and drink.

By 1970, tailgating had spread across the country and even north to Canada. Toronto's *Globe & Mail* newspaper notes, with a touch of puzzlement, the growth of the practice: "The game has become secondary to a potlatch ceremony called tailgate picknicking. . . . This . . . requires that the host participants outdo their neighbours in the quality and variety of food and drink and the elegance of serving accessories." Ten years later, Lisa Birnbach in *The Official Preppy Handbook* alleged that the tailgate was an essential ingredient to the game-day experience, ensuring that the modern fan was totally blitzed come kickoff: "Tailgate picnics, whiskey sours in the stadium, and the general complexity of the sport guarantee that nobody knows what is going on." Bizzell, OU's erstwhile teetotal president, would not have approved.

The next few decades would see tailgating grow into a "social movement." *The Ultimate Tailgater's Handbook* provides the modern tailgater with all kinds of practical advice. You can read about tailgating gear (charcoal versus gas grill; a portable generator, a must for the serious enthusiast; a first-aid kit, a responsible purchase); tailgater attire (the "loyal" female fan accessorizes with earrings and bracelets featuring her team's colors and/or logo); health and wellness (in hot weather "avoid eating heavy meals," which will "add heat to your body"; rather, "eat light foods and eat smaller portions more often"); tailgate setups ("basic" versus "intermediate" versus "serious"); and tailgating etiquette ("good sports" don't wear shirts with foul language, know the difference between "good-natured ribbing and obnoxious behavior," and "apologize in a nice manner after knocking over a tableful of food with an incomplete pass or a Frisbee"). For those struggling with what to bring to a tailgate, the handbook offers an abundance of recipes for food and drink (Joe's Jambalaya or green goddess dip, an apple martini or Frozen Gladiator).

Scholars have studied the tailgate as a social phenomenon. Tonya Williams Bradford and John F. Sherry Jr., from the University of California at Irvine and Notre Dame respectively, view the football tailgate as a means of transporting a "minimalist" version of one's home, minus the walls, to a public space on campus. A tailgate might include a kitchen, dining room, living room, bar set up, and even a patio. On site, tailgaters engage in most of the behaviors of domestic life. For Bradford and Sherry, the tailgate is a party, a site of "disinhibition and excess" for the participant who spends all week working, but also an opportunity for communal bonding in a modern society that isolates people instead of bringing them together. The weekend tailgate satisfies, to some extent, the need for belonging; it's a place of "reunion and homecoming, and thus a return to the extraordinary."

■ ■ ■

On game days in the fall, you can see John Hurd's tailgate once you leave Campus Corner, crossing over Boyd and using the sidewalk that leads to the entrance of Carpenter Hall. The tailgate is on the expanse of lawn between Parrington Oval and Asp. The night before the game, he claims the area with metal stakes and perimeter tape. Most tailgate spaces on campus are first-come, first-serve, while others can be reserved for a price. There are other tailgates around Hurd's, but his stands out. Looking at it from a distance, I find the inflatable tent strangely evocative. One second it reminds me of an old-school leather football helmet. Then it's just a white tent, with a dome shape to it. The tent has four sides and four openings, shaped like arches. There's a huge red OU on the front side facing Boyd.

Once you're inside the tent, it's like a living room, with three rows of red collapsible chairs on a red OU floor tarp. Given the dome shape of the tent, the space feels cavernous. Hurd informs me that the tent is thirty-three feet tall. Tailgaters stand in groups talking. A few lounge in chairs with a cold beverage, facing two stacked twenty-inch TVs, which are attached to a metal rig. The rig is a utility cart with wheels, with metal railing add-ons, which John engineered. By training and trade, he's an engineer (OU class of 1995). There are two different football games playing on the TVs, beneath which, on the cart's shelf, are two DIRECTV receivers, which connect to a satellite dish that sits on a converted red wagon just outside the tent. The satellite dish has been painted red. Superimposed on the red is a white OU logo.

To the right of the TVs is another converted cart, which hosts two 16,000-watt speakers. You don't appreciate the sound system until Hurd decides to play "Boomer Sooner" through it. He does this when OU scores and also, it seems, at random before the game, to get everyone riled up.

There are white foldout tables at the edges of the tent on which various foods and dishes, brought by attendees, are laid out. Occasionally, Hurd buys a few pizzas from nearby New York Pizza & Pasta, and sends a tailgater, equipped with a red wagon, to go and pick them up.

There's a large drum fan that circulates air and is popular during the hot afternoons. A converted generator powers the whole assembly.

But the crown jewel of Hurd's tailgate is the device he created to dispense beer from a keg. It seems to me, a mechanical doofus, an engineering marvel. He got the idea from Pinterest, of all places: in that version, a NASCAR racing helmet was somehow the conduit for beer.

The foundation of Hurd's version is a Sooner red mobility scooter, emblazoned with OU stickers, that makes the whole contraption somewhat easy to move. The whole device looks like something cooked up in a robotics laboratory. Extending from the base of the scooter is a long metal stem to which a metal platform is affixed, with holes to allow for the drainage of stray beer. An OU football helmet sits on the platform and features autographs of Sooner legends Barry Switzer, the Boz, and Bob Stoops. I watched Cale Gundy, who quarterbacked the Sooners in the seventies and then coached in different capacities, add his signature to the helmet before the Southern Methodist University game. John purchased the helmet at an OU Athletics auction for a couple hundred bucks. A metal carbon dioxide tank applies the pressure to move beer from the keg to a thermal insulated container beneath the helmet, which houses two hundred feet of stainless steel tubing, tightly wound in a circle, through which the beer travels. A red igloo barrel is secured to the stem with a metal hoop; the barrel is full of ice, which cools the water that gets pumped through the system and ultimately cools the beer to thirty-two degrees Fahrenheit. A special plastic cup is needed; a regular red Solo cup won't do. This cup has a magnetically sealed cap on the bottom, which allows for the passage of beer. The metal platform has a control panel where you can switch the machine on or off, select a cup size, and adjust the amount of beer dispensed. A light flashes if you've got an empty keg. Beneath the control panel, pasted to the front of the metal platform, is a playful but serious message for any tailgater who wishes to drink keg beer. It's serious because it costs money to buy the beer, and if you want to partake you should contribute financially. It's playful because it alludes to Coach Bud Wilkinson who famously placed a sign over the dressing room door at Memorial Stadium that read: "Play like a Champion Today." Hurd's version, which stretches across a strip of pigskin leather, reads, "PAY LIKE A CHAMPION TODAY." Clipped beneath the message, with a zip tie, is a

QR code encased in plastic that takes you to Hurd's Cash App account. Alternatively, for those with cash, there's a red donation box underneath the two TVs.

A plastic garbage can (with an OU logo on it, of course) sits next to the dispenser holding the keg.

Most of the tailgaters are Hurd's friends. Some have been coming for years. Others have tagged along with a regular attendee and are meeting Hurd for the first time. Still others are complete strangers—Sooner fans or visiting fans—who drop in to say hi, attracted by the whole setup, such is the friendly nature of tailgate culture. One of my many enjoyments during the 2023 season was watching newcomers experience the Sooner beer helmet for the first time. Their eyes would light up as if they were witnessing the most amazing magic trick. One second their plastic cup was empty, sitting atop an OU football helmet. The next, it was full of beer.

Hurd is a husky man in his late forties with short blond hair that gets spiky with sweat on game days. The back of one of the T-shirts he wears on Saturdays says: "We tailgate harder than your team plays." Growing up, he was a fan of Sooner football but didn't tailgate as a student in the nineties. The success of the Stoops era, after a period of struggle for the team, inspired him to start his tailgate in 2005. The setup was modest. His Chevy Tahoe transported a TV and a TV stand. After that first season, he asked himself, "What's going to be the new thing for the next year?" The answer: a trailer and grill. The tailgate kept evolving, with additions to make the tailgate bigger and better. "I try not to do anything half-ass," he says to me before the Iowa State game. "It's probably a little insane."

The set up and tear down, after so many years, is nearly an exact science. It takes an hour to do both.

"I bitch about it sometimes, but when you're sitting here with people, that makes it worth it," Hurd adds.

He sees the tailgate as "home base" for friends and families. After the weekend, he loves seeing the pictures that people post of his tailgate to social media.

Over the years, he's noticed an ebb and flow to tailgate attendance. It's not as "packed" as it used to be, and this season has a distinct feel to it. Hurd uses the word "anticlimactic" and thinks it has to do with OU's imminent move to the SEC: the signature conference in college football.

"There's a lot of looking forward to next season," he says.

The university is on the same wavelength. After shutting down Lindsey Street to tailgating in 2017, the administration opened it up again for the 2023 season and beyond. The goal, according to President Joseph Harroz Jr., is to excel in the tailgating arena as well as on the football field. He told *OU Daily*: "It's really a step on the way to our move to the SEC. . . . But the second step is going to be, as we go through this year, we're further studying what schools in the SEC do and analyzing the assets that we have to make sure that as we go into the SEC, as we go into not this football season, but the next football season, that what we have is hopefully the best in the SEC."

That's a tall order, given the festivities at Ole Miss's The Grove and LSU's Parade Grounds.

Hurd will be around for it, doing his part. He sees himself hosting his tailgate for another five to ten years.

Away from his tailgate, in his regular life, he is a full-time engineer with two daughters, one of whom attends OU. She's a sophomore majoring in biochemistry and often at the Hurd tailgate.

It's not hyperbole to say that Hurd is a talented guy armed with skills and interests. This season he started making custom "Oklahoma Sooners" straps for women's purses and bags. I've seen him deliver these custom straps, made from leather, to several women, and the reaction is always the same: instant love for the accessory.

More impressive is the charity work he does. Hurd used to own and operate a company that drilled wells for both water and ground source heat pumps. In 2005, he started learning about the need for clean water around the world. "I made a promise to myself that I was going to take a water well trip through an organization," he said, "and about a year later myself, along with thirteen or so fellow church members, went to El Salvador and put in our first well. We decided to go back the next year and the only openings were in Guatemala. I loved it, and we have been going back ever since."

Over the years, Hurd and his friends, in conjunction with a nonprofit called Asocaviva, have built close to forty wells, which should supply water to those communities for the next hundred years. The wells serve schools, churches, and medical clinics. What's more, Hurd trains locals so that they can do the drilling themselves; he donates the drill bits and other equipment required to do the work.

"What it means for these communities," Hurd says, "is that when we put a well in they don't have to buy water any more. Not only do we give them water, but we essentially give them half their wages back, as that is about what it costs to buy clean water."

■ ■ ■

In the early 2000s, a team of researchers from the University of Florida concluded that tailgaters were engaged in "serious leisure." The term comes from sociologist Robert A. Stebbins who used it to describe extreme hobbyists. He defined "casual leisure" as short-lived, passive, and pleasurable activity "requiring little or no special training to enjoy it." Riding a rollercoaster or watching TV is casual leisure. Its opposite requires the participant to take an active role; commitment is a key feature. Serious leisure is "the systematic pursuit of an amateur, hobbyist, or volunteer activity that is sufficiently substantial and interesting for the participant to find a career there in the acquisition and expression of its special skills and knowledge." Though Stebbins rendered no verdict on tailgaters, the researchers studying Florida Gator fans decided that these fans were very serious about their leisure. In plainer language than Stebbins, they summarize the commitment of Gator fans as well as the implications of their pastime. In so doing, the researchers describe tailgating football fans across the country:

> For fans of the University of Florida football team, being a Gator appears to be a central source of meaning and identity as evident in the clothes they wear, the adjectives they choose to describe themselves, and in some cases the color of the car they drive or the place they live. Some travel hundreds of miles to follow their team, to

> tailgate with their family and friends, and for some who are alumni of the University, football provides a link with their alma mater. No other sport in the U.S. seems to engender the same pre-game socializing (tailgating), rituals, and atmosphere as football.

The aforementioned scholars Bradford and Sherry suggest another intriguing aspect to the tailgate phenomenon that I witnessed firsthand on game day. They argue that the tailgate, like the home, offers relief from the consumerist rat race. In other words, in daily life, someone's always trying to sell you something. You get in your car and there are ads on the radio. You drive down the road and see company billboards. Public spaces are often designed with commercial intent; shops and restaurants seek your patronage as you walk around. By contrast, no one purchases food or drink at a house party; rather, everyone brings something: a potluck. Similarly, tailgates are domestic spaces for sharing, gift-giving, and reciprocity. Bradford and Sherry imply that the tailgate is a human-centered space where we can be our natural selves, free from coercion. The important thing isn't the "sale." Community and bonding are paramount.

I take their point. The game day tailgates I visited were sites of generosity and sharing. There might be a donation box, like Hurd's, to help with costs. But mostly I saw a free-for-all (the good kind). The dynamic changed once you walked over to Campus Corner or entered Memorial Stadium. Campus Corner was a thoroughfare of businesses. The permanent spots like Pickleman's and Chipotle were joined by pop-up vendors selling beer and margaritas, jerseys and memorabilia. "The Tailgate Tour," sponsored by Fox Sports, came to Campus Corner for the SMU game, bringing a slew of corporate booths. A Red Bull van had a DJ spinning records at an epic volume. Elaborate booths promoted Twisted Tea and Modelo. Once you got to your seat in the stadium, companies from around the metro area sponsored entertainments that took place between timeouts and other breaks in play. There was the Dental Depot Smile Cam, the Whataburger "What-a-toss," and the Diamonds Direct "Dance for your Diamonds." Corporate sponsors were prominently displayed around the stadium: Lowe's, Riverwind Casino, and OG&E.

The temptation might be to shrug at this. Advertising is a way of life in America. It's all just fun and games to complement the action on the field. Business and pleasure go side by side. But I think it's more consequential than that. I reached this conclusion after noticing other game day features at Memorial Stadium. For example, a military veteran was celebrated on field as the "Patriot of the Game" at every home game of the season. The OU track team was brought onto Owen Field to celebrate those members who had won Big 12 championships in the spring. I saw oversized donation checks delivered to representatives from the Special Olympics and Oklahoma Children's Hospital. For every home game, there was a customary flyover by the Blue Angels or some other military plane, accompanied by cheers from the crowd.

The entire spectacle—the game on the field, the advertising paired with entertainment, the acknowledgment and celebration of certain people and institutions—was a colorful stage show illustrating a way of life. Contrary to Bradford and Sherry, I didn't see the tailgate as divorced from the rituals in the stadium. The two were linked. In both spaces, the community's values were performed for everyone to acknowledge and appreciate. The community prioritized sporting excellence, the armed services, the vulnerable in society, and commerce. Based on what I'd seen and experienced tailgating, the community also cared about sharing, loyalty, and camaraderie.

There were aspects of the game day experience I found absurd; I shook my head a few times, baffled. How does one wrap his head around the spectacle of a giant shopping cart, the size of a monster truck, from which Tulsa cheerleaders launch T-shirts into a crowd of football fans (some amused, others indifferent)? At the same game, at halftime, I watched a "Bumper Ball" challenge sponsored by Raising Cane's in which fans donned an inflatable plastic suit to duel like sumo wrestlers. The epic collisions pleased the crowd to no end. The person left standing won a gift card for chicken.

Fandom can also be uncomfortable (the intense afternoon sun, a full bladder with a line at the porta potty, an upset stomach the next day).

But if you think of game day as a journey—leaving the ordinary for the extraordinary—it's easy to take the bad with the good, the pain with the pleasure, for five to seven games every year. Any worthwhile journey, after all, is full of adventure *and* difficulty.

You might quibble about some of the community's values, arguing that people shouldn't care so much about making money or drinking to excess or the military or winning at sports or even America. And it's a reality that many do object. They vote with their feet; they don't tailgate or go to Oklahoma football games.

Speaking for myself, I'm happy to waltz into a friendly tailgate for a shot of complimentary fireball to warm the belly, as I did on a cool November morning before the TCU game in 2023. I like the fellowship and laughter. I like the collective rallying around an institution I care about: the University of Oklahoma. By nature, I'm a solitary person, but I'm not so different from my fellow humans that I can do without the occasional get-together. In the fall, I like my Saturday adventures, with Hurd's tailgate as my second home.

▪ 6 ▪

RIDING WITH MR. OU

MR. OU, a superfan, texts me to say that he's going to feature in a music video. In fact, the filming of the video is about to take place; we should come check it out.

Jenn and I are tailgating ahead of the home game against Iowa State. The goal for today is to shadow Mr. OU, enter his world on game day. The music video shoot will happen at the Turnt Up Tailgate, on the lawn next to Carson Engineering Center and across the street from Campus Corner: a tailgate with a hip-hop vibe to it. For further context, a local rapper named CAJ and a local business owner, Corey Sutter, who goes by the moniker Scissorhands (he owns a string of barber shops in the OKC metro area), have produced an OU anthem called "Ready to Roll." They are shooting the video on game day because they want to include as many Sooner fans as possible.

At 2:45, Jenn and I leave John Hurd's tailgate and walk the short distance to Turnt Up. Though it's the last day of September, it still feels like summer: sunny with blue skies, ninety degrees.

Turnt Up has three tents; under one is a DJ booth, and at three o'clock Scissorhands gets on the microphone. He's wearing a red OU ball cap, a red OU T-shirt, and around his neck an oversized red chain from which dangles a large OU logo. He's holding a white hand towel, perhaps to wipe away sweat. As he informs people about the music video, a song starts to play in the background. "Ready to Roll" is less a hip-hop track than a chant with a repeatable chorus. It reminds me of the collaboration between Aerosmith and Run-DMC in the eighties, "Walk This Way"; both include a catchy guitar riff. But here, unlike in "Walk This Way," there's no rapping, just the looping chorus: "O-O-O-O-O-U. Sooners! Sooners are ready to roll!"

Mr. OU is standing in the grass, getting beat up by the sun. He's talking and taking pictures with people. Pink is his color for today. Breast cancer awareness is on the mind of Sooner Nation as Brent Venables's wife, Julie, was diagnosed with the disease in June. The cornerstone of Mr. OU's outfit is a fake pink mohawk, a foot tall on his head and held in place by a red OU visor. His Sooner football jersey is pink, with "Mr. OU" on the back along with the number one. He wears long, white basketball shorts on which are sewn breast cancer ribbons. On the right pants leg is "Boomer," on the left "Sooner." His socks are pink and pulled to his knees. His white high-top sneakers are painted pink on the sides. For some reason, he's wearing red wide-receiver gloves that must be hot in weather like this. Like Scissorhands, he's wearing an oversized OU chain.

Directed by Scissorhands, a group of people assembles at the corner of Asp and Boyd. A cameraman surfaces from out of nowhere, his video camera ensconced within a handheld rig. Scissorhands puts down the microphone to join the assembly. When he gets there, he sees that Mr. OU is still chatting and taking pictures with people.

"Antonio, get over here!" Scissorhands shouts.

"I have to take a picture with the kids!" Mr. OU replies.

"You ain't bigger than the program! We ain't filming a music video every day!"

Mr. OU joins the group of around twenty-five people, including the rapper CAJ and the superfans Señor OU and Boomer Jerry, both in matching red suits with the OU logo all over the pants and jacket (I wonder how, in costume, they can endure the heat; it gives new meaning to suffering for your team). Señor OU is wearing his trademark Sooners sombrero. Boomer Jerry has on a red pork pie hat. With "Ready to Roll" on a loop, the cameraman, in a crouch, films the group of fans as they bounce up and down, index fingers held aloft.

Jenn and I watch from a distance, comfortable as flies on a wall.

They move out into the intersection of Boyd and Asp where the road has been closed to traffic. The front line of the group consists of Mr. OU, the rapper CAJ, Scissorhands, and Señor OU, but their lieutenants, a crew of kids, are also there. As Scissorhands shouts "Boomer!" at the cameraman, slashing the air with his towel, a couple of kids shout "Yaaahhh!" while the other kids look around, perhaps for their parents. Mr. OU forms an "O" and then a "U" with his long arms. Then "Ready to Roll" is playing again, and everyone bounces around, chanting the chorus, as the cameraman moves in and out and side to side, shooting from various angles.

■ ■ ■

Antonio Record, aka Mr. OU, was born in Tulsa in March 1978 but grew up in Dallas. He was the only boy in a churchgoing family, which would come home on Sundays and watch Record arrange his teddy bears into an audience to which he preached the gospel. His grandmother thought Record, a likeable people person, was destined to become a preacher.

Though he was surrounded by gangs, Record managed to avoid that life. Instead, he focused on sports. In high school, he played basketball and dreamed of making it to the NBA. He got as far as Richland College in Dallas where he played for a season. It was during this time, his early twenties, that life got difficult. His mother and sister moved back to Tulsa, and he was on his own, trying to make a living. He got a job at Radio Shack; he was good with the customers. Then his girlfriend got pregnant. The stressors added up, and he made a mistake that led to an arrest and a court date. A judge gave him four years of probation.

Record found a job at the Hilton Anatole hotel in downtown Dallas where he often worked back-to-back shifts as a valet and bellman. His outgoing personality won him friends who offered him tickets to concerts and sporting events. In 2005, he attended his first Red River Rivalry game, which the Sooners lost to Vince Young's Longhorns. His first child, a daughter, was about to be born when he made another fateful choice. He wanted to be there for her birth, but the mother lived in Oklahoma. To leave Texas would violate his probation. Record took the risk. After his daughter's birth, he was back in Texas working when the authorities picked him up. The fallout was catastrophic; Record spent the next seven months incarcerated.

After his release, he went back to work and stayed out of trouble. By the time he was twenty-eight, he was father to two sons and two daughters. In 2015, at the age of thirty-five, he moved back to Tulsa to help take care of his grandparents. He met his biological father for the first time: a firefighter who came from a family of firefighters. His father had also organized the first ever Black rodeo in Tulsa. Record's life in Tulsa was as busy as it had been in Dallas. He got a good job at an aerospace company, NORDAM, but supplemented his income by waiting tables at Denny's and working the front desk at a Red Roof Inn. Long a Sooner fan, he found himself less than two hours away from Norman. He started driving down for football games. A vision of what he could be, as a Sooner fan, took shape in his imagination. More and more it started to feel like a calling. He wanted to be the "richest broke fan you'll ever meet."

His debut as Mr. OU happened during the 2018 season. By his own account, his outfit was "raggedy." He wore white cutoff jean shorts onto which he'd spray-painted "OU" in red letters with a black outline. His initial thought was to wear a mohawk that glowed in the dark, but he ended up spray-painting it red. Arm sleeves, sunglasses, and OU Chuck Taylors completed the outfit. At the game, Record roamed section one at Memorial Stadium, shouting encouragement at Kyler Murray and the team. He led chants of "Boomer Sooner." He seemed to be everywhere: up and down the concrete steps and across the front railing, the south end zone a stone's throw away. Fans couldn't help but notice, and they responded to his antics by joining in. At one point during the game, Record shouted, as if at the world at large, "You're about to know who I am!" The world got the message. That night he was featured on the local news.

The adrenaline ran through his veins for hours after the game, and when it finally dissipated he was left feeling exhausted but accomplished. He thought of the preachers from his youth, spent from a Sunday morning of sermons.

The experience was addictive. Record went to every remaining home football game that season but also branched out to ice hockey, baseball, and softball, whose teams showed their appreciation by giving him jerseys to wear.

By 2020, a move to Norman felt like the right thing to do. More than that, it felt preordained, as if it were God's plan. Once Record got to Norman, a friend helped him get a job as a janitor at OU, working nights. He did that for a year and a half before transferring over to the landscaping department where his daily tasks included caring for hedges and planting flowers and plants ("I like to see stuff grow and blossom up"). He used an edger and Weed eater to keep the lawns in his area sharp and aesthetically pleasing. He picked up trash on the ground.

If the work was routine and ordinary, his experiences as Mr. OU were anything but. He could be invited to as many as six tailgates on game day. OU fans plied him with beer. Kids ran up to him wanting a hug and picture. Away game tickets were offered. Often, he rode with OU fans to Saturday matchups in cities across the Big 12. He traveled to bowl games too. These excursions were full of fun and adventure, but they could be humbling as well. At the Kansas State game, a line formed of Wildcat fans who wanted to shake his hand. One of the fans said to him, "It was two games. Watching you and watching the game." After the Alamo Bowl win against Oregon in 2021, Record was in the stadium an additional three hours for pictures with fans. He didn't take a single bathroom break. A sympathetic vendor put a box on the floor to collect donations, and the fans obliged with enough money to pay his way back to Norman.

"It comes naturally," Record said to me. "Smiling and making people happy. I genuinely love people."

As Mr. OU, Record followed a specific code of conduct. It was OK to be loud, but he never disrespected the opposing team. Criticism of Sooner athletes was out of the question. OU fans were generous; they gave him tickets and even money. But he refused to take advantage of them. He would never charge money for a picture. "I don't want people to think I'm begging for anything," he said. However, if some company wanted to use him as a spokesperson he wouldn't say no. "I would love to do Mr. OU full-time," he added.

Service was at the core of his mission. For one OU softball fan living in Arkansas, Record got his hands on a softball and spent seven months collecting autographs from all the players plus Coach Patty Gasso. At home football games, he took up to two hundred pictures on his phone, posting many on his social media sites. Later, he got messages from fans who could no longer attend games. They thanked him for posting the photos; they got to live the experience through him.

I wanted to know about the negative sides of superfandom, but it was hard getting Record, a positive person, to talk about it. When I prodded him, he said that the "N" word had been directed at him a couple of times on his travels. One fan accused him of hogging the limelight: "You're getting too much TV time." However, Record was quick to push back against these experiences by saying that most fans, home and away, had treated him warmly.

One story in particular spoke to Record's relationship with Sooner Nation. To get him "ready for the SEC," fans had bought him a flamboyant game-day suit. Record showed me a couple of photos. Indeed, the outfit was impressive—he somehow looked like both a sports fanatic and an old school dandy—with a red, short-sleeved tuxedo jacket with coat tails and a crimson lapel. The front of the jacket was decorated with OU insignia while the back featured "BOOMER SOONER" and "MR. OU." All seven years that the Sooner football team won the national championship were listed, along with the message "CHASE FOR 8." The red knickerbocker shorts ended just below the knee and featured more Sooner insignia.

Life was good, but it wasn't all smooth sailing. A hip injury made Record waddle around because of the pain. By December 2022, he was in the hospital having hip replacement surgery. As Mr. OU, he didn't miss a beat. Soon after the surgery, he was at Lloyd Noble for OU–Texas basketball, moving slowly about the arena with a walker.

His biggest challenge, however, involved parenting. In his mid-forties, Record was father to a young child again. His son Jalen was ten months old. In his bid to juggle childcare, work, and fandom, Record found exhaustion, both physical and mental, a constant companion.

In the end, did he have any goals related to his superfandom? What did he want to get out of this?

Record's response made him sound like both an ordinary American tourist and an idealistic visionary. As an animal lover, he'd like to visit every zoo and aquarium in the United States while supporting his Sooners. He'd also like to create a nonprofit to benefit kids in Tulsa where he was born. He'd like to bring sports to them, including a softball field. "Sports help keep people's lives together," he said.

Record had another goal: earn enough college credits to transfer to the University of Oklahoma. It had long been his dream to graduate from OU and walk across that stage, diploma in hand.

▪ ▪ ▪

Jenn and I return to Hurd's tailgate for a while, but we are back at Turnt Up at five to grab Mr. OU and make our way to the stadium. The Pride of Oklahoma is coming east down Boyd and about to turn onto Asp. We walk down Asp, making it perhaps fifteen to twenty yards, before Mr. OU stops to satisfy a photo request. The person asking is a kid, and it's Jenn, not I, who notices that Mr. OU sets his cup of booze on the sidewalk behind him, out of the boy's line of sight.

"Around kids, he hides his drink," Jenn whispers.

We follow the band to a spot next to the Alumni Association tents located between Wagner and Price Halls. It's here that the band stops to play, surrounded by fans, some with their phones out recording. The song is an upbeat number, loud and brassy. We are on the sidewalk, approaching the scene, when Mr. OU notices a young fan in a wheelchair next to a lamp post. It's hard to tell his age; he could be eighteen or twenty-eight. He has brown hair and glasses. He's thin and wears a white OU T-shirt. Mr. OU walks up to the young man and lifts him half out of his wheelchair. One of Record's arms wraps around the young man's back. Together they groove to the Pride of Oklahoma, gazing into each other's eyes. Mr. OU holds up his index finger: There's only one Oklahoma. The young man does the same. Their faces reflect one another, showing pure joy.

The young man's parents are nearby, beaming.

I turn to Jenn and shake my head in wonder. It feels like something spiritual is taking place.

Gently, Mr. OU returns the young man to his chair. They share another moment of silent communion before Record turns, looking for Jenn and me. We continue down the sidewalk. We end up on Brooks Pedestrian Mall. It's busy, with fans everywhere, some queuing to get inside the stadium.

Jenn becomes Mr. OU's photographer, helping whenever he's stopped for a photo, which is every few yards. We make it to Jenkins and walk past the Heisman statues, the stadium on our right. Our destination is a friend's corporate tailgate. The bank where our friend Lydell Williams works has paid a lot of money to have a tailgate at every home game of the season, with food and drinks. Jenn and I are starving.

The bank's tailgate is along a row of corporate and university-associated tailgates on a strip of grass southeast of the stadium. When we get there, I look east and see the Everest Training Center. Williams greets us, and we introduce Mr. OU before heading to the spread of barbecue on a foldout table.

Mr. OU sits down in a collapsible chair. For a couple minutes he speaks with some friends of ours who have come over from Hurd's tailgate. Then he's quiet and appears a thousand miles away, slumped in the chair, without his sunglasses, the pink mohawk looking terribly out of place, given the exhausted expression on his face. A youthful man, he suddenly looks his age.

When we leave the tailgate, Mr. OU puts back on his sunglasses; the characteristic strut returns. He talks to people, strangers, as we head for the stadium, a few words of greeting, as if he's making his way through a house party.

We enter the stadium through a gate on the east side. Then we zig-zag through the crowd to reach the escalators. We keep moving and emerge through a section entrance, and I'm taken aback by our location. We're on a concrete platform: part of a ramp that leads from the playing field to the stands. There's a metal fence barrier to keep people from falling. We're behind the south end zone, which is painted crimson red with "OKLAHOMA" in white. I turn and look up toward the south stand; a sea of fans rises in tiered fashion. Out in front of thousands of people, I feel exposed. Mr. OU walks across the platform greeting a row of people, many of them in wheelchairs. This must be a section for disabled fans. He shakes hands, gives hugs, and poses for pictures.

The football team is about to make its entrance; players appear at the tunnel at the southeast corner of the end zone. They are maybe twenty yards away. Players shift from foot to foot with nervous energy. Some bounce on their toes, their red helmets bobbing. The Sooner Schooner, escorted by the RUF/NEKS and Lil' Sis, idles in front of the players. Music blasts from the sound system. When the signal is given, the Schooner, led by the ponies, races through a metal archway from which twin flames shoot into the sky. The heat strikes me in a wave. Then the players are running onto Owen Field, accompanied by smoke from a machine that swirls around and chases them for a few yards until they are clear of it. The crowd whistles, claps, and cheers.

As the Oklahoma special teams line up for the kick-off, we move across the top of the platform, and I feel as if I'm in the way, blocking the sight line of all those fans behind me. I'm glad when we finally leave for Mr. OU's seats, in the southwest corner of the stadium. When we get there, Record introduces Jenn and me to a motley and friendly gang of thirty- and forty-somethings. Throughout the game, whenever the Sooners score a touchdown, our neighbors spin around for high-fives.

Mr. OU disappears; he warned us that this would happen. He pops up below us, in the row closest to the field. Then he's behind the end zone again, interacting with fans.

Later, he tells me about his routine. After visiting fans behind the end zone, he'll head to the student section and then go see the Pride of Oklahoma. "I'll holler at them and hang out with them for a little bit," he says. "Then I'll work my way around until I can finally get to my seat."

The trip to his seat involves stopping and chatting with fans, taking pictures. Usually, the second half of the game has started by the time he reaches his seat. But even then he doesn't sit still. He climbs the stairs to talk with people, take pictures, and then he comes back down.

The game against Iowa State is competitive in the first half, with the Sooners pulling away by the end of the third quarter. With only a few minutes left in the fourth, Jenn and I decide to leave. Most of our new friends have already left, the outcome of the game decided. We don't know where Mr. OU has gone; we haven't seen him in a while. I tell Jenn that I'll text him later to thank him for the whole experience.

We leave through an exit on the west side of Memorial Stadium and go north on Asp against the tide of foot traffic. The night air is pleasant, and it feels great to move. At Brooks Pedestrian Mall, I look left and see Bizzell library, my favorite place on campus, gorgeous and collegiate in the dark. Bizzell is the ultimate symbol for the university, a repository for the knowledge and wisdom of our civilization. A contrarian voice in my head offers a different take: No, Memorial Stadium is the ultimate symbol. I wonder what William Bennett Bizzell, OU's fifth president, and David Ross Boyd, OU's first, would think of the balance between academics and athletics at their beloved institution. Boyd was a football fan. Both the library and stadium were built during Bizzell's reign. Then I think it's wasted energy to try and see the present through the eyes of the dead.

▪ ▪ ▪

I don't get the chance to sit down and talk to Record until December. I want to ask him about the moment with the fan in a wheelchair; for some reason I worry that he's forgotten about it. The football season, minus the bowl game, is over by then. The Sooners' last hurrah in the Big 12 has not ended the way the fans wanted. Consecutive losses to Kansas and Oklahoma State (in the last Bedlam, no less) have derailed the season, and the team was excluded from the Big 12 finale. To make matters infinitely worse, Texas has qualified for the College Football Playoffs for the first time and will face Washington on New Year's Day, with a spot in the national championship on the line. Our fate is the Alamo Bowl in San Antonio against fourteenth-ranked Arizona, which many fans feel is beneath us. It isn't even a New Year's bowl game!

I've seen Record a handful of times since Iowa State, in passing, at the rest of the home games for the season, a quick stop-and-chat. In October, I tagged along one morning as he went about his duties as a landscape worker at the university. There was a flower bed in front of McCasland Field House, his project for the day, and he backed a Kubota utility vehicle onto the sidewalk so that he could push dirt from the cargo bed onto the flower bed. He used a rake to spread the dirt and then took plastic pots of flowers and plants—yellow and purple pansies and green moneywort—from the back of the Kubota and lined them up on the sidewalk for planting. It was strange seeing Record in work garb. I was used to seeing him with his pink mohawk and athletic gear. That day in October, he wore work boots, brown Dickies pants, a red OU jacket, and a gray beanie. His work gloves were a fluorescent yellow. On his hands and knees, he planted a row of the tentacle-like moneywort where the flower bed met the sidewalk.

In early November, I learned through social media that Record had been in an accident at work. The Monday after the loss to Oklahoma State, his Kubota was struck by a car driven by a student on campus; Record was tossed from the UTV and hit his head on the ground, suffering a concussion. The Instagram post was of him at the hospital, lying on a gurney and wearing a neck brace.

He is fully recovered when I see him in December. I go to his apartment for the interview; it's easier this way because Jalen, his toddler, is with him. The apartment complex is less than five minutes' drive from campus. His unit stands out because of the presence of an OU flag. Impressively, Record has landscaped the flower bed next to his apartment.

He apologizes for the mess inside, but the living room is tidy. The TV is tuned to ESPN, with Jalen sitting on the couch. There's a little dog at Record's feet, a brown and white Pomeranian/chihuahua mix that sounds awful on paper, but Draco (named after the character in the Harry Potter books) is sweet and not yappy. Like any toddler, Jalen slides off the couch and waddles around; he has chubby cheeks and a constant smile. His head of thick, curly hair—sandy in color—is wild and impressive. There's

OU memorabilia on the walls, including framed and signed pictures of Adrian Peterson and Sam Bradford. A decorated Christmas tree is in the corner. I turn to my left and see a huge aquarium which looks designed for a reptile, with greenery and a basking light.

"That's my bearded dragon," Record says. We walk over to look, past the kitchen, and there's the lizard, gray and prehistoric, which he named Loki after the character in *Thor.* We hurry back to the living room where Jalen and the dog are in cahoots, intent on frenzy. Jalen circles precariously around the living room before hugging my leg. He looks up at me with an irrepressible grin.

It isn't long before Jalen tumbles, scaring himself in the process. He starts to cry. "Bottle time," Record says, scooping up his son in his arms. He takes the boy to another room, presumably to crib and bottle. Jalen quiets down.

When Record is back in the living room, sitting on the couch, I ask about the moments from the football season that stood out to him.

The Turnt Up Tailgate, where Records hangs out on game day, celebrated its eleventh anniversary this season, and its annual chili cook-off was memorable. They had a new winner this year.

OU's future in the SEC was a popular and recurring topic of conversation. Among the fans, there wasn't lot of sadness about leaving the Big 12. Instead, everyone looked to the future.

"If we make it to the Big 12 championship and win it, then that's fine, but if not we've got the SEC," Record says.

He's cautiously optimistic about our first season in the SEC, from a tailgating point of view, but at the same time thinks it will be a wake-up call. "I think it's going to be more packed," he says. "I think we're going to have more tents up. I think that after that first year we're gonna be ready, kind of like the first year of marriage. Let's see how this is gonna work. Now we know what we're dealing with. Now we can go onto the next year a little bit smoother."

Record thinks that Sooner fans will travel strong next season, enticed by the game-day atmosphere throughout the Deep South. Record plans on making it to every road game. "I don't know how, but I'm getting there," he says. "LSU is one of the spots I want to go to because I heard they had a lion or tiger that's right there when they [the players] come in."

The Grove—ten acres of party space, in the shade of oak trees, on the campus of Ole Miss—regularly attracts a hundred thousand fans; it's another must-see destination for Record.

Finally, I ask him about his encounter with the young fan in September.

"I guess the spirit takes over me," he says. "I have no idea what I do. It just comes and I do it, just like seeing an older lady walking down the steps by herself. I might get out of my seat and help her down. That was just one of those moments right there with that little boy. 'Hey, let's have some fun. I got you, buddy.' He was cool."

Such moments happen all the time, he adds. He'll catch sight of something that pulls him over in a magnetic way. Then he'll go over and "do his thing."

Record insists that he isn't motivated by ego or the need for praise. Rather, it's something innate in him. "That's just in my blood," he says. "That's how I was born and built."

He has a "three hundred and sixty kind of thing" where he can be talking to someone and feel the energy of another person, off to the side, who wants a picture with him. Of course, he always obliges.

He returns to the moment with the young fan. The parents got in touch with him on social media. This happens a lot, too. They thanked him for what he did. "You made his day," they wrote.

This new information only seems to support my interpretation: that the interaction between Record and the young man was unique and meaningful, that both got something from it. I come up with a term: transcendent communion. A holy moment in a secular space. Two people vibe with one another and connect, if only for a brief amount of time.

The skeptic in me wonders if I should play the journalist and investigate further. Is Mr. OU too good to be true? He says that the spirit, not ego, guides him. Can I trust him? I could interview people who know Record, searching for that dissenting voice. *He's not what he appears to be.* It's clear, based on what I already know, that he isn't a perfect person. He has a troubled past. He isn't a resounding financial success. His romantic relationships have been strained. If I look hard enough, I'll probably find more that, in a certain light, subtracts from his mystique. He's human, after all, like the rest of us, and it's true that the microscope, when applied to anyone, reveals and magnifies flaws and imperfections.

This feels like the worst approach to take, and besides I have evidence to the contrary. I've seen him with fans, friends, and coworkers. I've talked with him, one-on-one. He's not afraid to share his trials and tribulations. He's never boasted, never sounded prideful. He appears genuine to me: a man who's found his purpose, though his struggles are far from over.

The assertion sounds ridiculous, on the face of it, but nevertheless rings true: Fandom saved Record's life.

▪ 7 ▪

THE WOMEN PLAY TO WIN

THE FIRST PARENTS' TAILGATE of the OU women's 2023 soccer season happens on a Sunday afternoon in late August in unforgiving heat. It's easily a hundred degrees. Outside of John Crain Field, in the parking lot, a couple tables have been set up beneath the meager cover of trees. The tailgater can drink booze or soda or combine the two. There's also plenty to eat: Jimmy John's sandwiches, chips, and cookies. A few yards away are two cornhole boards, waiting for players. When Jenn and I get there, it's about an hour till kickoff. Oklahoma's opponent today is Oral Roberts University in the Sooners' second game of the season. My former student Cailey England will be in the starting lineup; in her senior season, she's been elected team captain again.

At the tailgate, we are meeting England's parents for the first time. Her mother, Laurisa, spots us as we walk up. She's fifty years old, with reddish-brown hair pulled back into a ponytail. The short sleeves of her white OU Soccer T-shirt have been rolled up, her shoulders exposed to the sun. Like her daughter, she has freckles sprinkled across her face. Laurisa welcomes us with a handshake and big smile. We talk for a couple minutes and then she's showing us around. First, we meet England's father, Aron.

He's fifty, works in software product management, and has short brown hair, a clean-shaven face, and an easygoing manner. Then we encounter a whirlwind of Sooner parents, each pair with a daughter on the team. Some have traveled from Texas, Florida, and Michigan. John and Judy Ramey are from Prosper, Texas, a suburb of Dallas. By trade, John's in telecoms sales. Their daughter Olivia, a sophomore, is the starting goalkeeper for the Sooners. John is clearly excited about the season to come. Thanks to Laurisa, the parents know I'm writing a book, and John asks me about the project. Then he holds up a finger as if he's remembered something. He says he'll be right back. A few minutes later, he returns holding something in his hand. At first glance, it appears to be a red and white rabbit's foot. But once he hands it to me, I see that it's something else, though I'm not quite sure what.

"I made these," John says.

It's a keychain in Sooner colors, made of red and white nylon strands woven together in a double helix and representing "OU DNA": one of the university's signature mottoes.

I'm humbled by the gift. Seemingly, the parents have already taken us in; Jenn and I are part of the tribe.

Two games of cornhole happen at the same time. An OU father and an Oral Roberts father, whose daughters know each other from the club soccer scene in Dallas, are pitted against one another. The loser will have to wear the gear of the other team during the whole game. The trash talk goes back and forth, just like the bean bags they toss. In the end, the OU father prevails, a fist thrown up in the air. Eventually, he walks over to his Oral Roberts counterpart with an OU ball cap in hand. The losing party shakes his head in resignation.

The soccer match has begun and we are inside the stadium when the Oral Roberts father makes his walk of shame, wearing the OU cap, in front of the bleachers where all the Sooner players' parents are sitting. The parents laugh. It's all in good fun.

The tiered bleachers in the stadium track with the south side of the soccer field. There are no bleachers on the north, east, or west sides. John Crain Field can hold up to 3,500 fans. Visiting fans usually occupy the left side of the bleachers, with home fans taking over the rest. The Sooner players' parents occupy the center portion, with most sitting near the top.

Jenn and I sit with England's parents at the top of the bleachers. I'm impressed by the size of the crowd for this nonconference game, with the summer heat hostile to everyone. The atmosphere resembles the one in Memorial Stadium during football games, just on a smaller scale. Music is played over the sound system to get the crowd going: Blur's "Song 2" and The White Stripes' "Seven Nation Army." The announcer provides occasional commentary. There's a video board that markets and hypes the soccer team, with clips of goals and other highlights. But also, like the video boards at Memorial Stadium, they advertise the other OU sports teams as well as OU sponsors. The RUF/NEKS and Lil' Sis are here, albeit in modest numbers. They're dressed in their trademark attire, the two young men in beige jeans and red, tucked-in shirts. One has a RUF/NEK paddle sticking out of his back pocket. The Lil' Sis member is wearing a red crimson dress, cinched at the waist, with brown boots. The outfits must be beyond uncomfortable in this weather, and the group looks deprived of its usual spirit.

Seeing England on the field puts my brain to work, and I make connections between the person in my classroom and the person competing on the pristine grass below. Visually, she's her mother's mini-me, with her reddish-brown hair pulled back and out of the way; the short sleeves of her jersey have been rolled up too. England is playing a new position; previous seasons she played in midfield but now she's in defense, surveying the field, talking to her teammates, and keeping an eye on Oral Roberts's attacking players. England seldom loses her one-on-one battles on the field; she's smart in her tactical positioning. When she gets physical, it's well-timed and effective: a vigorous shoulder barge to knock her opponent off-balance and win the ball. Her play on the pitch reminds me of how she was in the classroom: fully committed and well ahead of expectations.

Her mother seems to know everyone on the Sooner roster. She cheers for England, but she's also vocal about every other player, yelling names and providing encouragement. Laurisa tells us that she and Aron make it to almost every game, home and away; they'll reserve an Airbnb for a few days. After games, England joins them for a postgame meal—pizza in the Airbnb—and they'll do a postmortem, talking through England's and the team's performance.

Tonight, the Sooners go behind early, conceding a goal to the visitors. Their response is encouraging; they dominate possession and take shots on goal. The crowd—a mix of players' parents, OU students, and adult members of Sooner Nation—can sense a breakthrough, and the fans start to stomp on the bleachers, a rhythm to go along with the Sooners' momentum on the field. In the thirty-fourth minute, the equalizer finally arrives, and the scorer is another former student of mine, Leonie "Leo" Weber: an international student from Germany. It's amazing to me that OU recruits student-athletes from overseas. In fact, six of twenty-seven players on the women's soccer team are from countries outside of the United States.

It's an exciting game with goals from both teams, but the Sooners take charge in the second half. After striker Emma Hawkins makes it 4–2 in OU's favor, the Sooner players establish a line of communication with the fans. These are the players who aren't presently on the field. They stand in front of the players' dugout on the sideline opposite the bleachers and shout "Boomer!" From our seats, we shout "Sooner!" This call and response goes on for around thirty seconds; at the end of it, both players and fans applaud each other.

After the full-time whistle, the victorious Sooner team walks across the field to stand in front of the crowd, and everyone sings the "OU Chant," a recording of the anthem played over the sound system. Each Sooner has an index finger pointed toward the night sky.

■ ■ ■

England was born a triplet in Kirkland, Washington, in March 2002. When the children were six, the family moved to Dripping Springs, Texas. Laurisa describes her daughter as "always athletic and very competitive," with thigh muscles from the moment of birth. Her personality became apparent from a young age. England was quiet and shy, a rule-abider as well as a perfectionist. If she was going to do something, she wanted to do it right.

An incident from her sixth-grade year would enter family lore and speak to England's ambitions. When she contracted MRSA, a serious bacterial infection, in her right elbow, her parents took her to the children's hospital where the procedure involved cutting a hole to drain her arm. England insisted on no anesthetic, despite the considerable pain. Fascinated by her own illness and its treatment, she wanted to be fully awake to watch the whole procedure. An attending nurse told her, "Girl, you're going to be a doctor."

She played every sport that she could: gymnastics, swimming, soccer, basketball, and cross country. When high school came around, a decision had to be made. Which sport would she focus on? England chose soccer. It was the right decision; as she exceled on the field, college coaches began to recruit her. England and her parents traveled around the country, visiting schools. They went to Harvard, Rutgers, and the University of Pennsylvania. Since she was also a serious student, the right school would feature the right blend of athletics and academics.

No school felt right until she visited the University of Oklahoma. She fell in love with the campus. She liked the coach, and the training facilities for the soccer team were first-rate. OU Medical Center, an academic hospital, was in nearby Oklahoma City. Clearly, the university was committed to training doctors. What's more, Norman was only five hours away by car; her parents would be able to drive up for games. On England's visit to campus, she met some of the players and watched a training session. The intensity of the action, with players on the verge of throwing up, was another selling point. It signaled passion and commitment.

England arrived in Norman in fall 2020 on a full soccer scholarship. She joined a program that in its twenty-plus years of existence had struggled on the playing field. It had never won a regular season title nor a conference tournament title. England's next three years were a rollercoaster of experiences and emotions. For most freshmen, it's a challenge to make the field, but England worked hard and played significant minutes; highlights included scoring the winning goal against Kansas State in the season finale and being named to the Big 12 all-freshman team. In her second season,

England was named captain for the first time; the learning curve was steep. She had to come out of her shell to lead the team. With the Sooners needing a win against Iowa State to qualify for the Big 12 tournament, England bought sweat bands embroidered with the jersey number of every single player on the roster. Each player picked a teammate and wore the sweat band corresponding to her number. When your player was on the field, you cheered for her. In twenty-degree weather made worse by freezing rain, the Sooners pulled off a 1–0 victory. The sweat bands, England thought, played some role in bringing the team together.

Her junior year was the hardest. There was no team cohesion or identity, no trust between the coaches and players. Everything felt irreparably broken, and England, with her mental health in tatters, seriously considered transferring to another school.

She chose to stay. Many of her teammates didn't. New head coach Matt Mott brought new ideas and a healthier culture. He also brought in new players from the transfer portal. Once again, England was elected captain.

She was a student of mine in spring 2023. For years, I'd taught honors students, and for the most part they fit a certain mold. They were high-achieving and hard-working. They knew more about a range of intellectual topics than their peers in my "regular" classes, but it was also true that they were perhaps, on the whole, a little more neurotic. England was a supercharged version of the average honors student. There was no procrastination. As soon as a major assignment was announced, she got to work. She collaborated with me in person and through email, developing her ideas. She had me look at drafts of her essays, which were often longer than they needed to be. "Cailey, you're going to have to trim this down," I would say. England would look perplexed. But how? Everything she wanted to say was right there on the page.

Every minute of her day was filled with commitments related to soccer and academics. If she felt burdened by the weight of everything—the constant hustle—she didn't show it. There was work to do. There was the person England wanted to become, a physician, waiting (impatiently) for her in the future.

▪ ▪ ▪

The 2023 OU soccer season is full of dramatic, vivid, and revealing moments. The Sooners score eighteen goals in their first three games, all wins. Then, on a road trip, they lose three in a row and are held scoreless. At the next home game, John Ramey—the parent who gifted me the OU keychain—cuts a forlorn figure in the stands. His goalkeeper daughter Olivia has been benched after making a series of errors in those losses. When I talk to him, at halftime of the Murray State game in early September, John is philosophical. "We keep working through it," he says. "It's adversity. She has to figure out a way to fix it." At the same time, John is protective of his daughter. He isn't happy with the way the coaches are communicating with her. No coaching took place, he says. They just told her they were making a change. "I'm Olivia first, the team second," he adds.

The interaction only adds to a feeling I have: This all feels like an extension of the high school sports experience. The players' parents are the team's biggest fans. Notably, students come and watch the Sooners play, but they aren't huge soccer fans. Their identity isn't wrapped up in whether the Sooners win or not. Often, they leave at halftime. One international student, from Colombia, catches my ear at the Murray State game. After the Sooners score a spectacular goal to make it 3–1 in the second half, this student looks around him at the packed stands and then muses to his friend: "There's not enough celebrating for that goal. In Colombia they'd be screaming for ten minutes. Already there would be a shooting and two stabbings."

In much of the world, soccer is life and death. That's how seriously the world takes the sport. But in America it's different. College football is the sport with that high-stakes valence. This isn't to denigrate or dismiss OU soccer or its fans; it's just to say that in the United States *all* collegiate sports take a backseat to football (or basketball, depending on the school).

That said, I'm impressed by the variety of support for the women's soccer team. The OU drum line comes to most of the home games, sitting in two rows along the front, their beats a complement to the rhythm of play on the field. At halftime of one game, a contingent from the Pride of

Oklahoma performs on John Crain Field, with a twirler spinning batons. Similarly, the RUF/NEKS and Lil' Sis are a near constant presence, leading chants of "Boomer Sooner." Local boys and girls soccer teams come to the games, dressed in their uniforms. Along with the adult fans, they disparage the referee for calls that go against the Sooners.

Big 12 conference play begins in mid-September. The Sooners start strong with two wins and a draw. England scores a thumping header against Kansas State; her mother knows right away that she has scored (while I'm not completely sure). Laurisa jumps up and down, celebrating. Against the better teams in the Big 12, the Sooners struggle, with losses to Texas Tech, Central Florida, and West Virginia. October arrives, and it feels more like fall at the games. Jenn says to me in the stands, "Sports are really pleasant when the sun's not trying to murder you."

Texas comes to town in mid-October. The Longhorns are heavy favorites, nationally ranked with one of the top goal scorers in the country. Two thousand fans pack the stadium, the third largest crowd in OU soccer history, many holding up red soccer scarves with "Boomer Sooner" on them. From the first whistle, the Sooners are locked in, competing hard. They take the lead in the fifty-fifth minute thanks to a goal from senior Dani Wolfe, a transfer from Michigan. The deficit brings Texas to life; the Longhorns apply pressure but can't score. A couple minutes after the Longhorns are denied a goal for offsides, the Sooners score again, doubling their lead and proving that the night belongs to them.

The post-match scenes are epic. The players (including goalkeeper Olivia Ramey, who's been restored to the starting lineup) vent their frustrations about a season in which they've been inconsistent; they hug each other and exult. They aim the horns-down sign at the partisan crowd.

Unfortunately, the win isn't the springboard they are hoping for. The Sooners lose their last two regular season games, including Bedlam. They qualify for the Big 12 conference tournament and score some revenge, beating Oklahoma State in the first round. But they can't get past an excellent Brigham Young team (the Wildcats will make it all the way to the final four of the NCAA tournament). The 6–0 loss is the Sooners' worst of the season.

When I talk to her after the season, England is proud of her individual performances; she played nearly every minute of every game and in a new position too. "Adaptability" is a word that she uses. On the team front, there's frustration: With so many new faces—freshmen and transfers joining the veterans—and a new coaching staff, they didn't gel as quickly as they needed to. "I know we have the talent," England says. "We just haven't clicked on the field and created the product we wanted."

With her fourth year of collegiate soccer behind her, England has a decision to make. Because the COVID pandemic interrupted her freshman season, she's been granted another year of eligibility. Medical school calls out to her; she's eager to get started. On the other hand, her love for soccer is still strong; she likes this Sooner team and can see them evolving into next season. Once her collegiate career is over, there won't be any going back. Already, it's hard to imagine life without soccer; she's played the sport from the age of three. What's more, the next season will be Oklahoma's first in the SEC.

The opportunity, in the end, is too good to pass up. England decides to return to OU, as a graduate student, for one more season.

▪ ▪ ▪

If OU soccer is a program still trying to find itself, OU softball is a program much further along in its evolution. With deep roots and a winning tradition to rival any sports program, men's or women's, in the nation, head coach Patty Gasso's Sooners are the standard bearers in women's softball; in fall 2023, months away from the new season, they are a three-peat national champion. A fourth in a row seems more likely than out of the question, given the fact that the core of last year's team is returning. Gasso does not mince words; she calls her senior class of players the greatest senior class that collegiate softball has ever seen.

A moniker exists for the team culture that Gasso has developed and honed across the thirty years she's been at Oklahoma: "Championship Mindset." It's no secret what she prioritizes or how she's built the program. She's talked about the way the Sooners do things in interviews and at coaches' clinics. One of her lectures, in 2008, was recorded and sold as an instructional video called "How to Coach the Female Athlete." In it, Gasso is articulate, personable, and even funny. The substance of her lecture revolves around what she's learned about molding young women and fostering team chemistry. She argues that young women in the twenty-first century have a certain mindset, which requires adjustment. In an era when many of her players haven't worked a job and learned the "value of a dollar," Gasso instills in them a blue-collar ethic; she teaches them how to "earn" things. She treats her players like workers, making them punch in on an actual time clock when they arrive at practice. If a player practices well, she gets a dollar, which is stored in a team jar. If a player loafs, she clocks out and takes a "coffee break," for which she isn't paid. The team gets upset if they don't maximize their "pay" at the end of a "shift." The money in the jar goes toward the purchase of something they collectively want. One year, it was an XM satellite radio for the team bus.

About young women Gasso noticed something else: a lack of self-esteem and self-respect, which bred a lack of confidence. She teaches her players to stand up for themselves and what they believe in. On an interpersonal level, players learn the value of a firm handshake and looking people in the eye during conversations. Posture is important: how you hold yourself in public and how you walk down the street.

Some have called Gasso's approach—an amalgam of working-class ethics, pragmatic psychology, and best practices—her "secret sauce." Joe Castiglione, OU's athletics director since 1998, told *The Athletic*, "She's been exceptionally strong at melding and creating such chemistry."

The results have been astounding: seven national championships, including five in the past eight years. The team has had multiple winning streaks that boggle the mind: forty-one straight games in 2019, forty from 2020 to 2021, and forty from 2021 to 2022. The Sooners broke the NCAA softball record for consecutive wins in May 2023; the forty-eighth in a row came against Clemson in the postseason. With their triumph in the World Series, they are riding this streak into 2024: fifty-three and counting. (By way of comparison, Bud Wilkinson's towering Sooner football team won forty-seven straight games from 1953 to 1957, a record that likely won't be surpassed.)

The team has a mystique that inspires fear in opponents who are sometimes defeated, in a psychological sense, before the first pitch is even thrown. Because of its extraordinary success, the OU softball team is spoken about in the same breath as the OU football team. Softball players are legitimate celebrities on campus and in Norman.

■ ■ ■

No one in their right mind could have imagined this amount of success when the program was established in 1974. OU was responding, in part, to Congress's 1972 passage of Title IX, which established legal equity in the classroom and on the playing field for students in public education regardless of sex. OU's funding of women's sports began in the 1973–74 academic year; the initial budget for women's sports (which consisted of newly formed teams in basketball, track and field, volleyball, tennis, golf, swimming, and field hockey) was a modest $1,500.

Going back further in history, as context, OU's women have played organized sports like basketball since the early years of the twentieth century but weren't allowed a letterman's "O" sweater like the men. In 1914, the OU Women's Athletic Association tried to change that; their rallying cry was "O's for Women!" Their petitioning, however, fell on deaf ears; the "O" was reserved for intercollegiate athletics, so the argument went, and women were barred from such competition.

Marita Hynes, appointed OU softball coach in 1976, was paid an annual salary of $9,900, which was less than her salary as a high school coach, to lead both the softball and field hockey programs. *Sooner Magazine* in 2012 chronicled the many challenges facing Hynes. To make ends meet, Hynes worked as the scorekeeper for kids' baseball and softball games for four nights a week. For three nights a week, she umpired games in Oklahoma City, and on weekends she refereed basketball for five bucks a game. As softball coach of the Sooners, she had zero scholarship money to offer to players before 1977 when twelve full scholarships became available. Also in 1977, more than one uniform was offered to her softball players for the first time; now they had two. Furthermore, the team was provided transportation; before, they drove themselves to games. Now they got access to an OU-sponsored van.

After coaching for eight seasons, Hynes became coordinator of promotions within the athletics department. She advocated hard for women's sports at OU. When *The Oklahoman* wrote about Hynes on the eve of her retirement in 2003, after twenty-seven years of service, it detailed how Hynes fought for the big things like larger budgets and better facilities. But such was the imbalance between men's and women's sports she fought for the little things too, like office space or even a VCR. One of her major accomplishments was guiding the effort for a softball-specific stadium and complex, with a $1 million budget, which officially opened for play in 1998. (The stadium was renamed Marita Hynes Field in 2004.) Of course, her legacy is also tied to another project, which in 1994 made barely a ripple at all: Gasso's move to Norman. That year, when Athletics Director Donnie Duncan asked her to spearhead a coaching search, Hynes started calling her softball contacts from around the country. Maxine "Mickey" Davis, women's athletic director at Long Beach City College, fielded one of these calls and spoke glowingly about her softball coach, Patty Gasso. The name was familiar to Hynes, who remembered Gasso as the woman who once strode up at the Women's College World Series (WCWS) to introduce herself. Hynes invited Gasso to Norman for an interview. Later, in her evaluation of the candidate, Hynes used the words "calculated risk."

■ ■ ■

In fall 2023, the Sooner softball team plays a "Battle Series": six scrimmages that divide the players into three different squads which all play one another. Basically, it's a showcase with a serious purpose: Which athletes have the mettle to feature prominently for this team in the upcoming season? After the last scrimmage, on November 9, Coach Gasso speaks to the press; she's pleased with her pitching staff, especially Oklahoma State transfer Kelly Maxwell, who, after a period of adjustment, is finally "settled." The challenge this fall has been to meld the freshmen and transfers, a talented crew, with the returning seniors. Gasso admits that it's a process, in a sense, that's out of her hands. The team is stacked with repeat national champions—Kinzie Hansen, Alyssa Brito, Tiare Jennings, Jayda Coleman, and Rylie Boone—who have done the teaching so far. And the intense environment of the Battle Series has been another effective teacher.

For all that she has seen across the six scrimmages, Gasso isn't willing to show her cards. She insists that she still doesn't know her lineup: "You might ask me what I'm going to do and who's going to be playing where and I will not tell you because I do not know yet."

She does disclose that several newcomers, like freshmen Ella Parker and Kasidi Pickering, have made their mark and are in contention to start for the team. As a result, according to Gasso, the seniors are feeling the pressure: "They're a little bit tight because of that. They feel that pressure coming from others around them and that's good for us."

This feels calculated from the decorated coach: a bit of mind games for her own team. It's a reminder to her upperclassmen: Nothing is given; past accomplishments are in the past.

A mindset of willful amnesia—the past forgotten, the present omniscient—seems compulsory for any champions who wish to repeat their success. If that's the case, Gasso has done a tremendous job of forging players who live in the present, striving for excellence in every practice, every game. The culture of OU softball has proven itself. Consequently, the perks of winning have come streaming in. OU softball players are earning money through partnerships with Name, Image, and Likeness (NIL) collectives. Tiare Jennings inked a sponsorship deal with a local car dealership. In 2023, three Sooners were among the top five, in all of college softball, in terms of NIL value. The softball team has its own documentary series, *Championship Mindset*, which provides fans with an inside look at the team.

An obvious takeaway is that winning on the field brings success in other areas. To wit, the Sooners will move into a new stadium in the 2024 season. Love's Field, at a cost of $48 million, will be the premier college softball facility in the country. Winning seems to be the ultimate arbiter in determining a program's visibility, which makes sense. We live in a results-driven culture. OU athletics has a winning pedigree, and Sooner Nation expects to see Sooner teams on top. The renown and money must multiply the pressure ten-fold, especially for the OU softball team. They're the returning three-peat national champions. On a regular basis, they go on undefeated runs that make them look like giants among ordinary folk. Sooner softball fans expect more than winning; they expect domination. How will this team with its blend of veterans and fresh faces respond to the challenges that will no doubt greet them in the spring?

I'll be there, at Love's Field, to find out.

▪ 8 ▪

FAN TAXONOMY

Addendum

AFTER MY OWN game day experiences, I feel positioned to make a modest contribution to the taxonomy of football fans offered by *Sooner Magazine* in 1941. This first group I call the "Trolls." Often, the Trolls are visitors who sit among the home fans. Surrounded by Sooners, they are typically twenty-something males, alumni of the visiting school, and flush with the brazenness of youth. They arrive at Memorial Stadium already drunk (but somehow coolly composed) after spending hours in a Campus Corner bar where they endeared themselves to locals by telling jokes about Oklahomans. The age-old stereotypes found voice; Okies are poor, dumb, unfashionable, and miserable. The *Austin-American Statesman*, a newspaper read by some Trolls, printed jokes of this stripe on the eve of 2012's Red River Rivalry. At the risk of an eye roll from the reader, I'll share two. The first has to do with style: "The Oklahoma dress code isn't overly stuffy. In Oklahoma, elegant casual is a sleeveless T-shirt with fewer than three barbecue sauce stains on it."

Has the reader left this world because the above joke killed?

In the second one, Oklahomans find comfort and happiness sitting in the bleachers at the Cotton Bowl because it's a step up from their usual furnishings: "Heck, they'll pack the Cotton Bowl way before the game even starts and just sit there in the stands, like something's happening. This is because the furniture in the stadium is much fancier than the stuff they've got on the porch back home."

It's golden material—yes, I'm being sarcastic—and the Trolls are quick to produce it whenever they're feeling cocky or scared or wounded.

I remember such a Troll duo from the SMU game in September 2023. They looked like brothers (and were probably cohorts of the same fraternity), with the same short haircut, sunglasses, and blue Polo shirt: a mustang emblem, the SMU mascot, hovering over the heart. Furthering the mirror-image impression was the presence of a beer, held by each in his right hand. A few rows down from us, they insisted on standing throughout the game. OU scored a touchdown within the first five minutes, and when the Mustangs responded with a strong drive of their own, the pair of Trolls celebrated first downs with a dramatic extension of the arm, pointing down the field like a referee. The Sooner fans tolerated these men; after all, the game was in its early stages, and our defense eventually held them to a field goal.

Dillon Gabriel's offense stalled for the next two series, which caused frustration among the Sooner faithful. The Trolls hooted and high-fived, aware of the dynamic between the two teams. Oklahoma was ranked in the top twenty, a historic program known for winning. SMU had never been the same after receiving the "death penalty" in the late 1980s for illegal payments to players. On occasion, their football team would break into the top twenty-five, but it hadn't won a conference title in thirty-nine years. (This would change in 2023 as SMU topped the American Athletic Conference.) The Sooners were supposed to steamroll the Mustangs; as the home team struggled, the Trolls got louder and more demonstrative. There was a self-consciousness to their behavior; they reveled in being watched, in being the villain.

A second quarter touchdown extended the Sooner lead, putting the home crowd more at ease. However, a scoreless third quarter ended with SMU ominously on the move, aided by a pass interference call at midfield and a curious interference penalty on Brent Venables. SMU capitalized with a touchdown pass and then a successful two-point conversion.

Suddenly it was 14–11. The momentum of the game had shifted, and the entire stadium radiated with nervous frustration. Fans around us complained about the referees who were clearly against us. The SMU Trolls were ecstatic, the very picture of cocksure as they bobbed their heads and half-turned toward the hostile crowd behind them in a show of defiance and confrontation. Their sly dance of enmity had been going on for three-plus quarters now. It allowed for plausible deniability in case anyone called them out: "Who me? I'm not doing anything." Their performance was reaching its apotheosis; the reality on the field plus the Trolls' efforts had combined to toxic effect. A voice behind us, belonging to a woman, suddenly lashed out. "Shut up and sit the fuck down!" she shouted. "Assholes!"

I was reminded of an ironic piece of student writing from *The Sooner Yearbook* of 1981 about the downsides of fandom: "Were you ever offended by the foul language you heard? . . . Did you think you were going to sweat to death from the sweltering heat? If you've suffered from any of these symptoms, your condition is critical: You're a Sooner fan." It was certainly hot in Memorial Stadium, and foul language too was on display, not that it offended me. I heard enough of it and was even guilty of the profane from time to time.

I wanted to get a look at the Sooner who cussed out the Trolls. There was always tension between opposing fans, but each seemed to stay within a bubble as they cheered their respective team and booed the other. Certain polite lines were drawn, and most did not cross them. The fan behind us, animated by anger and fear ("We're going to lose to a team that should never beat us"), had said, "To hell with politeness," creating drama. I, an intrigued observer, was here for it.

Discreetly, I turned my head to the right and looked up. The culprit was sitting on the row directly behind us. I was shocked. The woman with the foul mouth was a gray-haired senior citizen. I whispered this fact to Jenn, whose eyes widened. "Don't look," I pleaded.

The Trolls pretended that they had heard something untoward but knew not the source, their heads swiveling and their faces blank in mock wonder and ignorance. They said nothing in response to the angry Sooner fan.

There's a certain amount of bravery and risk attached to the Troll. After all, in a crowd of eighty-five thousand at Memorial Stadium, Trolls are a distinct minority. As their team frustrates the favored home team, their acts of fandom are commonplace enough—shouts of "Let's go!" and fist pumps and high-fives—but in this context their actions are exaggerated to maximally impact the opposing fans around them. In other words, it's a performance, an amplification of their normal behavior. This is all unmitigated fun, provided that their team continues to excel in the role of spoiler. Unfortunately for the SMU Trolls, the fun didn't last.

The Sooners found rhythm and a sense of urgency, with Gabriel driving the offense for seventy-five yards and a touchdown to give OU a ten-point cushion. Less than three minutes later, we scored another touchdown, and it was all but over. Quickly the game had swung.

But this wasn't a happy crowd. Relief and disappointment were part of the equation. Sooner fans were not convinced by this team. Yes, it was early in the season, but we should be trouncing the likes of SMU. Our Big 12 opponents, especially Texas, would prove a taller task. We weren't ready.

There were rumblings of this order, and as the other SMU fans, twenty-somethings scattered around us, began to leave, a few OU fans suddenly discovered their own inner troll.

"Daddy's money can't buy you a win!" one guy shouted, which made a lot of Sooners laugh. Of course, he was invoking the stereotype that SMU, a private school, was attended by the privileged children of wealthy Dallas socialites. (Was he not aware that OU had its own cohort of privileged children from Dallas as students?) It wasn't clear if the targets heard. A young, auburn-haired woman in red shorts and a blue T-shirt, a victim of too much drink, held onto the railing, and each of her downward steps looked perilous. Trailing behind was her unconcerned boyfriend.

I had to give the SMU Trolls credit; they stayed put. They were quiet now but kept standing. They were noncompliant to the end.

■ ■ ■

My taxonomy includes a character I call the "Scapegoater or Voice of the People." From a seat in the stands, this fan verbally points the finger, identifies what's gone wrong on the field, and proposes answers. Because of the medium of communication (the voice) and the context (the stadium, amid tens of thousands), this fan is not given to nuance or elaboration. Their criticism is more bark than soliloquy. The referees are a time-honored target of their ire. Additionally, each season a Sooner coach is branded as the problem writ large. For several years, through the coaching eras of Bob Stoops and Lincoln Riley, that unlucky person was the defensive coordinator (Mike Stoops anyone?). In 2023, it was offensive coordinator Jeff Lebby. Despite our quarterback Dillon Gabriel putting up big numbers and becoming a Heisman Trophy candidate, the offense often sputtered, with too many three-and-out series. Our first loss of the season, dashing our playoff hopes, happened against Kansas in late October, and the Scapegoater, in the game's aftermath, blamed Lebby (not without merit). An interception by the OU defense with 2:30 left in the fourth quarter convinced many Sooner fans that the game was won. Our lead stood precariously at 33–32. With only one first down standing in our way to victory, Lebby and the offense ran the ball three straight times for net negative yardage. The entire series lasted less than thirty seconds, forcing the Sooners to punt and giving Kansas more than two minutes to drive down the field for the winning score, which they did. At subsequent games, at home, the Scapegoater went to work. When the offense struggled, the Scapegoater shouted, "Lebby out!" or "Lebby, you suck!" Fans around him laughed and nodded their head. Sometimes the Scapegoater was so disgusted that it was merely the coach's last name he spat from his lips, with the utmost derision attached to it. Though I could not see him, I imagined the Scapegoater lifting his eyes and shaking a fist at the heavens, as if Lebby were a supernatural force that could not be stopped.

Another system of fandom derives its name from that the fact that its members are eager for the attention of others. (This might be said, however, about all such systems.) "Catwalk" fans are members of the student body, at a juncture of boldness as well as insecurity in their young lives. They crave affirmation, the approval of the crowd. The whole pageantry of game day, from the tailgate to the game itself to the late-night bar hop, is an opportunity to be seen. The coeds often travel in packs. The whole campus becomes their runway. I remember one such coed, blond and long-legged, striding down Brooks Pedestrian Mall before the game against Central Florida in October. She wore a sleeveless black top, blue jean shorts, and cowboy boots. The way she walked, with her hips swinging back and forth, made her look like a supremely confident superhero; she was on her way to face the Final Boss. Young men put themselves on display too. Some are partial to wearing the red and white striped overalls, no shirt underneath, that's been a sartorial tradition at OU for decades. Others can be seen in face and/or body paint in the student section. Still others (young men, that is) will go topless for the stadium "Flex Cam," praying that their gym time has been worthwhile. For those who prefer that you notice their sense of humor rather than their biceps, there's a system variant: the "Jesters." A good example was found in the student section during the 2023 season. Armed with a small whiteboard and dry erase markers, these students earned minor celebrity with their sardonic game commentary. In the home opener against Arkansas State, they trolled the visiting team's kicker after two missed field goals. The crowd laughed at the whiteboard message displayed on the video boards at Memorial Stadium: "ARK ST KICKER TRYOUT 8 AM MON." At the SMU game, the Jesters were briefer even than a haiku. On their whiteboard was a play on words, mocking the visitors' name: "SM-EW."

I hate to end this chapter by referencing fans from another school, but there's something about the moment, which happened after the SMU game, that stays with me. It feels both disposable and profound, throw-away but emblematic. Jenn and I were part of the stream of fans leaving Memorial Stadium and walking north on Jenkins. The street was blocked off, so people walked in the middle of Jenkins as well as on the sidewalks, heading toward their tailgate or car. It was suddenly dark outside; the game had ended and so had the day. In the distance was Sarkeys Energy Center, the tallest building on campus: rectangular and plain, without ornament. In front of Jenn and I walked a couple of young men, SMU fans; they could have been the Trolls who goaded us for much of the game, but they were not. They wore SMU colors and were probably still students. They walked soberly, without wobble, with almost the air of young philosophers on a stroll. They were quiet, perhaps reflecting on the loss or on loss in general. Then one of them said, apropos of nothing, "At least we don't live in Norman."

The other young man said nothing in reply; he nodded his head. A beat later, he pushed the speaker into a hedgerow that ran along the sidewalk. Jenn and I didn't break stride; we walked around the SMU fan still standing. Once past him, I turned my head around to gawk at the spectacle: the one kid devoured by the hedge, the other admiring his handiwork. Both SMU fans were laughing.

At least we don't live in Norman.

How many times, over the decades, had losing fans (I call them the Disgruntled Visitor) uttered those bitter words? An attempt to assuage the pain, embarrassment, and shame of loss. We lost to you, but your town sucks, which means that you suck.

They were fighting words and made me kind of mad. I recalled some of the Okie jokes that continued to make the rounds (*an Okie divorce is like a tornado: loud, angry and someone is gonna lose their trailer home*). But what could I do to retaliate? There was nothing. Boys will be boys. Trolls will do their thing. And violence was neither advisable nor legal.

As I write this, though, I see myself as a Sooner vigilante from the 1920s or a member of the Deep Dark Mystery Club, tasked with protecting the university. Put another way, I am here to defend the honor of OU, Norman, and the state of Oklahoma. Armed with a well-worn paddle, regulation in size, I'm chasing those SMU boys down Main Street. I'm chasing them out of our town.

In its second season, the football team at the University of Oklahoma played two games in fall 1896 against Norman high school students, winning by scores of 12–0 and 16–4. The next year, English professor Vernon Parrington arrived in Norman, transforming the team with training methods and tactics learned from his time at Harvard University. *Photo courtesy of Western History Collections, Special Research Collections, University of Oklahoma Libraries, OU Collection #887.*

A ticket booth stands beside the entrance to Boyd Field in 1914. Named after David Ross Boyd, the university's first president, the field was built in 1905, west of the Field House, with a grandstand and bleachers for five hundred fans. A thick hedge along the perimeter kept the ticketless from watching the action. *Photo courtesy of Western History Collections, Special Research Collections, University of Oklahoma Libraries, Mrs. Buford D. Monnet Collection #40.*

The Ruf Neks, an all-male spirit group founded in 1915, wield their paddles and conduct a "Frosh Gauntlet" south of the Field House in October 1927. Paddling was a form of corporal punishment used by upperclassmen to teach and control "yearlings." The widespread and controversial practice was banned by the university soon after this photo was taken. *Photo courtesy of Western History Collections, Special Research Collections, University of Oklahoma Libraries, Roy E. Heffner Collection #P109.*

Lloyd Burgess Curtis (*above, standing behind the bass drum*) poses with the first all-student pep band at the University of Oklahoma in 1905. During football games at Boyd Field, Curtis and the band sat in the wooden bleachers playing "Boomer Sooner" and "light marches" and tried to "make as much noise as possible." *Photo courtesy of Western History Collections, Special Research Collections, University of Oklahoma Libraries, Richard Conkling Collection #2.*

The Ruf Neks lead a "snake dance" at the intersection of Boyd and Asp in fall 1940. Pep rallies would start on campus but then move to Campus Corner where students built a bonfire, with the Pride of Oklahoma playing "pep songs" in the background. Firefighters would show up to douse the flames. *Photo courtesy of Western History Collections, Special Research Collections, University of Oklahoma Libraries, OUPS Collection #13681.*

Football coach Bennie Owen (*right*) poses with two of his players. He angles his body to the right and away from the camera presumably to hide his missing arm, which was lost in a 1907 hunting accident. The pioneering coach came to Norman in 1905, leading the team to its first-ever victory over Texas. He retired from coaching in 1926 after guiding the Sooners to four undefeated seasons and three conference championships. *Photo courtesy of Western History Collections, Special Research Collections, University of Oklahoma Libraries, OU Collection #4*

Oklahoma Memorial Stadium—also called Owen Field, after the football coach—is under construction in early 1925. The west stand (capacity: sixteen thousand) is a work in progress and will be finished just a few months later, in October, for the home opener against Drake University. Below the stadium is land where the South Oval will take shape, with the first buildings erected in the 1930s. *Photo courtesy of Western History Collections, Special Research Collections, University of Oklahoma Libraries, OU Collection # 1112.*

Students escort OU president William Bennett Bizzell from his house on Boyd Street on a cold November night in 1938. A crowd of students, celebrating a Sooner football victory the day before that clinched the Big 6 Conference title, asked Bizzell to cancel Monday's classes. The president's refusal caused a student "riot" the next day. *Photo courtesy of Western History Collections, Special Research Collections, University of Oklahoma Libraries, OUPS Collection #2454.*

(opposite top) Mex, a Staffordshire bull terrier, was brought to the university in 1919 by Mott Keys, a US Army veteran. For the next decade, Mex won campus fame as a sports mascot, honorary assistant coach, and member of several student organizations. He survived a murder attempt—the malefactor who poisoned him was never caught—and escaped a kidnapper. *Photo courtesy of Western History Collections, Special Research Collections, University of Oklahoma Libraries, OU Collection #1192.*

(opposite bottom) The Ruf Neks and Jazz Hounds, a male spirit group, form a funeral procession for Mex after the mascot's death in April 1928. After a viewing of the body at the Kappa Sigma house, the procession of students walked with Mex's casket—singing pep songs along the way—to a spot just north of Memorial Stadium where Mex was then buried. The exact location of his grave is not known. *Photo courtesy of Western History Collections, Special Research Collections, University of Oklahoma Libraries, Roy E. Heffner Collection # P739.*

Students dance on a countertop at a Campus Corner drugstore at the end of the "stormiest day in OU history" in November 1938. Earlier, bands of students defied president Bizzell and barged into classrooms, convincing professors to cancel class. The Sooners had won the conference title, and students felt more committed to celebration than their studies. *Photo courtesy of Western History Collections, Special Research Collections, University of Oklahoma Libraries, OUPS Collection #2462.*

Morris Tenenbaum (*center*), OU's first superfan, conducts business with two fraternity brothers in the late 1940s. A tailor by trade, Tenenbaum roamed the campus, buying clothes from cash-strapped students and then reselling them. For several decades and a succession of football coaches, he guarded the practice field during the week and the locker room at Owen Field on game days. *Photo courtesy of Western History Collections, Special Research Collections, University of Oklahoma Libraries, OUPS Collection #26539.*

SOON
Best

As OU's first African American football player on scholarship, Prentice Gautt displayed astonishing maturity and poise, encountering racism on the playing field as well as on campus. He was a talented athlete and diligent student, winning the MVP award in the 1959 Orange Bowl and earning Academic All-American honors in his senior season. *Photo courtesy of Western History Collections, Special Research Collections, University of Oklahoma Libraries, OU Collection #1082.*

(opposite top) Students wave at the camera before driving to Dallas for the Red River Rivalry in October 1957. The Friday before OU–Texas was dubbed "Migration Day" as thousands drove south on US 77 for a weekend of football and revelry. Larry LeVieux, class of 1955, compared the crowds in downtown Dallas to a swarm of ants: "They were everywhere; in the streets, in hotels, restaurants, night clubs and private homes." *Photo courtesy of Western History Collections, Special Research Collections, University of Oklahoma Libraries, OU Collection #1607.*

(opposite bottom) Jubilant Sooner fans swarm the field at the Cotton Bowl and tear down a goalpost after a razor-thin 14–13 victory over Texas in 1951. Coach "Bud" Wilkinson's team won the school its first national championship the season before, and the decade would bring more glory: a forty-seven-game win streak and two more national championships. *Photo courtesy of Western History Collections, Special Research Collections, University of Oklahoma Libraries, OU Collection #15919.*

Members of the OU spirit squad—a Ruf Nek, cheerleader Jessie McDowell, and "Little Red" Phil Waller—walk onto Owen Field before a football game circa 1960. Little Red became OU's official mascot in the early 1960s but was such a controversial figure that the university banned performers in "Indian costume" in 1973. *Photo courtesy of Western History Collections, Special Research Collections, University of Oklahoma Libraries, OU Collection #1826.*

Cecil Samara, the "World's Biggest OU Fan," stands next to the Big Red Rocket on a game day in the early 1990s. The Rocket was a 1923 Ford Model T renovated to embody Sooner Spirit. Samara drove the slow-moving vehicle—its top speed was thirty-five miles per hour—to home and away games as well as to Dallas for OU–Texas and Miami for the Orange Bowl. *Photo courtesy of Lisa Hall.*

The Sooner Schooner, driven by a Ruf Nek, charges onto Owen Field at a football game in the early 1990s. The modified Conestoga wagon, pulled by a duo of Welsh ponies named Boomer and Sooner, made its debut in September 1964 during a home game with the University of Southern California. It became the official school mascot in 1980. *Photo courtesy of Lisa Hall.*

Mike Vickrey, an army veteran and general contractor, fell in love with OU at an early age. He parks "the Beast," a converted school bus covered in Sooner decor, on Boyd Street for home football games. A trailer addition provides a space with benches and a TV where fellow tailgaters can sit, socialize, and watch the game. *Photo courtesy of Rosa Guardiola.*

Cailey England played on the OU women's soccer team for five seasons (2019–24), serving as captain and breaking several program records. She was recognized as a scholar-athlete in both the Big 12 and SEC and started medical school in fall 2025. *Photo courtesy of Camille Whitehead.*

Rylie Boone swings at a pitch at Love's Field during the 2024 season. The new stadium cost $48 million to build and stands as a visual reminder of how far the softball program has come: The team in the eighties and nineties played its games in a public park. In 2024, the Sooners won their fourth national championship in a row under head coach Patty Gasso, bringing the program's total to eight. *Photo courtesy of Chad Hamilton.*

Carrie Henderson relaxes at her tailgate in the parking lot of Oklahoma City's Devon Park during the 2025 Women's College World Series. Henderson played catcher for the Sooner softball team in the 1980s and, as a season ticket holder at Love's Field, travels from her home in Bixby to Norman to watch the women play. *Photo courtesy of Rosa Guardiola.*

Antonio Record, aka Mr. OU, began his journey as a superfan in 2018. The designation feels more like a calling than a hobby for the Tulsa-born Record, who hopes one day to graduate from the university. Across a variety of sports, Mr. OU can be found in the stands cheering on the Sooners. *Photo courtesy of Ladonna Shaffer.*

(opposite top) John Hurd's beer dispenser is a popular attraction at his tailgate on the lawn in front of Carpenter Hall. An engineer, OU class of 1995, Hurd used a variety of materials to build the dispenser including a mobility scooter, OU football helmet, CO_2 tank, and stainless-steel tubing. *Photo courtesy of Rosa Guardiola.*

(opposite bottom) Fans hang out at John Hurd's tailgate before Oklahoma hosts Alabama in November 2024. The three tents were specially ordered to mark OU's first season in the SEC. In their best performance of a disappointing season, the Sooners upset the Crimson Tide, with hundreds of students rushing Owen Field to celebrate. *Photo courtesy of Rosa Guardiola.*

Part III

■ ■ ■

SPIRIT

9

BROTHERHOOD OF THE UNSHAVEN

THE YEAR 1915 was a special one for Sooner football. Bennie Owen's speedsters, considered the fastest team in the Southwest conference, won all ten games, including a nailbiter with Texas 14–13 in front of eleven thousand fans at the Texas State Fair. Before the rivalry game, a local businessman collaborated with OU "yell master" Charles Leslie High to ensure that the football team would be supported in Dallas like never before. D. L. Larsh, manager of the Norman Milling & Grain Company, paid the thousand dollars to reserve a special train to carry High and more than a hundred "Sooners and Sooner supporters" to the game. On the side of the train was a sign that read, "BEAT TEXAS." Eleven hundred well-wishers, unable to make the trip, assembled at the Santa Fe train station to say goodbye. Among the riders were twenty-three members of the OU pep band, which played for the crowd on the platform the same selection of tunes that they would later play at the game "to hearten the Sooner warriors and dismay the Longhorns." This would be the first year the band traveled to support the Varsity at OU–Texas.

Two months later, at a Sooner basketball game, another act of spirit transpired whose reverberations are still felt today. This act was categorically different from the one that took place in October, with the band. The

OU basketball team was playing in-state antagonist Oklahoma A&M in the Gymnasium, a "little frame building" located where Memorial Union stands today. Among the crowd was a group of Varsity football players who, shall we say, were intoxicated with Sooner pride. Accounts vary as to what happened. *Sooner Magazine* in 1938 reported that a passerby, strolling past the building, noticed the boisterous young men and remarked, "Oh you roughnecks," before walking away. A video posted to OU's official Facebook page in 2019 presents the episode differently. In this version, a fellow Sooner fan, sitting in the stands, was so irritated by the football players that she yelled at them: "Sit down and be quiet you roughnecks!"

Contrary to the stories above, I found evidence in the student newspaper to suggest that the group was around, generating spirit, at least four weeks prior to that December basketball game. The students involved couldn't have been football players since their "stunt" happened at the Varsity's game against Kansas on October 30, 1915, at Boyd Field. It's likely that aforementioned yell master High, the group's founder and the first ever "Head Nek" (he was also known as His Majesty King Jazzum), led the proceedings. The *University Oklahoman* reported that on the day the "Rough Necks" joined the "Freshman, Juniors, and Seniors . . . down from the rooter's [*sic*] bleachers and took possession of the field between halves, the classmen staging a monster snake dance." The students on the field, according to the newspaper, numbered close to a thousand. Thanks in part to the spirit shown by students and alumni in the stands, the Sooners prevailed over the Jayhawkers 23–14.

The spelling of the spirit group's name has varied considerably over the past hundred-plus years. At first, they were the Rough Necks. By 1919, they appeared in *The Oklahoma Daily* as the Ruf Neks, as if to emphasize that they were not rule followers, even when it came to spelling. Other formulations found their way into the newspaper, *Sooner Magazine*, and then online: Ruf-Neks or Ruff Neks or RUF/NEKS. In this book, I call them the "Ruf Neks" until we get to the modern day. The reader will see why later.

By the 1920s, the group's form and function had been worked out. Dressed in white "duck" pants and red corduroy shirts, they existed to exalt both the university and the football team. In the beginning, they didn't travel to support the Varsity; the Ruf Neks were responsible for leading the "razzum" and organizing "stunts" at home games. Such halftime stunts included symbolic burial of opponents—the Kansas Jayhawkers and Missouri Tigers were frequent victims—and the formation of an "OU" on Boyd Field alongside members of the band. When Washington University visited Norman in October 1921, the Ruf Neks showed their hospitality by driving a wagon (a precursor to the Sooner Schooner) onto Boyd Field; two members stood on the wagon wringing out clothes to dramatize "taking the Wash out of Washington."

The Ruf Neks were a competent bunch, put in charge of organizing pep rallies and even the homecoming parade. And the aforementioned stunts were tame enough. But there's no question the Ruf Neks exhibited a rough and tumble nature, and quickly they developed a reputation. One Ruf Nek, in 1920, was none too happy when someone outed him to his hometown newspaper. When the young man's father read that his son had become a member of the group, he promptly sent a letter, the message of which was relayed to *The Oklahoma Daily*: "I got a letter from the old man telling me that I could just cut that out or he would cut me off. He said the reason he sent me to college was to get me out of the ruf nek crowd at home."

When *The Oklahoma Daily* admonished the upperclassmen in October 1921 for lagging behind the freshmen in the spirit department, its editors also published a threat from the Ruf Neks. The problem, according to the newspaper, was that too many students were bringing a date to the game: "A man with a date at his side feels ungallant if he turns away from her and lets loose his lungs with a good husky yell, or if he loses the thread of her tea-room conversation when he watches whether Tarz Marsh is going to snag down this next pass." The solution was to bring back an old rule banning dates on game day; there should be no coupling at Boyd Field. As a result, the *Daily* was sure that the upperclassmen, compared to "stags herded into their own pasture," would then "feel free to tear loose with their hells and horns." A "deeper bellowing" would issue from their collective maw. If anyone was found to violate this rule, the Ruf Neks would be on hand with their paddles to dish out punishment. The short editorial titled "A DATELESS SOONER IS A ROOTING SOONER" ended with a note of support: "Go to it, Ruf Neks, the school is with you."

Paddling became a controversial subject in the twenties and got the Ruf Neks in trouble. It was the first time the group was sanctioned by the university, but it wouldn't be the last.

Sooner Magazine offers proof that paddling was on people's minds. A short article in the November 1929 issue lamented the fact that not a single bookstore existed in Norman. The writer then jested that, though you couldn't buy a book, you'd have no trouble finding that instrument of discipline used by schoolmasters and Ruf Neks alike: "About all you can sell in Norman are paddles." In the same issue, a letter to the editor, from an OU alumnus, lands emphatically on one side of the corporal punishment debate. I. G. Richardson, class of 1917, was responding to the university's recent ban on the paddling of freshmen. Before, paddling was rampant. Richardson, a firm believer in the maxim "spare the rod, spoil the child," views his own experience with paddling at OU as character-building:

> I believe that more good was accomplished during my four years at the university in developing real "he-men" by the use of the paddle, than any other method of instruction which our modern universities offer. I know of many raw-boned freshmen, fresh from the "sticks," who have developed into very successful businessmen because they were disciplined in their freshmen year at college.

The Ruf Neks would have agreed with the sentiment, and they used the paddle freely and publicly. It was part of their initiation rites for incoming members, and it was wielded in the stands at Boyd Field. One of their traditions, chronicled and denounced in *Sooner Magazine*, involved the public paddling of a willing student who, for this act of endurance, earned an "honor" beneath his picture in the college yearbook. Before a "large and interested crowd" on Campus Corner, a "beefy Nek" would put the "neophyte" through hell. One time, a coed in the crowd nearly lost her eye to a splinter flying forth from a paddle, such was the force of the beating. The Ruf Neks did themselves no favors by operating with a spirit of defiance. According to reports, they refused to show their tickets at the gate to Boyd Field; instead, they simply rushed the gate and went through. During one such occurrence, a boy was hit on the head with a paddle, suffering a serious injury.

Such incidents angered the public, newspapers, and administration, and they played a role in the eventual ban on paddling. Not that the Ruf Neks paid heed.

In 1929, they were hauled before faculty and regents for a meeting to determine their fate. *Sooner Magazine* published an account of the proceedings. The committee had found out about a recent initiation ceremony, which involved paddles, pledges, and a drive to the countryside. Though the committee could not determine with absolute certainty whether the paddles had been deployed, thus breaking the no-paddling rule, the faculty and regents used the testimony of the Ruf Neks against them as a conclusive nail in the coffin. When the Ruf Neks admitted that paddling was central to their identity, the committee reasoned that since paddling was now outlawed it made no sense to allow the group to continue: "The abandonment of the paddling practice virtually destroys the only feature and traditions of these organizations worth while and that unless this practice can be continued there is little inducement to continue the orders."

Formally, the Ruf Neks (along with the male spirit group the Jazz Hounds) were abolished in September 1929. Any students found guilty of trying to revive the group would be expelled by the university.

Local newspapers such as *The Oklahoma City Times* and *The Daily Oklahoman*, which had published scathing columns about the Ruf Neks, were no doubt pleased with the punishment. Frank Buttram, president of the regents, told *The Norman Transcript* that abolition of these troublesome groups was a progressive move that kept the university in lock step with its peers nationwide. He thought that OU would have no problem creating a replacement pep group:

> The University of Oklahoma will have as much school spirit as ever. Traditions will not be forgotten simply because fifty-seven boys are barred from swinging paddles on freshmen. Traditions amount

> to more than this obsolete form of fun. The whole student body will be a pep organization. Ten or twelve peppy fellows, dressed in appropriate loud colors, will be chosen to lead yells at the football games. That is done at all the large universities.

Not everyone, however, was pleased. Less than a month after the Ruf Neks were banned, on a Thursday night, a group of three hundred freshmen caused a ruckus downtown, according to *Sooner Magazine*. The freshmen "built a bonfire, invaded the Sooner theater and took some cigars, etc[.], from several drugstores." The publication reported that Norman business owners lamented the absence of the Ruf Neks, who, it was thought, would have kept the freshmen in line.

The two spirit groups were reinstated in March 1932, the explanation for their revival escaping this researcher's efforts. The '89-ers, the replacement pep squad endorsed by the board of regents, went the way of the dodo. Ruf Nek pledges, forty in number, were seen marching around campus with their "rope encircled waists and bewhiskered male mugs." Red and white ribbons were attached to their clothing, and the pledges chanted their traditional refrain of "Ruf Tuf Ruf Tuf Ruf Tuf."

Ruf Nek traditions developed over time. Some of the following continue to exist, in one form or another. Pledges grew out beards for the first three weeks of their four-week pledge-ship (hence, the Ruf Neks' alternative name, the Royal Order of the Unshaven). After week three, they shaved ceremonially in front of a crowd of students on Campus Corner. The pledges could use their own razors, but the senior members of the club supplied them with a "secret-formula shaving cream," *The Oklahoma Daily* reported. Sticking with the theme of shaving, the Ruf Nek president abstained from the practice if the Sooners lost a ball game. He couldn't pick up a razor until after the Sooners had won again. The "Fadada" chant, full of nonsense words like a nursery rhyme ("Deton boten doten / Raddy daddy / Do hey . . . ") was spoken before the start of every home game. After leading the football team onto the field, the Ruf Neks sprinted a hundred yards and slid like baseball players around the goalpost where they pounded the grass with their paddles and said the Fadada chant to chase off evil spirits along with any snakes or "critters" that might be hiding. Before and during big football games, the Ruf Neks served as campus security guards. For example, the night before OU–Texas and Bedlam, they patrolled campus buildings to protect against vandals. Once, after a loss to Nebraska in the 1970s, they congregated around the goal posts on Owen Field to keep visiting fans from tearing them down. Since 1983, the week before OU–Texas, the Ruf Neks have applied a fresh coat of paint to the "BEAT THE HELL OUT OF TEXAS" street art that decorates the walkway east of Elm between Ellison and Farzaneh Halls.

▪ ▪ ▪

Predictably, the Ruf Neks were in trouble again in 1933 and then again two years later. They were suspended until the next regents' meeting for using a "profane" yell on the field at halftime of the homecoming game against Kansas. They promised the regents "to be good," but then, in 1935, the Ruf Neks allegedly broke that promise. The student paper reported that on "Migration Day" to Dallas for the Red River Rivalry, they were "charged with leading and inciting the trainload of students to destructive violence." Windows were broken, causing $150 in damage.

The Second World War broke up the Ruf Neks in 1943, but they were back on campus three years later. In 1947, firing a shotgun to celebrate Sooner touchdowns came into practice. *The Oklahoma Daily* referred to the Ruf Neks' shotgun as "Big Ben" or "old blunderbuss." Cecil Morris, starting right guard and co-captain of the football team, said he only heard two sounds during the 1955 season: his quarterback's voice and the Ruf Neks' shotgun blasts. According to Ruf Nek lore (I could find no research corroborating the story), their shotguns got the attention of the FBI in 1958 after OU–Texas. For some reason, the federal government seized the guns (one account blamed a tattling Texas fan who claimed the shotguns were of illegal length). All but one of the shotguns the Ruf Neks got back. The lone shotgun, kept by the government, was then donated to the Smithsonian Institution in Washington, DC, such was the historic and cultural value of the artifact, where it still (allegedly) resides. My investigation into the matter—a phone call to the Smithsonian followed by an email—went nowhere. I picture "old blunderbuss" stored in a crate in a dark basement room of the Smithsonian, radiating heat. It's just begging to be fired again.

■ ■ ■

Lil' Sis is known as the female offshoot of the Ruf Neks, but the organization was preceded by a group called the Ruffettes. In September 1947, an article in *The Oklahoma Daily* announced the group's formation and detailed its first meeting where sixty "coeds" chose a name and a committee to draft the group's constitution, which would likely resemble that of the Ruf Neks. The Ruffettes' uniform was also decided: white sweaters and red skirts. Across the front of the sweater the group's name would appear in red letters. When President Harry Truman rode a train into Norman for a campaign stop in September 1948, the Ruffettes were one of the spirit groups that performed for the crowd of fifteen thousand ahead of Truman's arrival. They were side by side with the Ruf Neks the following month, holding "flaming torches" as they visited the Greek houses, collecting students, en route to Memorial Stadium where a pep rally was about to take place.

The Ruffettes disappear from the student newspaper after 1949, leaving one to assume that the group fizzled out through lack of interest. The story picks up again in September 1972. After expressing interest in joining the Ruf Neks, Kathy Armstrong, a freshman from Oklahoma City, and Susan Blend, a freshman from Houston, started doing the things associated with pledging the spirit group. They attended the annual rush smoker, bought a uniform, and sold eyeshades at football games (the latter had long been a practice of Ruf Nek pledges to raise funds for the group). At the first pledge meeting, they were given mixed messages. They would be allowed to participate in some activities, but no promises about membership could be given. Tom Watson, assistant Ruf Nek pledge trainer, admitted as much at a later court hearing presided over by the University of Oklahoma Students Association (UOSA). He said to the court, "We told them from the beginning we didn't know what their status was, but we would find out."

In early October, Armstrong and Blend heard from the Ruf Neks that they weren't eligible to join the group, after which the women filed a complaint with UOSA seeking reimbursement for the uniforms they had purchased and eyeshades sold. Bill Burnham, a law student who represented Armstrong and Blend at the initial hearing, argued that the Ruf Neks should be considered a student organization and thus subject to the student code of conduct, which prohibited discrimination on the basis of sex. The Ruf Neks had violated the code.

In early December, the student court released its verdict, siding with Armstrong and Blend and ordering the spirit group to stop discriminating by the fall semester or face a ban from Owen Field. The Ruf Neks appealed, arguing that they were a private group and not a student group; thus, they could discriminate if they wanted to. In April 1973, their appeal was turned down by the OU Judicial Tribunal. In that same year, a female branch of the Ruf Neks was born: Lil' Sis.

The two groups held joint meetings and cohosted rush events, but it was clear the Ruf Neks and Lil' Sis weren't on equal footing. Several activities were off limits. Lil' Sis could not be on the field during football games; they sat in the stands. They were not involved with the Sooner Schooner at all. The shotguns were fired by the Ruf Neks only. Lil' Sis cheered alongside their male counterparts at pep rallies. They participated in fund-raising projects and community events, such as an annual Easter egg hunt for children at the Jane Brooks School for the Deaf in Chickasha.

Lil' Sis's evolution happened slowly. In 1989, members rode in the Sooner Schooner on touchdown celebrations for the first time. In October 2000, they emulated the Ruf Neks in a negative sense, making headlines for a hazing incident. During a pledge event called "Paddle Night," three Lil' Sis pledges were plied with alcohol at houses where Ruf Neks and Lil' Sis members resided. One pledge was so intoxicated she was rushed to the hospital and treated for alcohol poisoning. Lil' Sis was suspended as a result. In 2003, as the group celebrated its thirtieth anniversary, its nine members declared to *The Oklahoma Daily* that they continued to pivot around three core principles: strength, sisterhood, and tradition. Jaclyn Williams, Lil' Sis president, said that prejudices and stereotypes about them persisted. Naysayers asserted that hazing was rife in the group. Cynics claimed that Lil' Sis had little reason to exist; they were simply riding on the Ruf Neks' coattails. Kandis Murdock, Lil' Sis vice president, brought up tensions with the Ruf Neks. She said that the men were actively excluding them from traditions such as riding in the Schooner and painting the "Beat the Hell Out of Texas" street art on campus.

Khaliliah Smith, a former Lil' Sis president, was blunt in her assessment of the relationship between the two spirit groups. She said, "The discrimination we were fighting in 1973 is the same discrimination we're fighting now. . . . All those years they've tried to destroy us, but we're still here, and we'll continue to be here."

The Ruf Neks did little to dispel this characterization. Their president Jim Allred told the student newspaper, "The only thing we have in common is that we share the same name."

Obviously, the two groups had their issues. However, an epic collaboration between the Ruf Neks and Lil' Sis in 1991 showed what they were capable of. In February, the two presidents of the respective groups sneaked into the elevator shaft of Monnet Hall on a Friday night, waited for everyone to leave, and then, in red and white colors, painted a giant Ruf Nek paddle. There on the wall of the elevator shaft, it reached four stories in height. One of the painters, Lil' Sis president Robin Stroud, told *The Oklahoma Daily* in 2005 that their purpose was to leave a hidden treasure for future members to discover. "Only one or two pledge classes in 1991 and 1992 got to see it," Stroud said. "We knew that once it got discovered it would get closed down."

According to Jacquelyn Slater Reese, librarian for the Western History Collections in Monnet Hall, the infamous paddle painting still exists; no one, however, is allowed to see it for obvious safety reasons.

In the 2010s, the pace of change within the two spirit groups accelerated. Certain members of Lil' Sis started asking questions: Why don't we have our own ceremonial shotgun? Why hasn't a woman ever driven the Sooner Schooner?

The shotgun came first. Debuting at the annual spring game in April 2019, it was dubbed "Trailblazer" and painted red and white, with

"1973"—the year of Lil' Sis's founding—on the gunstock. Three years later, Lil' Sis were part of the Ruf Nek "gun line" for the first time: three members, each with a .410 shotgun, firing into the Norman sky.

The question of driving the Schooner arose at a Lil' Sis meeting in 2019. Darby Dean, Lil' Sis president, described the moment to *The Oklahoman*. She said to the other members, "I don't know why we're not driving the Schooner. . . . We're shooting shotguns. We're doing these things. Why aren't we driving?"

The following summer, while at home in Texas, she was invited onto a Zoom call with Phil O'Neill, director of Spirit Squads for OU Athletics, who informed her that she'd been selected to train as a driver. According to an interview in *The Oklahoman*, Dean spent sixty hours in the fall getting to know the Schooner as well as ponies Boomer and Sooner. This included practice runs on the farm and in the parking lot of Lloyd Noble Center before graduating to practice runs on Owen Field.

The Thursday before Bedlam in November 2020, Dean was told that she'd be driving the Sooner Schooner at the game. In the second quarter, after a Sooner field goal, Dean held the reins as the wagon darted into the north endzone. She thought the ponies were moving a little slowly, perhaps tired from an active first quarter. But once they made the turn they sped up. The Schooner was moving very quickly as it approached the tunnel following its successful run. Dean and her passenger, Ryan Ard, each raised an arm in a victory salute. Back in the tunnel, with the ponies cooling off, Ard and Dean engaged in an old ritual, exclusive to drivers of the Sooner Schooner. On the left arm of Dean's crimson dress was placed a ceremonial patch, featuring the wagon and one of the ponies.

■ ■ ■

Before I go forward with my account of the Ruf Neks, I should be clear about something. It's not my intention to simply catalog the group's bad behavior. Of course, they reveled in their mischief, but they were more than their bad boy image suggested. Members participated wholly in campus life, assuming a variety of roles and going on to professional success. Wesley I. Nunn, a founding member of the Ruf Neks, was business manager and sports editor of the student newspaper *The University Oklahoman*. Along with the paper's editor, Nunn was responsible in 1916 for turning it into a daily, which they retitled *The Oklahoma Daily*, a remarkable feat given their resources at the time. After graduation, Nunn worked in the oil business for decades as an advertising executive. He stayed connected to his alma mater while living in Chicago, serving as a member of OU's Athletic Council and a member of the executive board of the University of Oklahoma Association.

Many Ruf Neks stayed local following graduation. They became valuable members of the community: dentist, high school teacher, college dean, city councilman.

Fast-forwarding to the present, the group remains civic-minded. Dakota Page, class of 2025, told the OU Foundation website that service was the most rewarding part of his career. He cited Saturdays in the fall, with all their varied excitements: "People always ask, 'What's your favorite part of game day?' and I could say the shotguns or the Schooner and ponies, but mine really is the Fan Fest, taking photos with the fans and talking with them." Service also meant giving back to the Cherokee community to which Page belonged. An architect in training, Page hoped to one day write an architecture book in the Cherokee language, which he learned in his youth, to "help provide a pillar of education in the field for future generations of Cherokee architects."

Groups with longevity serve as a barometer for society. Through study of the group, one sees how society has changed. This is certainly true with the Ruf Neks, who gradually evolved with the times. At one shameful end you have Charles Leslie High, OU's first "pep manager" as well as founder of the Ruf Neks in 1915. High was a proverbial man about campus, popular and involved. A talented singer, High regularly performed in campus minstrel shows in black face. Such shows were commonplace in America in the nineteenth and twentieth centuries and illustrated the country's racial stratification. Initially, I was shocked to see High's performances advertised in *The Oklahoma Daily*; given the realities of racial segregation at the time, I shouldn't have been.

At the other end, you have Jared Bush. In 2019, he became the first African American to drive the Sooner Schooner. As fate would have it, this was also the infamous ride that saw the Schooner crash for a second time in its history. I learned something about the aftermath of that crash in an interview with John Carter, a Ruf Nek who graduated from OU in 2023. Carter drove the Schooner and helped train other drivers. He told me that Bush received death threats on social media. These haters—unhinged, to say the least—blamed Bush for the crash since he was the one driving. While Bush was on Campus Corner on a Saturday night, following the crash, people in passing cars shouted the N-word at him. (There's also a lesson here about the persistence of racism in American culture.) Carter and his fellow Ruf Neks rallied around their brother, and Bush refused to quit. After a period of re-training, he took the reins again, and for the next two years "crushed every run he did after that."

Carter called Bush a "warrior" and "legend" for the way he bounced back. Additionally, he said that Bush's comeback changed his outlook on life. For the way Bush embodied the Ruf Nek spirit, Carter thought Bush should go down in history "as the most famous Ruf Nek."

■ ■ ■

In the late twentieth century, hazing continued to be at the center of the Ruf Neks' troubles with the powers-that-be. The group was suspended in October 1981 following accusations from several ex-pledges. At a subsequent hearing with the OU administration board, counsel for the Ruf Neks argued that hazing was ill-defined in the OU Student Code of Conduct. Furthermore, it was argued that the ex-pledges' allegations were untrue. The board ruled against the Ruf Neks, whose suspension was made indefinite. After reviewing the evidence, Jack Stout, vice president for Student Affairs, said it was "the most blatant case of hazing I have encountered in my fifteen years at OU." The allegations make for difficult reading. Former pledges testified that various substances were put in their mouths: bourbon, chewing tobacco, snuff, beets, and hot peppers. With their mouths stuffed, they were forced to exercise. When one pledge threw up, he was allegedly made to do pushups in his own vomit. At least two pledges went to the hospital for treatment.

The questions are inevitable: What purpose does hazing serve? Why do human beings do it?

Anthropologists and psychologists have noted that hazing takes place in human societies around the world. Social psychologist Brock Bastian, from the University of Melbourne, along with other researchers, concluded in 2014 that collectively experienced pain acts like "social glue" binding the participants and promoting cooperation. In his 2024 study of an American college fraternity, anthropologist Aldo Cimino, from Kent State University, argued that hazing serves as a "commitment-selection strategy." In other words, it tests a pledge's commitment and resolve. Is this the kind of person who will stick around and be useful? Or will he bolt at the first sign of adversity, thereby failing to contribute to the group? In such a dynamic, the group takes precedence over the individual. If the social scientists are correct, humans appear hardwired for rituals that are difficult and even painful; these rituals are used for selection. Passing the test is a ticket to belonging.

That said, there's no denying the harm that can result from hazing: post-traumatic stress disorder, substance abuse, depression, and even death (seventeen fraternity pledges died in this country between 2010 and 2017). To make matters worse, psychologist and hazing expert Susan Lipkins argues that hazing has only gotten more "brutal" in the twenty-first century, with the sadism cranked up to new levels. Such acts have included severe beatings, abuse of pledges' genital area, "butt-chugging" of alcohol, and even the use of stun guns. A 2014 report by the Association for the Study of Higher Education found that 73 percent of college students in Greek life had been hazed during their pledge-ship.

While rituals of endurance, such as hazing, might have a biological component, it's also true that culture plays a role. Plenty of people want to stop the practice, with at least forty-four states passing anti-hazing laws, but others, including powerful alumni, want hazing to continue because they believe in it. According to Sam (the pseudonym for a senior officer in a national fraternity), the practice "works." His defense of hazing, an echo of the aforementioned academic scholarship, can be found in the 2019 book *Fraternity: An Inside Look at a Year of College Boys Becoming Men*: "Hazing creates an unusually strong bond between people who weather tough times together, and the toughness also creates the illusion of reaching a worthwhile goal. It increases the value of the letters because you've undergone such a hard process of obtaining them."

Whatever the prevailing sentiment about hazing held by OU alumni and students, the University of Oklahoma has long taken a dim view of the practice and, in the Ruf Neks' case, struggled to get a handle on things.

After the Ruf Neks' 1981 suspension, the university formed an ad hoc committee to study how the spirit group might be reformed. Two public forums were held. Alumni added their voices, making phone calls to the likes of Leon Cross, assistant athletic director, in support of the Ruf Neks. In June 1982, the committee's ruling, full of requirements, was published in *The Oklahoma Daily*. The old pledge system was discarded. The Ruf Neks would fall under the supervision of the office of Student Affairs and particularly a three-member advisory board. In terms of joining the group, a pledge must meet physical fitness standards (the ability to jog from Campus Corner to Memorial Stadium, the ability to sprint a hundred-yard dash, and the ability to walk up and down the stadium steps to sell eyeshades). Pledges and members must observe "field etiquette": no swearing or obscene gestures while on Owen Field. The successful pledge must also possess knowledge of OU and Ruf Nek history. There was now a no-drinking policy while on duty with the Ruf Neks, and all members would have to sign an anti-hazing statement at their initiation ceremony.

The Ruf Neks resumed their regular duties in the fall. The oversight, however, was not permanent. Into the twenty-first century, the Ruf Neks got their autonomy back, with some arguing that the group received preferential treatment from OU president David Boren. *The Oklahoma Daily* characterized the group as one that "boozed and hazed with impunity." In October 2007, anonymous calls to the university's anti-hazing hotline led to another official investigation of the Ruf Neks. As a result, twenty-five members were banned for a year from football games and other university events. Another consequence was that, starting in the spring, the Ruf

Neks would fall under the control of the athletic department. They were now an official student organization.

In retrospect, this seems a watershed moment when change could not be denied or thwarted any longer. Indeed, after 2007, the Ruf Neks disappear as a frequent punching bag of the student newspaper.

When I talked to John Carter, the recently graduated Ruf Nek, his words seemed to corroborate this notion that the group—at 109 years old, the oldest male spirit organization in America—was a changed entity. I asked about hazing, and Carter was categorically against it, calling the practice "unprofessional" and "irrelevant." He said other things, which sent the message that this new generation of Ruf Neks was different from the old. He spoke with both an air of idealism, in line with the politics of our time, as well as an air of pragmatism. Concerning the latter, he said that he and his colleagues were mindful of posterity: "We want to do what's best for the club because we want to be around for the next one hundred years and we need to conform to whatever that standard's going to be." Carter praised Lil' Sis and spoke in glowing terms about their hard-won advances. The antagonism that characterized the groups' relationship for decades seemed no longer present. As if in illustration of this, Carter shared that he fell in love with a member of Lil' Sis; they're married now. In fact, she was his passenger in his first official ride on Owen Field.

I wanted to hear from current members of the Ruf Neks and Lil' Sis, but when I inquired, I ran into a bureaucratic wall. Phil O'Neill, director of OU Spirit Squads, told me that the group was not available to the media. This sent a clear message and made me think of public relations. I thought of "branding."

Considering the Ruf Neks' anarchic and colorful history, it made me sad to think that, in a sense, they were now a "managed" group, closely monitored by the university. (The 2010s, I would argue, are when the Ruf Neks became the RUF/NEKS, a polished and inoffensive student club.) But at the same time, it was impossible to argue that many of the recent changes hadn't been necessary and righteous. I was in two minds about the whole thing, and after a while I figured out the source of my ambivalence. Americans love a good rebel; the trope is part of our cultural heritage.

For whatever reasons, we fall in love with real-life baddies like Bonnie and Clyde and Al Capone, despite their crimes and misdeeds. Audiences cheered and swooned over James Dean in *Rebel Without a Cause*. In Soonerland, former star linebacker Brian "the Boz" Bosworth defied convention with his rebellious haircut (a hybrid style combining the Mohawk, flat top, and mullet) while delighting fans with his take-no-prisoners approach to football and life. He was banned from the 1987 Orange Bowl after testing positive for steroids. He called the NCAA "communists" for allegedly ruling over student-athletes with an iron fist. Decades after his playing days in the 1980s, Sooner Nation continues to adore "the Boz."

For many years, the Ruf Neks belonged in this rebel category, attracting loyalty and sympathy among the fans and even university administrators. They've been tremendously popular. Though a subdued force in the present, the group retains its bad-boy aura, and for this and other reasons (firing their shotguns, driving the Sooner Schooner, and leading the "razzum") the RUF/NEKS will continue to play an essential role in fandom at the University of Oklahoma.

A question emerges: Can a tiger change its stripes? A fictional character swims in my imagination too: Alex, from Stanley Kubrick's *A Clockwork Orange*. At the end of the classic 1971 film, the charismatic anti-hero's eyes roll back into his head after he convinces his captors that he's been rehabilitated. He's no longer a danger to society. But as he imagines his old perverse delights (and anticipates new ones), the audience hears his ironic voiceover, "I was cured all right."

A part of me hopes that, like Alex, the RUF/NEKS will never be cured.

▪ 10 ▪

TWO MASCOTS

IN 1916, Mott Keys and Hutton Bellah were soldiers in the US Army stationed at Fort Sill in Lawton, Oklahoma, when they found a stray, sickly puppy—white with brown spots—on the street and smuggled him onto base. A fellow soldier, by the name of Blakely, was a horse trainer and pledged to make the stray "one of the smartest dogs in the army." Months later, Keys and Bellah brought the dog as they traveled south to a military base in San Benito, a Texas border town a few miles from the Rio Grande. Along the way, they decided to rename the Staffordshire bull terrier "Mexico." (According to the American Kennel Club, members of this breed have a head that "is short and broad, with pronounced cheek muscles, and the tight-fitting coat comes in several colors. Staffords still resemble the pugnacious brawlers who once ruled England's fighting pits. But today's responsible breeders are producing sweet-natured, eager-to-please Staffords with a reputation for being patient companions to the whole family.") Mex was with the two soldiers for a year on the border before accompanying Bellah to Camp Bowie in Texas ahead of a deployment to France with the army's Thirty-Sixth Division. The United States was about to enter the First World War. While Bellah served overseas from 1918 to 1919, Mex lived in Hollis, Oklahoma, with Bellah's parents.

Keys never went overseas. Released from the military, he matriculated to the University of Oklahoma in fall 1919. On the way there, he picked up Mex. Thereafter, the dog began his illustrious tenure on campus.

Mex was a joiner. In his nine years at the university, he was initiated into Kappa Sigma, Phi Beta Kappa, Sigma Delta Chi, Red Red Rose, Quo Vadis, Battle Ax, Zeta Bigma, and the Deep Dark Mystery Club. Mex was a "rooter" for all the athletic teams—earning Varsity letters for golf, tennis, baseball, and basketball—but it was on the football field where he made his biggest mark. Clad in a crimson sweater, Mex patrolled the sidelines at football games. Observers said he cheered Sooner touchdowns with his bark. Mex was also a security guard trained to keep other dogs off the practice field. At one Tuesday session, Mex charged a large bulldog "weighing twenty pounds more than himself" that got too close to the players. *The Oklahoma Daily* reported on the near clash: "The big dog recognized Mex's right on the Owen field and realized he was a visitor and did not fight the famous Sooner hound." For his contributions to the team, Coach Owen made Mex an honorary member of the coaching staff.

Just days after the confrontation with the bulldog, in September 1921, Mex landed on the front page of *The Oklahoma Daily* for a more serious reason. The headline read: "Poisoning Arouses Ire of Sooner Dog Lovers; Big Reward Offered." Mex, along with two other dogs, had been poisoned. One of the dogs died, but thanks to a veterinarian's help and a strong constitution Mex survived. Determined to find the perpetrator, Sooner fans pledged to "make Norman too hot for the guilty man," but the search, with no leads available, went nowhere.

Mex made a full recovery and returned to his duties as Sooner mascot. He loomed large in the imagination of those on campus. In November 1922, the *Daily* published a comic sketch that saw Mex as part of a rowdy cast of characters. He chases after and bites a Ruf Nek whose beard makes him unrecognizable. Mex mistakes the Ruf Nek for "a Jayhawker, Tiger or Aggie spy."

Mex's life took another dramatic turn on a road trip to Des Moines, Iowa, with the football team in late October 1924. As the players switched trains in Lawrence, Kansas, Mex couldn't be coaxed to come aboard. One account said that Mex bolted to chase after a cat. Dressed only in his "night apparel," the captain of the team ran after the bull terrier but got called back to the train, which was about to depart. The team had to leave Mex to fend for himself. Some argued that Mex's absence affected the Sooners' play on Saturday; they lost badly, 28–0 to Drake University. The missing dog became a topic of conversation on radio and in newspapers; a reward was offered for his safe return. Five days after Mex ran off, Kappa Sigma fraternity, Mex's custodians, fielded a phone call from Arkansas City, Kansas. A local dog catcher had rescued Mex from a man who intended to keep him. A front-page headline in Wednesday's *Daily* announced: "The Lost Is Found! Mex Once More Is in Hands of Friends." The student newspaper then declared it would be collecting reward money for John Carter, the dog catcher, described as a "poor, hard-working man" who wasn't paid a salary by the city for his services.

Old age sidelined Mex in 1925. With "dull tooth and wheezy bark," he leisurely spent his days on the lawn of the Kappa Sigma house, but in fall 1926 he made a comeback. Wearing his patented sweater, a ten-year-old Mex was present for the first game of the season, a home win against Arkansas.

Mex officially retired as mascot in late 1927. In March 1928, an "ailing" Mex was sent to an animal hospital in Oklahoma City where his caretakers adjusted his diet. The changes seemed to work; he looked healthier on his return to Norman six weeks later, but this may have been wishful thinking. On Monday, April 30, the house of Kappa Sigma became a site of mourning. Mex had passed away: "Men of the fraternity, big and muscular men, cried. When they talked of Mex, their voices were somewhat choked. They knew that never again would Mex be there to do tricks for them, or to lead the parades of the Ruf Neks at football games between the two halves."

The funeral took place two days later. Early in the afternoon, Kappa Sigma hosted a viewing of Mex's body: "Throngs of silent men and women students filled the living room of the Kappa Sigma house and passed one by one before the casket." Then the procession began. The Jazz Hounds walked in a line, wearing their trademark outfits: a cardigan of red and white vertical stripes, with a bow tie fixed at the neck. The Ruf Neks, crimson shirts tucked into white duck trousers, marched next to them, each member with his hands on the shoulders of the man in front of him. Both groups took turns chanting their pep songs while a large group of students trailed behind, talking in whispers.

The procession stopped at an open grave, which had been dug just north of Memorial Stadium. A prairie wind blew as a Kappa Sigma brother recited the eulogy, recounting Mex's life and adventures. Students at the rear of the crowd complained that they couldn't see what was happening. A handful fought their way to the front. While fraternity brothers lowered the pine box holding Mex's remains into the grave, a student played "Taps" on a cornet. The shoveling of dirt onto the casket signaled the end of the ceremony. Students turned from the gravesite and, talking again in normal voices, walked toward the "campus coca-cola dispensaries."

■ ■ ■

The Ruf Neks planned to memorialize Mex with a marble statue to sit above the Sooner dugout in Memorial Stadium. During Mex's later years, they started a fundraising drive for the statue, but their plan never came to fruition.

Mex's original owners went on to mixed fortunes.

Mott Keys, who rescued Mex from homelessness, sent a telegram upon hearing of the dog's death: "Tho [*sic*] just a dog, he attained the highest in his dog life. A more understanding friend, man never possessed. Thirteen years of love and loyalty unsullied and unbroken by an almost human understanding and faithfulness. He gave his best. I could wish for myself, no kinder epitaph than for my dog."

Keys had been a proverbial "man on campus" in the 1920s. Like his dog, he was a joiner. While studying journalism and law, he was a member of Kappa Sigma, student council, Young Democrats, and the Deep Dark Mystery Club. He was president of the inter-fraternity council and the able coordinator of fraternity and sorority dances. Furthermore, he was known for his business acumen; he opened a tailor shop in Norman in 1921 that he later sold. So entrenched was he in the social and academic life of the university that he was often teased in *The Oklahoma Daily*. He'd been a student for so long that some called him the "campus papa" and predicted that "he could stay in school at least ten more years."

Eventually, Keys graduated and started a decades-long career in the insurance business. He published a magazine called the *Oklahoma Insurer.*

Mex's other owner, Hutton Bellah, suffered a fate that sounds taken from the pages of a crime novel. The start of his career was auspicious. After reuniting with Keys and Mex at the University of Oklahoma, the World War I veteran graduated in 1923 with a degree in journalism and joined the faculty as an assistant professor. He left to become the editor and publisher of the *Altus Times-Democrat*; for the last half of the twenties, he was a well-respected figure in journalism in southwestern Oklahoma. The last phase of his life, with its bizarre and tragic turn, was reported by the *Kansas City Star.* In 1929, Bellah moved with his wife and child to Los Angeles after selling his interest in the Altus newspaper. Significant financial losses, precipitated by that year's historic crash of the stock market, seemed to trigger a breakdown. Bellah abandoned his family after Christmas. The following month, in January 1930, *Sooner Magazine* published a tribute to Mex penned by Bellah ("He never forgot a former Sooner and no matter how many years one might fail to show up for homecoming—Mex always met him with a delighted wag of his stump tail and graciously kissed his hand"). A month later, Bellah's second child was born in his absence. He moved to Madison, Wisconsin, living under a pseudonym, William A. Lee., and married a woman finishing her degree at the University of Wisconsin. The couple relocated to Arizona where Bellah continued his newspaper career, purchasing a majority stake in the *Yuma Sentinel.* He wrote for and edited the paper. An old colleague of Bellah's in Oklahoma, Harrington Wimberley, happened to be a reader of the *Sentinel.* The style and voice of William A. Lee's writing reminded him of Bellah's work. Wimberley's hunch led him to make some inquiries, which soon caught the attention of Bellah. It was thought that the threat of exposure drove Bellah to suicide. He shot himself in the head, leaving a note for his second wife: "I can't go on. I am sorry. I am not all bad."

While they were both significant contributors to campus life, Keys and Bellah have all but disappeared from memory. Their impressions on the university are faint. Mex, on the other hand, endures. He shows up in the *OU Daily* as both legend and trivia. Often the writers get the history wrong. They say that Mex is buried within Memorial Stadium when, according to the *Daily* article reporting on his funeral in 1928, he was buried north of the stadium. They describe him as a bulldog when in fact he was a bull terrier. Mex has become a character in a ghost story too. Over the years, groundskeepers reported hearing a dog's howling in the stadium. Naysayers blamed the wind. It's Oklahoma after all. But the groundskeepers insisted that the nights in question were windless. Richard Zielinski, director of choral activities in OU's School of Music, kept a ceramic statue of Mex on the corner of his desk. OU fans have named their dogs after Mex. The bull terrier even has his own X account where he comments on Sooner sports; incidentally, he was blocked by former head football coach Lincoln Riley.

In a hallway on the second floor of the Physical Sciences Building hangs a black-and-white photograph of Mex's funeral procession. The solemnity of the occasion is etched across the young faces of the Jazz Hounds and Ruf Neks, leaving no doubt as to what has happened: They've lost a dear friend. I first gazed at this photograph when I started teaching at OU. Who was this dog to deserve such a farewell? Then I looked at it again once I began researching and writing this book. I've come to know Mex. He was loyal and devoted, traveling with the football team for every away game from 1919 to 1925. He was tough, brave, and resilient. Lounging in the grass in the sunshine, he knew how to take it easy.

▪ ▪ ▪

Before he went overseas in 1953 to serve in the Korean War, M. S. "Doc" Bartlett, a physician from Sapulpa, found himself daydreaming about a new mascot for his alma mater. He told *Sooner Magazine* in 1998 that he thought about the Land Rush and the settlers who rode Conestoga wagons into Indian Territory, searching for their new home. By 1955, when he was released from the service, he had a design in mind. His older brother, Charley, once a varsity football player under Bennie Owen, arranged a meeting with Sooner assistant football coach Gomer Jones who, in turn, arranged a meeting with administrators. Backed up by Jones's enthusiasm, Dr. Bartlett pitched the idea of ponies leading a wagon onto Owen Field—"a mascot that symbolized the settling of Oklahoma Territory and the pioneering spirit of the '89ers"—to celebrate Sooner scores. While it took considerable time for the administration to decide, Charley was all in from the start. He and Dr. Bartlett purchased a pair of white Shetland ponies from a dealer in Kansas and built a version of the "schooner."

In 1964, the Bartlett brothers finally got the green light. At a late September home game against the University of Southern California, the ponies "Boomer" and "Sooner" pulled a "miniature prairie schooner" onto Owen Field accompanied by the Ruf Neks. As seen in an *Oklahoma Daily* article the following week, it was already being called the "Sooner Schooner," and there was already a plan in place for the new mascot. It would appear at every home game and "Norman football activities," and every October it would travel with the football team to Dallas for OU–Texas. The Ruf Nek homecoming queen, sophomore Vicki McNeeley from Norman, sat inside the wagon where she got a clear-eyed view of the ponies. "I just can't believe that horses can be so small," she told the *Daily*. "The only way I can tell them apart is that Boomer has freckles on his nose."

A week later, the Schooner was part of the Norman festivities ahead of OU–Texas weekend. A parade of vehicles, including a fire truck and Ruf Neks on motor scooters, snaked around campus ending at the Pi Kappa Alpha parking lot where a pep rally took place, with the Schooner at its center. The Ruf Nek president, Dennis Deakins, stood in the wagon, which had its cover pulled back, and delivered a fiery speech.

The next day, the Sooner Schooner and ponies were loaded onto a trailer for the journey to Dallas. During halftime of the game, which the Sooners lost 28–7, OU's new mascot was introduced to the Cotton Bowl crowd.

A routine was established. During the football season, the ponies stayed in Norman at the polo stables of a former OU football player. The Ruf Neks were responsible for training and caring for them. In the offseason, Boomer and Sooner lived on a farm in Sapulpa.

An accident during homecoming week 1965 broke Ruf Nek hearts and sent them scrambling for a solution: Sooner, their four-year-old pony, died suddenly of a broken neck suffered while trying to get over a fence. Mickey Cotton, a sophomore Ruf Nek from Mounds, spent the Friday night before the homecoming game against Kansas training the new Sooner, acquired from the same farm as his predecessor. “It takes a lot of work to train them,” Cotton told *The Oklahoma Daily*. “They have to learn to pull and turn together and to listen for their commands when the crowd gets noisy.”

When OU beat Texas 18–9 the following year, it was the first time in eight seasons—since the heyday of the Wilkinson era—that the Sooners had won the big rivalry game. Understandably, Sooner fans were ecstatic; they rushed the Cotton Bowl field, tore down one goalpost, and loaded part of it onto the Sooner Schooner for transport back to Norman.

The Schooner was a hit with students and fans, and it wasn’t long before its likeness appeared everywhere: on the front cover of the school directory, on checkbooks from the local bank, and of course on T-shirts. In 1980, it was named the official school mascot.

However, the Schooner went from hero to zero in 1985 when, according to some fans, it cost the football team a national championship.

Second-ranked Oklahoma was facing fourth-ranked Washington in the 1985 Orange Bowl. In a close game, tied 14–14 early in the fourth quarter, Oklahoma’s offense had positioned itself for a field goal—from twenty-two yards, a chip shot—to take the lead. Kicker Tim Lashar sent the ball through the uprights, which triggered the band to play “Boomer Sooner.” It also brought onto the field the Sooner Schooner for its celebratory arc. The Schooner’s dash onto the field, however, was not swift. A wet grass field at Miami’s Orange Bowl Stadium caused the wagon to get stuck, and the referees took notice. In a YouTube video of that game’s highlights, the Schooner labors on its turn, heckled by nearby Washington players who jump, point, and yell at the mascot. Boomer and Sooner take slow-motion steps, accustomed to the artificial turf of Owen Field. For its interminable time on the field, the Schooner is flagged for a penalty for the first time in its twenty-one-year history: fifteen yards for unsportsmanlike conduct. A second penalty on the play, for illegal procedure, pushes the ball back even farther and makes Lashar’s second effort from forty-two yards a dicey situation. The ensuing kick is duly blocked, the climax of a disastrous sequence. Though a subsequent field goal gives OU a 17–14 lead, Washington scores two touchdowns to win the game and knock the Sooners from title contention. "The Sooner Schooner Game," as the matchup came to be called, was boiled down to that moment in the fourth quarter when a blunder from the mascot arguably shifted the momentum of the contest.

Articulating the wrath of Sooner Nation, a columnist from *The Oklahoma Daily* included in his list of predictions for 1985 a terrible fate for both the Schooner and its caretakers: "The Sooner Schooner will be tinder for the first bonfire of the new year. By student vote, the Ruf/Neks will have to sit in the schooner while it burns."

▪ ▪ ▪

For those involved in the mascot's operation, things could turn scary in the blink of an eye. A Ruf Nek was injured in October 1990 when he was struck by the Sooner Schooner on its return to the northeast tunnel of Memorial Stadium after an OU touchdown. Ruf Nek president Brian Amy was running alongside the charging wagon and shouting at people in the crowded tunnel to get out of the way. As the Schooner veered toward him and another Ruf Nek, Amy "pushed the pledge out of the way [of the Schooner] to the right . . . [and] as he fell, his leg swept mine out." Amy fell too, with his right leg in the wrong place at the wrong time; it was run over by a wagon wheel, resulting in a broken fibula that required, in surgery, a steel plate and pins as well as a bone graft.

One Ruf Nek driver called the ponies "unpredictable," and so they proved on a Saturday in November 1997 when, on their way to collect the Ruf Nek queen, they bolted down Chautauqua Avenue, swerved several times, and then jumped the curb in front of the Kappa Alpha Theta house. The driver, Jeremy Karbowski, was flung from the wagon, injuring his ankle. Boomer and Sooner kept going, and the wagon collided with a lamppost, causing enough damage to shut down the Schooner for the rest of the football season. The Ruf Neks on hand managed to catch up to the horses and calm them down. Said an eyewitness from the sorority house,

"Someone honked their car horn and it must have spooked the horses. They ran onto our lawn and hit a lamppost. The horses' bits pulled back so much they made their mouths bleed."

The Sooner Schooner has crashed twice on Owen Field. Given the inevitability of human and animal error, plus the voluminous number of touchdowns scored by the Sooners since 1964, it's a surprise that it hasn't happened more often. I've watched both crashes on YouTube. The first occurred in October 1993, with some blaming the artificial turf, which would be replaced with natural grass the following season. Driver Scott Gibson is standing casually in the seat with reins in hand as the ponies make their turn. Given the tight angle of the turn, the wagon starts to tilt and then momentum takes over. As the wagon tumbles, Gibson leaps away, landing on his feet before doing a sideways roll. He suffers a bruised knee and hairline fracture of his left forearm in the accident. Before things went haywire, the Ruf Nek queen, Jean Connelly, was happily sitting in the front seat, swinging a white paddle. You can't see her, in the video, as the Schooner crashes to the turf. Luckily, her injuries are minor: a bruised hip and sore neck. A Ruf Nek named Ryan Wray sitting in the back of the wagon, his legs dangling, had been holding a flagpole with a large red OU flag. He lands hard on his hip, his face colliding with the canopy, then scrambles out of the wreck. Wray sustains a cut above his right eye.

Gibson told *The Oklahoma Daily* afterward, "The horses were moving faster than they normally do. . . . They didn't turn wide enough. The next thing I knew, I was on the turf."

Reporting on the incident a few days later, the student newspaper quipped that during the game, a disastrous loss to Colorado, the Sooners only had one turnover: the Sooner Schooner.

The second crash happened in an era of high-definition TV and social media. Therefore, the fallout was different, with abundant footage of the crash as well as commentary galore from internet trolls. OU was playing West Virginia in mid-October 2019 on a sunny day. Everything looks normal as the Schooner leaves the stadium's northeast tunnel, with a Ruf Nek driving and a Lil' Sis in the passenger seat, twirling a paddle in her left hand. An American flag, secured to the back of the wagon, flaps in the wind. A host of Ruf Neks and Lil' Sis members run next to the wagon as it makes its way onto Owen Field. The ponies look motivated and energetic in their charge. You can hear the crowd's welcome as the Schooner reaches the fifteen-yard line and begins to turn. Quickly things go south. Like in 1993, the turn is too sharp. For a split second, the wagon balances on the wheels on its right side as if it's performing a trick; then it tumbles over. From the Fox broadcast booth come the words, "Oh my goodness." Driver and passenger are thrown to the grass, and a lot of debris—it's impossible to tell what it is—flies out the back of the wagon, scattering on the field. Boomer and Sooner continue to gallop forward, pulling the undercarriage, which has been separated from the wagon bed.

Then the TV angle changes; we see a replay of the debacle as if we are standing in the north end zone. It's a worm's-eye view, more intimate and violent. Gus Johnson, Fox's play-by-play announcer, narrates the crash as if it were part of the game. "Watch her ability to roll," he says about the Lil' Sis (Abby Redick-Harris) thrown from the wagon. "When she hits the ground, nice roll! That's what they teach you in jujitsu." Though you can't see their faces, you know that the crash victims feel dazed by the way they remain on the turf.

I watch the YouTube video over and over as if I'm inspecting the Zapruder film of Kennedy's assassination. Right away I wonder about the path taken by the Schooner, which seemed to turn a little early. I watch other videos and see that I may be onto something. On other successful runs, the twenty-yard line, not the fifteen, is the place where the Schooner turns. Is the 2019 crash a result of driver or pony error? Is it just one of those things that happen when you put humans and animals together?

The Oklahoma Daily interviewed a Ruf Nek alumnus, Adam Burnett, who called the accident a "fluke." In his four years as part of the spirit group, Burnett helped to maintain the Schooner: "I've put that exact Schooner together a thousand times. . . . I've painted it, pushed it. I've also seen those drivers drive it in more parades and walking around showing it off . . . and dude, it's a fluke that happened."

Still, he went on to blame a perfect storm of circumstances: wet grass and a tight turn from the ponies, which made the wheels drag. It also led to a piece of wood called the "tongue," which sat between the ponies, moving into a bad angle. These things precipitated the crash.

Such was the media furor that the university released a statement of its own, attributing the crash to unequal "weight distribution among riders in the rear of the wagon." In simpler terms, the back of the wagon was heavier than the front. It was a matter of physics.

The internet commentariat, of course, went wild with jokes, memes, and criticism. *Wired* magazine recruited a physicist to explain what happened. ("So the Sooner Schooner was indeed accelerating, simply because it was turning. Also, you might notice that right before the crash, the horses seem to take a sharper turn. That reduces the radius of curvature and increases the centripetal acceleration. But why did it tip over? Torque!") Even the animal rights group PETA chimed in. Its Twitter account read: "Exploiting animals for sports is unnecessary & incredibly dangerous for animals AND humans.@OU_Football: KEEP HORSES OFF THE FIELD."

In the end, no one riding in the Schooner was seriously injured, and the ponies were okay too. The wagon, however, was in such poor shape it had to be retired. An updated version, with an improved and safer design, was unveiled in June 2020 ahead of the new season. It featured "heavier running gear, wider wheelbase, hydraulic brakes, lowered driver seat and more space." At the time of writing, the safety record of this version of the Sooner Schooner—so far, historically, four different wagons have been used—looks like this: thirty-one straight home games without an accident.

▪ 11 ▪

THE PRIDE OF OKLAHOMA

THE FIRST BAND to play at football games at the University of Oklahoma was an improvised group of students and townies, with the latter providing most of the all-male musicians. From 1901 to 1903, the band assembled in the fall, played at home games, and then parted ways once the season was over.

An officially sanctioned school band was started in 1904, though its illustrious moniker—the Pride of Oklahoma—wouldn't be used until 1936. The impetus came from a recently matriculated student, Lloyd Burgess Curtis, a cornet player and graduate of the Haskell Institute: a boarding school for Native American children in Lawrence, Kansas. Curtis moved to Norman, with his family, to study engineering. The young man, an avid musician, asked two music professors about the existence of an official school band. When he heard that there wasn't one, Curtis received permission to start a band composed solely of OU students. Those early days are chronicled in an unpublished manuscript—*100 Years of Pride 1904–2004: A Documented History of the Pride of Oklahoma Marching Band*—written and compiled by Terri Cooter, a former Pride member and ex-president of the OU Alumni Band Association. She includes a quote from Curtis about the band, which in the beginning was entirely self-sufficient: "We'd get together after school hours and play together possibly, and probably, at different places over town where they [student band members] lived. They had room enough, and after a few rehearsals we got ahold of a little music that the music department picked up for us. We'd go out for some of the ball games and had quite a time."

"Boomer Sooner," composed in 1905 by OU student Arthur M. Alden, became a staple of the early band's repertoire. In the first version of the song, Alden authored the lyrics but borrowed the melody from a Yale University song called "Boola Boola." The opening stanza invokes two of the primary agents of the 1889 Land Run. The second stanza simply repeats the territory's name—Oklahoma wouldn't become an official state for another two years—and then name-drops the university.

Boomer Sooner, Boomer Sooner
Boomer Sooner, Boomer Sooner
Boomer Sooner, Boomer Sooner
Boomer Sooner, OK U!

Oklahoma, Oklahoma
Oklahoma, Oklahoma
Oklahoma, Oklahoma
Oklahoma, OK U!

In 1906, Alden added a third stanza; again, he borrowed from an existing collegiate song: University of North Carolina's "I'm a Tarheel Born." Here, Alden's lyrics are more sophisticated than those in the previous two stanzas; in a rhyming couplet, they express a sentiment familiar to anyone who's fallen in love with their alma mater. The sentiment was already strong on the Norman campus, less than twenty years after the university's founding.

I'm a Sooner born and Sooner bred
and when I die, I'll be Sooner dead
Rah Oklahoma, Rah Oklahoma
Rah Oklahoma, OK U!

The OU band, consisting of sixteen young men, was a year old before it was outfitted with uniforms: military style with form-fitting coats, snap-bill hats, and non-pleated trousers. The trim on the uniform was crimson and cream. Curtis's band sat in the wooden bleachers at football games. Curtis's goal was to "make as much noise as possible." The band played "Boomer Sooner" or "light marches" after the football team scored. There was no marching on the field before the game or at halftime.

By 1911, the band was expanding with Curtis, now a graduate student in electrical engineering, still in charge. There was a shortage in money and uniforms, however, so about half of the musicians wore business suits at performances. The band played at OU sporting events, school parades, and political events. There were also concert performances at the Seawell Opera House on Main Street (the location of present-day Mister Robert Fine Furniture & Design) to raise funds so that the band could accompany the football team on its travels. Shirttail parades, before football games, were a popular way to drum up spirit, and the band was at the forefront of such shenanigans, which saw students donning the nightshirts they wore in the privacy of their bedrooms. On one such occasion, in late October 1911, nearly the entire student body—roughly four hundred students—participated in the shirttail parade on a Thursday night before the Washburn game, assembling in front of the library at 7:20 P.M. and then, led by the band, parading around Norman streets for the next three hours. According to a vivid account in *The Umpire*, there was much "howling" from the crowd and the singing of songs, and the event ended with a bonfire lit in the middle of the street just east of the railroad tracks where students took part in a "war dance." The student newspaper gave the university band, tireless in its efforts, ample credit for the fun of that night: "The University band was out and lead [*sic*] the procession the whole evening. In fact, it was the most important factor of the whole affair and aided greatly in making the shirt tail parade the entire success that it was."

After thrashing Washburn 37–0, the Varsity beat Missouri and then, for the first time in nine years, defeated Kansas 3–0 in Lawrence amid a November snowstorm. At chapel on Monday morning, a rally was held to celebrate the team, back from Lawrence, with hundreds of students, faculty, and townspeople in attendance. Interim president Julien Monnet gave a speech before the band played "Boomer Sooner," with students singing along. Afterward, the football team was carried out on the shoulders of students and placed in a "tallyho," a kind of carriage usually pulled by horses. This time, however, OU freshmen provided the horsepower. Band members sat beside the victorious team and played music as students labored to pull the tallyho to Main Street for a second rally. When everyone reached Main Street, the players took turns thanking the crowd for their support. Then they urged fans to come to the next game, which would be played at home, against Northwestern Oklahoma State.

▪ ▪ ▪

After Curtis left his position in 1915, a succession of band directors followed, each working to evolve his team of musicians. William R. Wehrend, in 1929, was the first full-time faculty member hired to direct the band. A showman and disciplinarian, he stayed in the job until 1945. His methodical approach was described in the November 1941 issue of *Sooner Magazine*. The work to produce a halftime show of music and marching was a collaboration between Wehrend and his second in command, Leonard Haug. In his office, surrounded by instruments, Wehrend worked on the music, jotting down notes on paper and whistling under his breath. For his part, Haug had created a small-scale model of Owen Field, resting on an assembly of chairs, on which he gazed while moving around 153 toy soldiers that represented members of the band. Musicians received "mimeographed" copies of both the music and the marching formations. On Tuesdays and Thursdays, Wehrend gathered the band together for practice on a field south of Richards Hall and west of the stadium. For two hours, the band worked to mesh the music and marching. The time spent on the practice field was only part of the more than twenty hours of intense practice weekly, all leading to a six-minute demonstration on Saturdays of teamwork and precision that sent a "thrill down your spine." The OU band would cover "the gridiron with an intricate and flowing pattern of color, with spirited music flowing down the crisp autumn wind."

The on-field pageantry of a Wehrend-led band, however, told an incomplete story; like their football-playing counterparts, Pride members faced adversity and discomfort from a variety of circumstances. Most of it was only mildly unpleasant or inconvenient, like an ill-fitting uniform or travel delays or overnight stays on a crowded train. In a recollection from Cooter's unpublished manuscript, Pride alumnus Harold C. Frantzen (1933–36) recalled performing at the Cotton Bowl for OU–Texas, a game where temperatures often soared; his wool uniform was suffocating and "smelly from too many twenty-five cent cleanings." What's more, zippers weren't a uniform feature; the front of his coat popped open and stayed that way. On a more serious note, Frantzen said that a cohort fainted from the heat of that day. Ken English, a drum major from 1941–42, remembered a rainy game with Santa Clara where the Pride marched on a flooded field; with every step, their feet sank several inches in the mud. "I'm sure the band ruined lots of uniforms that day," he said.

In 1934, things took a grave turn on a trip to support the Varsity in Washington, DC. The morning after the Thanksgiving Day game with George Washington University, which was so rain-soaked that the band couldn't perform at halftime, the ninety-eight members of the band boarded three buses in the dark. Just a few minutes later, the lead bus crested a hill before the student driver lost control; the bus crashed into a ditch, ending up on its side and chopping down a utility pole. While most of the riders suffered only minor injuries—cuts and bruises—others weren't so lucky. One student, emerging from the wreckage, unwittingly touched a downed power line; sparks flew from his head. He was knocked unconscious, and a couple of students, with their wits about them, administered CPR, likely saving his life. The student driver sustained a broken arm in the crash while two others suffered very serious injuries: a fractured skull and broken pelvis. Miraculously, no one died.

Diffferent scenarios were floated to explain the cause of the accident, but it seems that no one was eager to assign blame.

This dark incident aside, it must be said that membership in the band, while requiring hard work and dedication, also translated into fun and adventure. On the way to Dallas for OU–Texas in 1938, the band stopped in Denton where it practiced its halftime show before heading to a dinner and dance with students from Texas State College for Women. According to band member Bob Swift, whose story appears in Cooter's unpublished manuscript, he and his peers were each paired with a coed, of senior status, from the college. Swift was intimidated by his date's senior standing. "I loved women and dates, but I was scared to death of such older seniors," he said. "It showed about midnight when I took my date back to her dorm well before the others." A couple months later, Swift was with the band in Miami, Florida, for the first bowl game in OU's history. The 10–0 Sooners were set to face Tennessee in the Orange Bowl. Before the game on New Year's Day, Swift and his compatriots stayed in motels, soaking up the sun on Miami beaches during the day. At night, they gathered in the motel lobby to play the piano and sing songs like "Moon Over Miami," to the delight of tourists.

Frantzen, who endured the boiling sun at the Cotton Bowl, remembered the band's summer tour of Oklahoma, the purpose of which was to entertain the state's citizens during a bleak time. The Great Depression brought economic hardship and caused a mass exodus of people, with close to half a million Oklahomans leaving the state in the 1930s. In old buses whose reliability was questionable, Franzten and company traveled to all corners of the state down dirt roads and across risky bridges. If a bridge looked particularly unsafe, the students disembarked and then watched as the bus crawled across. Then they walked across themselves before boarding the bus again. The band played concerts for the poor and the well-off, staying overnight in palatial homes with servants as well as in simple homes on remote Indian reservations. "We were always treated very well," Frantzen said, "and enjoyed every moment of every trip."

Women joined the band for the first time in 1936; their uniform included long white skirts instead of pants because of the strict sartorial guidelines, based on gender, of the day. After the rules changed on membership, the number of women in the Pride steadily increased. By the following decade, more than forty were members.

The 1930s also saw the birth of the "OU Chant," which became, like "Boomer Sooner," a standard in the band's oeuvre and part of the pregame experience at Memorial Stadium. The songwriter was a singer and graduate of OU, Jessie Lone Clarkson Gilkey, who returned to campus in 1937 to join the music faculty. At the urging of students in the Women's Choral Club, who wanted a school song to "make them starry-eyed," Gilkey got to work after an evening out with different student groups, including the band and Ruf Neks. They ended up at the Monterey Restaurant on Boyd (now called the Mont), a short walk from campus, where Gilkey and students continued to have a good time. More than fifty years later, Gilkey reminisced about that night to *Sooner Magazine*. "We were there until all hours, just singing and eating," she said. "Then I went home, sat down half asleep at the piano and scratched the words down. Not in a minute, but just leisurely sitting there."

The chant is markedly different from the many yells written through the decades to excite fans during games. Gilkey's composition is contemplative and poignant: a testimonial to student experience. How many generations of Sooners have been seduced by the beauty of OU's campus? On the night she wrote the lyrics, Gilkey had earlier walked out of Holmberg Hall and noticed her surroundings: the maple trees, the green lawn, and the red brick arches on Parrington Oval, all of which inspired the "Chant":

> O-K-L-A-H-O-M-A
> Our chant rolls on and on!
> Thousands strong
> Join heart and song
> In Alma Mater's praise—
> Of campus beautiful by day
> and night,
> Of colors proudly gleaming Red
> and White,
> 'Neath a western sky
> OU's chant will never die.
> Live on, University.

The final lines embody the hope and wish that OU will live on, no matter the vagaries of time and circumstance, long after the student leaves to tackle the rest of life. Implicit in the chant is the melancholy notion that time is fleeting; for people, it's finite. However, the University of Oklahoma is an institution, not a human, and thus can carry on. Any singer of the chant, who feels bonded to OU, can take heart from this fact, for a part of the person—the soul—lives on with the institution.

Once Gilkey finished writing the "OU Chant," it was heard by just a few in her inner circle. A year later, however, she shared it with OU's alumni secretary who, in turn, was looking for an OU-themed song to share with an Oklahoma City radio station. The chant quickly grew in popularity, with the Pride adding it to the repertoire. Not only that, it became part of the band's culture. Members recited it before group meals and at official functions. On one occasion, however, the band embarrassed itself as members, in 1965, flubbed the lines at a dinner in Dallas the night before the Red River Rivalry game, with "distinguished guests" in the room. Robert Witten witnessed the debacle as a freshman in the band; he remembered the humiliation in Gene Braught's face as the band director realized that his charges didn't know the words to the song. "The result was an angry speech by the director at the next Monday's band practice, followed by 'choir practice' each day for the next two weeks where we were required to learn the song," Witten said. "I only remember the band singing the Chant one more time that year in public. . . . But let me tell you, we had it down cold."

In the 1950s, under the directorship of Haug, who took over from Wehrend, the Pride earned plaudits on the national stage as Coach Wilkinson's Sooners dominated on the gridiron. The culmination of the band's rise was its performance at the Cherry Blossom Parade in Washington, DC, in 1961. The parade, an annual event recognizing the 1912 gift of three thousand cherry trees from Tokyo's mayor, featured a competition, with a panel of judges deciding the winner. In 1961, two hundred performers—floats, cars, marching bands, an ensemble of clowns, and ROTC drill teams, among others—vied for the grand prize. The Pride was not an official competitor; for whatever reason, director Haug had not entered them as such. On a crisp spring morning, 250,000 people lined the parade route. The Pride, wearing red uniforms, marched with discipline and pomp down the street, the rising sun glinting off the musicians' instruments. They played the tunes that celebrated their state and university: "Fight for OKU," "OK Oklahoma," and "Oklahoma!" From his vantage point in the grandstand, Director Haug watched the band's approach, the music mingling with the enthusiasm of the crowd. He later told the *Norman Transcript*: "As the band marched past the reviewing stand, it looked and sounded—how shall I say it?—tremendously convincing. Its playing was superb. Its posture and alignment couldn't have been better. And everywhere, from everyone, it seemed, came a thrilling roar of ovation."

That night, the band did not attend the awards ceremony in downtown. Instead, without a curfew, members explored the nightlife of the nation's capital. When a few returned to the hotel from their adventures, well into the evening, they discovered a trophy, shaped like the Washington Monument, waiting for them at reception. Despite not entering the competition as an official contestant, the Pride had performed so brilliantly the judges felt compelled to award them the grand prize.

▪ ▪ ▪

The Pride could be a diplomatic force, its function the cultivation of comradeship, across eras when competitiveness, in collegiate athletics, was increasing exponentially. When Oklahoma faced powerhouse Notre Dame for the first time in 1952, in South Bend, the band saluted its hosts by playing the university's famed "Victory March." Ten years later, the teams faced off again, this time in Norman, and at halftime the Pride played while forming the likeness of Saint Patrick, an important figure in Catholicism. Even against Texas, Oklahoma's fiercest foe, the Pride could "play nice." Dr. William H. Reiff, a member of the band in the late thirties, recalled in *Sooner Magazine* participating in "a little friendly competition" in Dallas before the rivalry game. All the piccolo players and drummers from both sides got together to form a "fife and drum corps." Decades later, the Pride was once again feeling magnanimous when, at halftime of the 1968 game, it serenaded Texas fans with renditions of classic Longhorn tunes, including "The Eyes of Texas" and "The Yellow Rose of Texas."

The Pride, however, wasn't always in a giving mood. The band enjoyed needling Texas fans; once, it accomplished this by playing "The Eyes of Texas" as a funeral dirge.

At the end of the day, the band was committed to a single cause: supporting the Sooners. Often, it played an integral role in inspiring the team. Lewis Hardage, coach of the Sooners when they visited George Washington in 1934, described an intimidating atmosphere in the stadium, full of vocal home fans who wanted to see OU fail. "You feel as if you're surrounded by the enemy and haven't a friend in the world, until suddenly, just before time for the game to start, your own band marches onto the field playing your favorite college song," he said. "If that doesn't give a football player an urge to play his best, nothing else can."

Opposing coaches paid tribute to the Pride as well. At a game in Norman in October 1957, during Oklahoma's historic win streak, Colorado's head coach Dal Ward gave credit to an "enthusiastic" bass drummer in OU's drum line for interfering with a Buffalo drive. It happened in the third quarter with the ball on the Oklahoma seven-yard line. On a third down and two, David Miller of Claremore, Oklahoma, started "beating the hell" out of his bass drum. The racket produced by the drum made Colorado's center hike the ball early; the Buffalos were penalized for illegal procedure. After the game, which OU won 14–13, Coach Ward said, "I'll always remember that bass drummer in the Oklahoma band pounding harder and harder when our players pleaded for silence. This cost us a touchdown in the third period."

I talked to Miller, the bass drummer, in 2025. By then, he was in his late eighties, a retired science teacher living in Norman. His hobbies, in retirement, included following women's sports at OU, especially gymnastics and basketball, and marble painting. The two hobbies came together for several years as Miller would gift each OU gymnast and basketball player a personalized marble with her name, class year, and OU painted on it.

Recalling the Colorado game sixty-seven years later, Miller said that he and his bass drum had made such an impression that they got moved from the stands to the Sooner sideline for the next home game, against Notre

Dame. Alas, Miller proved no talisman; despite beating on his drum with the same vigor, college football's greatest win streak ended at forty-seven games as the "Fighting Irish" defeated the Sooners 7–0.

Sometime later—it could have been weeks or months—Miller happened upon Bud Wilkinson as the Pride member was walking west on Brooks Street toward the stadium. The coach was walking in the other direction. Both recognized the other. "Bud, I want you to know that I did not win that game for you," the young Miller said, referring to Colorado, tongue in cheek.

Wilkinson replied, in the same playful vein, "I know damn good and well you didn't."

The Pride was there for the birth of Sooner Magic in November 1976. Though Oklahoma, after winning two consecutive national titles under Barry Switzer, wasn't in contention for a three-peat, the Sooners could secure a share of the Big 8 title with a win against Nebraska, in Lincoln, in the final conference game. Conditions were miserable for everyone involved, including the band: thirty degrees but the windchill made it feel like zero. Mark Jones played with the Pride that day and wrote about his memories decades later on the Killer Nashville website: "It was the kind of cold that stiffened the valves and keys on your horn and froze your breath. We stood in formation, half-frozen but loud, and played Boomer Sooner until our lips were numb."

The Cornhuskers led 17–7 as the fourth quarter began. Elvis Peacock's touchdown run for fifty-one yards cut the lead to 17–13 (the two-point attempt failed), and the Sooner defense forced a turnover on downs deep in its own territory, giving the offense an opportunity to win the game with 3:30 left on the clock. With the Pride blasting "Boomer Sooner" at every opportunity, two trick plays involving high-risk passes—in an era when the Sooner offense ran the ball almost exclusively—brought the Sooners within touching distance of the goal line, with under a minute to go. On the very next play, Peacock scored again to put the Sooners ahead for good: a win against the odds. Entrenched with the Pride, Jones the horn player went wild in those last few minutes: "We hollered through chattering teeth as two flea-flicker plays broke the game open, and we won. Those were the kinds of victories you never forgot."

The circumstances of the Nebraska win provided the ingredients for Sooner Magic, generally defined as an invisible force that takes charge when Oklahoma teams, in all sports, face tremendous adversity with time running out in the game. Sooner Magic propels Sooner teams to an improbable win. It's a divine force that speaks to the university's privileged place in the universe: We are favored by the gods. Innumerable instances of Sooner Magic have transpired in Sooner sports history, but the term entered the lexicon after the Nebraska win in 1976.

The most celebrated case of Pride support happened at Bedlam in 1983. The band was under the guidance of Gene "Coach" Thrailkill, and a loss for the Sooners seemed imminent early in the fourth quarter, with the team down 20–3. The band was sitting in the stands behind the endzone, with Thrailkill standing on the field behind the goal posts directing the music. OSU police came over and asked to see the director's sideline pass, which Thrailkill didn't have. He'd been told that he didn't need one. The police, unsympathetic, told him that he would have to leave. An incensed Thrailkill said, "I'm not going anywhere. You're going to have to remove me." With the police calling his bluff, Thrailkill turned to his band and instructed them to start playing "Boomer Sooner" and not to stop until the team was ahead. For the next hour, the band was indefatigable. By some estimates, the OU fight song was played at least three hundred times, with musicians rotating in and out to get rest. When OU quarterback Danny Bradley was under center, the Pride played "Boomer Sooner" quietly. When OSU had the ball, the Pride played at full volume. (Such was the impact of the Pride's performance that the NCAA would later ban the playing of music while either team was preparing to snap the ball.) The Sooners responded by clawing their way back into the game. An onside kick, recovered by Oklahoma, gave the offense a final chance with time running out and the score 20–18. The offense drove to the OSU twenty-nine, putting kicker Tim Lashar in position for a forty-six-yard field goal attempt, which he duly converted, with nerves of steel, to give the

Sooners the lead. The OU defense stifled the Pokes on their last desperate drive, and the miracle comeback, yet another example of Sooner Magic, became a reality. When it was over, the Sooner benches cleared. Players, coaches, and support staff ran to the end zone to celebrate with the Pride.

Brian Britt was a freshman in the band that day and described the scene as "pandemonium." The excitement was something he'd never experienced before. "As a freshman snare drummer from Durant, Oklahoma," he said, "that was probably the most important thing I'd ever been a part of in my life up to that point. Just to feel like you were a part of something bigger than yourself was really cool."

On Monday after the game, flyers were posted around campus requesting the band's presence at Owen Field. Decades later, Britt told local news station KOCO that he felt dread when he saw the summons. "We'd never meet in the stadium unless it was raining," he said. "Somebody did something they weren't supposed to do, and we're in trouble."

His instincts proved incorrect, however, as head coach Barry Switzer had something other than reproach in mind. In fact, he wanted to celebrate the Pride's role in the weekend's victory. Once the band was gathered in the stadium, Switzer handed over a game ball with a dedication on it. The writing on the ball said: "The Day 'The Pride' Won."

Britt would go on to make marching bands his life's work. For fifteen years he worked in Oklahoma and Texas high schools and universities. When Thrailkill retired in 2001, after thirty years of service, Britt applied for the vacancy and, in his words, "somehow got the job." His first stint lasted until 2013 when a career change appealed to him. He moved to Dallas to direct fine arts for a school district. Less than two years later, however, he was back at OU at the request of President David Boren. His tenure carries on today. The game ball from 1983's Bedlam resides in his office.

Part IV

A COACH AND HER DIAMOND

▪ 12 ▪

THE FOUR-PEAT, PART I

IN EARLY MARCH 2024, Miami of Ohio comes close to ending OU softball's win streak—at sixty-six games and counting, Oklahoma had eclipsed the old record of forty-seven, held by Arizona, long ago—and wrecking the Sooners' debut at Love's Field. A back-and-forth game is tied 7–7 at the bottom of the seventh inning until senior catcher Kinzie Hansen homers to end things. The home crowd can sigh with relief before watching OU thrash Liberty 8–0 in the second game of the doubleheader.

The next day, Jenn and I buy general admission tickets for two games against Louisiana and Liberty. After parking at Lloyd Noble, we walk to the stadium next door. Farther north is Marita Hynes Field, and across Jenkins sits Reaves Park. You can stand in one spot, surveying the scene, and capture in panoramic view the different eras of OU softball.

An expanse of dirt lies in front of the south perimeter of Love's Field. The stadium isn't completely finished. Apparently, the locker rooms aren't available; the players will use the ones at Marita Hynes until April. The facade of Love's Field is an act of continuity: the same red brick found on campus buildings and at Memorial Stadium forms the shell. An arch rises, enclosing a black wrought iron gate. The stadium has a retro feel to it, like those new baseball stadiums that embody the traditional and modern at the same time. We follow the stream of fans to gate one where the normal security measures are in place: metal detectors staffed with security personnel. Everything is orderly. Beyond security are kiosks where you line up again to scan your tickets. Then you go through the gates and into the stadium.

The concourse is spacious, but with foot traffic coming from all directions it's a little overwhelming. We follow the people in front of us. Along one brick wall there's a listing, by year, of OU's seven national championships. We see concessions and a store for OU gear. But it's the green of the field that attracts us the most. We walk to the edge of the concourse, beyond which is tiered seating, and gaze out at the immaculate playing field. Bands of light and dark green grass, an effect of the mowing process, extend from the brown dirt of the infield. A red padded wall borders the back end of the field; the left side presents, in chronological order, the seven championships: a likeness of the trophy along with the year and "National Champions" in cursive writing. On the wall in center field it says "SOONERS" in white. To the right of that, nearly in the right field corner, is a Women's College World Series (WCWS) emblem, next to which are three columns of numbers: the years the Sooners went to the World Series. The years colored gold are those they walked away as champions. On the grass in center field there's a red, interlocking "OU."

The whole scene pops with newness, as vivid a picture as anything found on a television these days—4K resolution—except that we're looking at real life and not a screen.

Sandwiched between outfield bleachers is a rectangle full of landscaped greenery: evergreen shrubs. And above that is an eye-catching feature: a scoreboard in the shape of the state of Oklahoma. The idea came from athletic director Joe Castiglione. "Love's Field," with a heart symbol, sits atop the scoreboard to let everyone know that none of this would have been possible without the $12 million donated by the Love family, which owns Love's Travel Stops and Country Stores.

The new stadium has seating for more than four thousand fans, more than double the capacity of Marita Hynes Field. The sheer size of the complex, at 44,000 square feet, outdoes its predecessor (15,168 square feet) too.

There are other stark differences indicating how far the program has come. In its tribute to Marita Hynes Field in 2023, *OU Daily* reported that a chain-link fence instead of a wall once formed the boundary of the field. What's more, the fence was so short—four feet tall—that fans could easily lean over it. To protect outfield players trying to rob batters of home runs, metal piping topped the fence. A wooden wall replaced the fence in 2000, but the new boundary posed its own dangers. Once, a center fielder on the opposing team, chasing a fly ball, ran into the wall, knocking herself out. Permanent seating could be found behind home plate, but elsewhere, including beyond the outfield, benches were brought in to accommodate fans.

The dugouts didn't have a bathroom, so players would have to return to the locker room where the combination of tile floors and players' cleats meant that slips and falls were a universal experience.

It's not yet spring, and so there's a late-morning chill in the air. The skies are a clear blue, and there's a slight wind, which makes me wonder: How much of a factor is wind in softball? It must affect the flight of the ball off the bat. Can it affect pitchers?

Sophomore Kierston Deal, wearing a protective face mask, is in the pitching circle for the Sooners. From the start, she and her colleagues are all over the Ragin' Cajuns, scoring three in the first inning and four in the second. Also in the second inning, with the bases loaded, OU's defense turns a double play to end the threat; the speed and athleticism of the players dazzle the eye.

Jenn and I watch the action from a spot at the rim of the stadium, with third base and the pitching circle in our line of sight. To our right, and barely visible, is the batter at home plate, bathed in shadow. It's not a satisfying view, but with our general admission tickets we don't have a choice.

Oklahoma is up 8–0 after the fifth inning when the run-ahead rule comes into play. The Sooners are long-term specialists of ending games early thanks to this rule, which extends "mercy" to a team that's losing soundly. In 2022, across sixty-two games, Oklahoma run-ruled opponents forty-one times.

The second game of the doubleheader turns into another runaway win for the Sooners, this time against Liberty University.

▪ ▪ ▪

Gasso's instructional video "How to Coach the Female Athlete" leaves out one vital ingredient, the Christian faith, which has been more visible in recent years, with both Gasso and her players talking about it in the media. It wasn't always that way. In an interview with the *Sports Spectrum* podcast in 2023, Gasso admits that in her early days at OU she was afraid to bring up her faith because, after all, her employer was a public institution where a separation of church and state was presumed.

Gasso won her first national championship in 2000, but it was far from smooth sailing after that. She admits she struggled with the pressures of coaching and parenthood. She felt she was failing at both. With a second national championship not forthcoming, she worried about getting fired. She would come home late from work and try to read her young sons a bedtime story only to fade quickly. The boys read to her instead. Gasso was close to burnout.

In 2010, she says she got a wake-up call from God. His message was: "You're doing this wrong. You're not here to win games. You're here to win souls."

Everything changed from that point, on and off the field. A culture of faith and devotion blossomed within the team, led by the players. A second national title came in 2013. Then the Sooners won back-to-back titles in 2016 and 2017. With winning comes expectation and thus pressure. But Gasso's teams appeared to handle the pressure well. You hear the team described in a certain way. They play with such freedom and without fear. How is that possible in a high-stakes sports culture where even collegiate players are under the microscope?

The answer seems to be rooted in their faith. What matters most is not winning but service to God. Gasso uses vivid imagery to draw a distinction between two states of being: happiness and fulfillment. Happiness is associated with winning; it's fleeting. A player wins a national championship and the confetti rains down, the trophy finally in her hands.

But the next day comes and the fanfare is all gone. The player finds herself alone. Fulfillment, on the other hand, is a process of "becoming" centered around faith. Gasso described this mindset to the *Sports Spectrum* podcast: "Who are we becoming? The direction that we are going. How do we grow as women? How do we grow in our faith? How do we find that path so that when the lights do go off my life is still working toward fulfillment rather than that one shot of happiness that can leave you very unhappy soon after?"

The evidence that a lot of her players have bought in is all around. For example, during her decorated tenure at OU, short stop Grace Lyons started a custom in which players from both teams came together to pray once the game was over. This was put to the test when arch nemesis Texas ended the Sooners' forty-game win streak in April 2022. Despite the sting of loss, Lyons and her teammates didn't hesitate; they circled up with the Longhorns and prayed.

Bible verses appear in the locker room, printed out and placed on players' lockers. They can also be found on players' visors. Most players attend pregame chapel, and as a team before games they circle up in the locker room for the reciting of a prayer or Bible verse.

Players are bullish in speaking about their faith in interviews. At a press conference during the 2023 WCWS, a reporter asked a trio of Sooner players about cultivating joy and keeping anxiety at bay. All three players talked about Christianity.

Jayda Coleman said that though she won a national title with the Sooners her freshman year she didn't feel joy until she found Christ. "It's what makes our team so strong," she added. "We're not afraid to lose because it's not the end of the world if we do lose. Yes, obviously, we worked our butts off to be here and we want to win, but it's not the end of the world because our life is in Christ and that's all that matters."

The unabashed declaration of their faith, shown at this press conference, went viral on the internet, with many people (including NFL quarterback Derek Carr) saluting the women for their honesty and commitment. Not everyone, of course, was complimentary. In online spaces like Reddit, users debated Christianity in sports, especially softball. Some saw a culture of coercion and conformity. The most radical voices compared Oklahoma softball to a Christian cult.

Gasso insists that faith isn't a prerequisite for joining her team. A skeptic might say that the team culture and identity—by this point, three decades in the making—has already been established, with faith as a central tenet. Gasso herself said as much in 2023, stating that the program "kind of runs itself." She added, "Before a player even comes in they know what we're about. They know our expectations. We're blue collar, hard-working, humble. Fearless. I try to empower them as young women. And [we're] also bringing into the fold the faith-based."

■ ■ ■

An astonishing thing happens on Sunday, the opening weekend at Love's Field. Against the same Louisiana team they run-ruled twenty-four hours prior, the Sooners find themselves in a dogfight, with their seventy-one-game win streak on the line. Pitcher Kelly Maxwell, who controversially transferred from Oklahoma State during the offseason, can't find a rhythm, and Louisiana jumps out to a 3–0 lead; it looks grim in the seventh with the visitors holding on at 4–2, but then the Sooners, in clutch fashion, tie the game, forcing extra innings. Regrettably, it's a false dawn. The Cajun bats come alive in the eighth, and Gasso's team can't keep up. The Sooners lose 7–5.

The Oklahoman calls the team "unrecognizable" in its write-up of the game, an error-prone affair in which the Sooners "beat themselves."

I wonder about the pressure of sustaining such a historic run. Is it a good thing that they lost and so early in the season? Now they won't have the streak to worry about.

"We are human," Gasso says in the postgame press conference. "We are human beings. That's what happened today."

■ ■ ■

Jenn and I are back at Love's Field the following Saturday for the opening weekend of conference play. Iowa State is the visitor. This time, wanting a better view, I've purchased tickets with actual seats (it's not a cheap event;

tickets on StubHub start at fifty dollars for the outfield bleachers and over a hundred for closer seats). Our friends Lenny and Kelly have joined us. We sit along the first-base line. It's a beautiful day, with the sun shining, and we peel off layers of clothing as the game progresses. Before the first pitch, the Sooners huddle up and, as a unit, shift from left to right, back and forth, chanting, "OU! OU!"

Maxwell is the starting pitcher. As I scan the field, looking at the Sooner defense, it's impossible to ignore their physiques. It's more apparent from our vantage point today; last week, we looked down on the action. The Sooner women (for the most part) are tall and muscular: physical specimens. Jenni Carlson of *The Oklahoman* wrote about their "Peloton legs" in 2022. A strength and conditioning coach, Dayne Sommer, worked the players hard in the weight room, developing their leg and core strength. The result was both aesthetic and effective. Pitchers were throwing harder, hitters striking the ball farther.

No trace of Maxwell's struggles last Sunday is showing up today. Her pitches crash into Hansen's mitt with a loud thud as the sellout crowd follows along with a chant of "O-O-O-O-U!" One wonders if Hansen soaks her catching hand in Epsom salts after these outings. Maxwell faces down Iowa State's batters with aplomb: a routine first inning with two strikeouts. I notice something on the field I've never noticed before. After each out, there's a chain reaction of movement that flows from one defensive player to the next. A shimmy of the shoulders or a little dance. It's not a random thing. It seems coordinated.

I've never seen this in baseball. I ponder it for the entire game. Is it a form of communication? A means to stay connected as a team when gaps in physical space, some large, exist between the players?

Something else gives me food for thought, though it's not the first time I've noticed the phenomenon. The players from both dugouts chant things. This is unique to softball; their male counterparts in baseball certainly don't do it. There's a stoicism in baseball in line with traditional American masculinity. By contrast, softball players are animated and exuberant; they remind me of a European soccer crowd that sings throughout the match. Somehow, a softball player is both player and fan, and though I can't make out the words the chants seem to serve different purposes: to support teammates and unnerve the opposition.

(As fate would have it, freshman sensation Kasidi Pickering is later a student of mine in fall 2024. She tells me that the synchronized dugout cheering, composed by the team and often centering around a player's nickname, is done to hype the batter and "keep everyone engaged." The gestures performed by Sooners playing defense, a dance or handshake, serve a similar purpose. They are meant to be fun and energizing. Two of Pickering's derive from Michael Jackson dance moves: the toe stand and shoulder shimmy.)

The Sooner bats finally come to life. Runs in the third and fourth innings are enough, and Maxwell pitches a complete game shutout. Our tickets are only for the first half of the double header, and so we have to give up our seats; a few hours later, the Sooners run-rule the Cyclones 11–2.

The Sooners complete the series sweep of Iowa State on Sunday. Two days later, the OU Board of Regents approves a plan for a bronze statue of Coach Gasso to stand in front of gate one at Love's Field. The same sculptor who made statues of Heisman Trophy winners Baker Mayfield and Kyler Murray is overseeing the Gasso statue, expected to be unveiled later this year. Gasso will join Bennie Owen, Bud Wilkinson, Barry Switzer, and Bob Stoops as the only OU coaches immortalized in bronze.

▪ ▪ ▪

Through the rest of March, the Sooners dominate the opposition as if to prove the loss to Louisiana was just a blip. That said, they haven't faced elite competition yet. This changes when they travel to Austin in early April to face Texas, ranked fourth in the country.

It's accurate to describe the two teams as rivals, but it's also true that the rivalry has been one-sided for many years now. The last time Texas beat OU in a conference series was 2009.

Still, I predict close games, and Friday's match up delivers. Maxwell, established as the Sooner number one with a record of 10–0, has four strikeouts already by the second inning. Jayda Coleman stars on the offensive side; her single in the third gives OU the lead. Then, in the fifth, she homers with runners on base to put the Sooners up 5–0. The Longhorns threaten to make a game of it, with two runs in the seventh, but Maxwell stands firm.

The status quo has been upheld, for now.

Sooner momentum carries into game two where they take an early lead. However, it's a much tighter game than the first. Texas pitcher Citaly Gutierrez is a force, and we lose 2–1. Game three is an echo of game two; we lose by the same score.

The statistics are telling. The Sooners batted .260 in the series. Until this weekend, their batting average was a nation-leading .394. Over three games, they scored only seven runs, their lowest run total since the three-game series was introduced to the Big 12 in 2012.

Gasso's championship teams *produced* in high-pressure moments when the game was on the line. The series loss to Texas feels indicative of where the season will go. I start to catastrophize. In Soonerland, I'm not alone. Online, aggrieved fans place the loss at Gasso's feet. I'm surprised at some of the vitriol; it shows that nothing—not even seven national championships, including three in a row—makes a Sooner coach immune to criticism. I recall a telling passage from George Lynn Cross's memoir *Presidents Can't Punt*. Cross was OU president during Wilkinson's remarkable run in the fifties; the man, as erudite as they come, was also an ardent Sooner fan, accompanying the football team wherever it played. After the Sooners upended Maryland in the 1954 Orange Bowl (the Terrapins were a six-point favorite and already declared national champions), Cross and his wife, Cleo, were at the after-party when they came upon an inconsolable Maryland fan, already drunk on bourbon and water. "I just don't understand it," the man lamented. "We're supposed to be the greatest team in the nation, and we get beat in the Orange Bowl."

After trying (and failing) to reason with the man, Cross and his wife left the table to allow him to stew. Despite a "satisfying evening," the OU president found himself musing on college sports and an increasingly obsessive and irrational fan base. He writes, "I had the disquieting thought that probably both teams had too many fans of this kind—that they were the major cause of the problems that bedeviled intercollegiate athletics."

■ ■ ■

Gasso's team rebounds from the weekend "disaster," taking out its frustrations on hapless Wichita State on Tuesday. Two days later, the Sooners return to conference play for an at-home series with BYU. I'm at Love's Field for the game and sitting along the third-base line, close to the offensive side of things. Before Maxwell opens the game with the first pitch, her teammates (Rylie Boone, Alyssa Brito, and Tiare Jennings) are horsing around on the field. They're pretending to *be* Maxwell, pantomiming the underhanded pitching motion that has tormented opponents all season. I glance at the sky, an unbroken powder blue, and a flock of geese passes in V formation. I take it as a good omen; V means victory, right?

I'm surrounded by women who know each other. To my right sits a woman and (I'm guessing) her partner; the two appear to be in their fifties. One wears a red OU hoodie, the other a black one. Both women are wearing OU baseball caps, with their ponytails poking through the rear closure. In front of us is another female couple, older than my neighbors, their hairstyles short and sprinkled with black and gray. To my left is a woman in her forties who's been joined by her niece: an OU senior who, I overhear, is applying to medical school.

It becomes clear that they are softball regulars and a tight-knit group. They talk about their 2022 trip to Hawaii where they watched Jocelyn Alo, the Sooner softball legend, break the home run record. "The Commissioner was our driver and nearly killed us," one of them says; the others laugh.

The Commissioner is the nickname of one of the women sitting in front of us. The others are known as the "Committee." The Commissioner has brought two sets of flag pennants to keep track of two important statistics: strikeouts and home runs. When Maxwell, who is celebrating her birthday today, fans a BYU batter to end the top of the first inning, the Commissioner hangs a pennant, emblazoned with a "K" for strikeout, on the railing in front of her. Four more times tonight, Maxwell's efforts will earn a pennant. The Commissioner gets to display the home run pennant as early as the second inning when Coleman homers to left field, scoring base runners Boone and Alynah Torres too. Coach Gasso, in a black hoodie and her trademark white visor, patrols the third-base line, looking on with stoic approval.

For the defense in the third inning everything is routine; three batters come to the plate and fail to reach base. The Commissioner is busy again as freshman Pickering strikes the ball cleanly for a solo home run in the bottom of the third. OU leads 4–0.

I've taken notice of the vibe in our seating area. An interloper of sorts, I'm in the middle of these women who all know each other, and I've stayed quiet, occasionally taking notes, while they banter, comment on the game, and tell stories. They seem to grow more comfortable with my presence. As I sit there quietly, they're talking around and past me; occasionally, an arm shoots out close to my face. Then I see another arm from the other side; the women are gesturing in animated fashion. Caught in between them, I'm like a tree or statue: part of the scenery, practically ignored.

Between innings there's a kids' race on inflatable horses. Then there's a fan giveaway, sponsored by the Tex-Mex restaurant Chuy's, and when it's announced that our section of the stadium has won the prize the Commissioner and Committee cheer the news; one of them says she's never won anything in her life.

Maxwell continues her dominance in the top of the fourth. The Commissioner notices the fact that BYU's batters have failed to get a hit.

"She's got a no-hitter going," the Commissioner says.

"You're not supposed to say that, dude."

"I've jinxed it." The Commissioner sounds contrite.

A young woman in an OU polo shirt walks down the steps along our section to deliver our prize: Chuy's coupons, which get passed down. Chuy's, a "Proud Sponsor of OU Athletics," has gifted us a free taco "with purchase." We have to buy something in order to get something. I'm not the only one in our area that feels cheated.

Our shared grievance breaks the silence between the Commissioner, the Committee, and me. I start a conversation with my neighbor. She tells me that she and her partner have been coming to OU softball games for years; in high school, in the eighties, she played the sport herself. I ask if she goes to any other sports. Is she an OU football fan?

She shakes her head. "Only softball and women's basketball," she says.

I want to know what she thinks about the series loss to Texas. She mulls it over for a second before sharing the question with the others;

they take turns chiming in. Everyone agrees that there's an issue with hitting. The reason: It's hard to say. The players are just not swinging. It could be a psychological thing. At the plate they look like they lack confidence. Gasso is trying out different batting orders, so that could be affecting their rhythm. My neighbors don't act especially worried, like they've been through this before with the team.

At the top of the fifth, the jinx comes to fruition. The Cougars get a base hit and just like that Maxwell's no-hitter is gone. The Committee lets the Commissioner have it with a collective glare and then some words of rebuke.

Playing spoiler is about as good as it gets for BYU today. The Sooners score four in the bottom of the fifth to run-rule the visitors. It's capped off by a three-run homer from Sanders. Along the third-base line, we're in perfect position to see it. As the ball comes off Sanders's bat with a loud crack, we watch it streak past us in the air like a meteorite that's entered the earth's atmosphere. It's visual poetry.

■ ■ ■

I'm befuddled when the next day the Sooners lose game two in convincing fashion. Oklahoma pitchers, minus Maxwell, prove vulnerable while the BYU bats, silent the night before, are very loud indeed. The nine runs against Gasso's team are the most given up by OU since early in 2020. On offense, the Sooners put plenty of runners on base but leave them stranded. Batters aren't delivering in crucial moments.

The Jekyll and Hyde turnaround worries me. Previous teams, during the three-peat, were close to unbeatable. Already in 2024 the Sooners have lost four games. The 2021 team lost four all season; the 2022 team lost three. In 2023, there was a single blemish on the Sooners' record.

They bounce back, as they tend to do, the next day, taking the series against BYU. The team then goes on a run, winning eight in a row, but I think I speak for Sooner Nation when I say I don't trust this team.

The same vulnerabilities resurface when Oklahoma State comes to town and at the worst possible time (at least to my addled fan brain). It's the conference finale as well as the last Bedlam to be played beneath the Big

12 banner (the two teams will continue with Bedlam despite OU's move to the SEC). Oklahoma takes an early lead in game one, but the Sooner bats are quiet for much of the night; they leave eight base runners stranded. The stage is set for Maxwell, pitching against her former team, but her performance is off. In four innings, she gives up four hits and three runs. Kierston Deal comes on to help, but things get exponentially worse. The Pokes double their run total: the final score, 6–3.

In game two, the Sooners get done to them what they've been doing to teams for years. Bad weather suspends play for three hours. When play resumes, the pitchers keep it scoreless for three innings; Oklahoma breaks the tie in the bottom of the fourth; they trade runs in the fifth. But then the Cowboys open the floodgates in the sixth, scoring five runs. The stats tell a story; the visitors out-hit OU 10–5 and produce four homers.

Oklahoma wins game three, but does it matter? The series has been lost. So has the conference title, which goes to someone (Texas, no less) other than Oklahoma for the first time since 2011.

The Big 12 tournament starts in a week, and after that, for those teams that qualify, the NCAA tournament. It seems outrageous to consider, but could the Sooners stumble at any of the stages before the WCWS? (The last time the Sooners failed to advance to the WCWS was 2015.) You have the conference tournament, then Regionals and Super Regionals. It goes without saying: A bad performance can end your season. Ominously, Gasso's 2024 team has shown in six losses that it's not invincible. And its rivals are very good, Texas especially.

Sports fans are readers of tea leaves and only happy to try and predict the future. Sports fans are also suspicious of Hollywood endings, especially regarding their own team. My gut tells me that the four-peat will be a dream deferred.

▪ 13 ▪

THE FOUR-PEAT, PART II

CARRIE HENDERSON drives a white Toyota 4Runner with a red pinstripe down the side. On the back quarter panel of the large SUV is a "Boomer Sooner" sticker, which once garnered a stranger's attention while the fifty-nine-year-old was pumping gas at a service station.

"You must be a Sooner fan," the man said.

"No, I'm a Sooner," Henderson replied.

For her, there's a difference. "Once you've lived it and been a part of it, it's always with you," she says. "Once it's in you, you live it and breathe it."

Henderson grew up in small-town Bixby, just south of Tulsa, in a sports-crazed family. On Saturdays in the fall, they always listened to Sooner football on the radio.

She and her brother were athletes. They played baseball together with the neighborhood kids until she got older and started playing softball with the girls. Henderson was good enough that colleges began to recruit her in the early 1980s. The idea of going to college was like a foreign concept that she couldn't wrap her head around. A self-described "country girl," she figured that after high school she would get married, start a family, and work a job.

Then the University of Oklahoma called, with assistant coach Mary Williams inviting Henderson to Norman for a tryout. The softball team needed a catcher.

A week after the tryout, Williams called again; this time, she made Henderson an offer: a partial scholarship to play softball for OU. Proving that she was more than just a simple "country girl," Henderson told the Sooner assistant coach that Northeastern State University, in Tahlequah, had offered a full ride with the opportunity to play any position she wanted. The statement was true; Henderson would never lie. At the same time, she knew she held a bargaining chip. On the spot, Williams upgraded the offer to a full scholarship.

Henderson didn't actually meet Marita Hynes, the head coach for whom she would soon play, until after the tryout and scholarship offer. The moment stands out vividly in her mind, even forty-plus years later. Henderson was playing at an under-eighteen national tournament in Las Cruces, New Mexico, and had just hit a home run. When she rounded third base, she saw a woman she didn't know jumping up and down, part of the group welcoming her home. "Who is this woman?" Henderson wondered. It was Hynes, head coach of the Sooners.

The Norman campus, during her first semester, felt huge and a million miles from home. An academic adviser put her in classes that didn't conflict with softball practice. There was study hall to attend. The whole experience was like a dream.

"There was not a day that I didn't get up and come out of the door and think, 'I can't believe I'm here,'" Henderson says.

At games in Reaves Park, bleachers were scarce and so were fans. She and her teammates had to put up and take down the fences that the Little League kids used for practice. There was no locker room for the players. Looking back, it was far from glamorous, but at the time, as young women, they didn't know any better. In fact, they thought they had it made. Someone did the team's practice laundry for them. They got to travel to California to play; it was the first time Henderson had ever been on a plane. Once they were on the West Coast, Hynes was ever mindful of her players' financial situation; some came from poor or working-class households. Coach Hynes made sure to distribute the per diem allowance each morning, so that her players could buy what they wanted or needed throughout the day.

"She took care of us like nobody's business," Henderson says.

In the 1980s, the Sooner softball team was not the powerhouse it is today, and there was little pressure on players to win championships. Still, there were standards to be met. Hynes insisted that they play and behave with integrity; she never let them forget that they were representing the University of Oklahoma. For their part, Henderson and her teammates felt an immense pride wearing the Sooner uniform. Across four seasons, Henderson would come to the plate with bat in hand and look along the third-base line where Hynes was standing. The two would lock eyes, and Henderson felt a surge of confidence; she saw a coach who believed in her.

She graduated from OU in 1986 with a bachelor's degree in recreation and rehabilitation. For a decade, Henderson worked at the Kimberly-Clark paper plant in Jenks. Then, at thirty-five, she and her husband had twin boys, and she stopped working to stay at home with them. When they were of school age, she got a job working in their school.

Life threw at her several monumental challenges. In 2012, when the boys were twelve, her husband passed. Then she became her parents' caretaker, a responsibility that lasted until their passing in 2019. But there was also joy. The twins, both musicians, matriculated to OU where they joined the student logistics team for the Pride of Oklahoma. Basically, they were like roadies for the band, helping members set up for practices and on game days. After graduation, one became a police officer and the other, a trained pilot, stayed at OU to teach aviation. Now an empty nester, Henderson went to work with her brother at a metal fabrication shop in Bixby.

For many years, while working and raising kids, she couldn't afford to go to Sooner games. In 2000, Henderson could finally purchase season tickets for football. While she cheered on the softball team as it developed into an elite program, she didn't start attending games regularly until 2023 when she bought a season ticket from a friend for a seat behind home plate at Marita Hynes Field. When it came to getting season tickets for Love's Field, Henderson was far down on the waiting list but managed to get four tickets in the outfield bleachers. She was there for opening day with other softball alumni to get an early look at the ballpark. Coach Gasso gave a speech, and the current team was there too. It made Henderson feel good to think she was part of this: the program's history.

Hynes, her old coach, came to town for the ceremony as well. The two have been friends since Henderson's playing days. Hynes, who retired in 2003, has lived in New Mexico for many years now, but occasionally drives back to Norman or Oklahoma City to watch the softball team. When she does, she always checks in with friends, Henderson included.

During the 2024 season, Henderson's been to almost every home game and even traveled to her first away game: against Kansas in March. On game days, she'll drive down, with her dogs, to Norman where she owns a house; one of the twins lives there. She drops off the dogs and then drives to the ballpark to tailgate; often, she and her friends are out in the parking lot several hours before the game. Sooner fans walk by and strike up conversations.

As the postseason begins, Henderson is philosophical about the Sooners' difficult regular season. She understands, as a former player, how hard the sport is. The weight of expectations, carried by this program, makes the pressure even worse. Knowing this, she never gets down on the team. She believes in them, even when they lose—especially when they lose. She thinks the series losses to Texas and Oklahoma State may turn out to be blessings in disguise.

▪ ▪ ▪

At the Big 12 tournament in May, the Sooners look like a revitalized team. They steamroll Kansas 10–1 and then run-rule BYU. The matchup for the championship game is the one Henderson and her friends want: a second go-around with Texas. Ironically, the roles have been reversed. Texas is ranked number one in the country and favored to win. Their ace, Citlaly Gutierrez, is back to torment Sooner batters again. Nevertheless, everyone at Henderson's tailgate feels confident; the series loss in the regular season was a close contest in the Longhorns' backyard. We're in the postseason now, where OU excels, and in friendly territory, Oklahoma City.

Oklahoma corrects what went wrong against the Longhorns in April; the batters come alive with runners in scoring position, and Maxwell, in the circle, allows just a single run in five innings. The Sooners get their revenge, 5–1, and take home the Big 12 tournament trophy.

Six days later, Regionals begin, with Love's Field as one of the host venues. Henderson isn't too worried about this stage, given the caliber of opponent. The Sooners prove her correct; Cleveland State is both shut out and run-ruled. Oregon goes down in two games. Oklahoma progresses to Super Regionals.

The next opponent is fourteenth-ranked Florida State, a rematch of the Women's College World Series championship series the year before. Henderson harbors an active dislike for the Seminole team. There's a swagger about Florida State that gets on her nerves. She finds herself in player mode, a mindset she sported as a collegiate athlete. Back then, circumstances might conspire to hamper her focus before a game. The weather was miserable, cold or rainy, or she might have been exhausted from traveling, with mid-terms or finals looming. With a game on the horizon, Henderson would find something about her opponents to fixate on. "Sometimes in order to compete at a high level I found it helped to pick out something that irritated me about the other team," she says. In 2024, she's doing this again; Florida State's catcher has long, false eyelashes that "creep her out." It may sound ridiculous to act this way, but Henderson insists it's part of sports at the highest level.

OU and Florida State are long-time adversaries, two programs of the highest caliber, having played each other in the WCWS the past two years. Love's Field hosts this year's matchup. Game one is a blowout, 11–3, with Sooner bats making up for an off night from Maxwell. The second game, a must-win for Florida State, is a battle. Sooner pitchers Kierston Deal and Nicole May face adversity, but with defensive help from their teammates they prevail. Freshmen Parker and Pickering prove invaluable, with critical hits that score runs. Oklahoma wins 4–2 to advance to the WCWS.

■ ■ ■

For Henderson and friends, the WCWS is a weeklong celebration but also an act of endurance; by the following Wednesday, after a week of tailgating and spectating, everyone will be exhausted. They claim their area in a corner of the parking lot at Devon Park in Oklahoma City on Tuesday, a couple days before the first game of the tournament, stringing together eight canopies to form a tent city. Among the items inside are portable drum fans, gas-powered generators, jumbo ice chests, and big-screen TVs. But arguably the most arresting feature is a poster that hangs on the adjacent fence, facing the sidewalk. It's such a stand-out item that throughout the week fans will stop to laugh and take a picture; it makes a great backdrop for Sooner fans especially.

The poster's subject is the Longhorn head coach, Mike White, and it doesn't present him in his finest moment. Henderson was inspired to create the poster after remembering an incident from the Big 12 tournament in 2022. White got tossed from the game after arguing with the umpire over two controversial calls. As he exited the field, the Texas coach turned around and shot his middle finger at the umpire.

Henderson admits she has zero respect for White. On top of this incident, she cites past comments that "implied things" about Coach Gasso's recruitment methods.

To make the poster, she screen-grabbed the image of White flipping off the umpire from TV. Then she took the image to Walgreens to get it blown up and printed off. From the beginning of the WCWS till the day before its finale, Henderson's poster hangs on the fence, a magnet for anyone who dislikes the Texas Longhorns. She takes it down each night to protect it from thieves.

As far as on-field matters go, Henderson prepares herself for an extremely tough tournament. First, there's the weight of history. No program in softball has ever won four titles in a row. Second, the competition is stiff, with UCLA, stacked with fine athletes, a particular worry.

Six days after the Super Regional, the Sooners are clicking offensively and defensively when they take on the seventh-ranked Duke Blue Devils in their first game of the WCWS.

As she will throughout the tournament, Henderson sits in a section of the stadium to the right of the catcher and along the first-base line. Her seat, pretty much level with the field, offers an exceptional view of the action. Unfortunately, she's experiencing a reunion of sorts with a University of Washington fan who sat in front of her the year before. Henderson can't believe her bad luck. The Washington fan, presumably in her sixties, is with friends but last year was with her husband and son. The husband commented on every pitch thrown, regardless of the team and pitcher, while the son scribbled in a scorebook, documenting the game. The family hated the Sooner softball team. Washington hasn't made the WCWS this year. Is the woman only here in the hope of witnessing a Sooner collapse? Where are her husband and son? Henderson can't believe she feels this way, but she'd rather be sitting close to Texas fans than this woman.

By the third inning, the Sooners lead the Blue Devils 4–1. The momentum of the game, by the fourth, is irreversibly in their favor, and Oklahoma run-rules Duke in the sixth inning, the final score 9–1.

If anyone can boast of dominance in softball, alongside OU, it's the UCLA Bruins whose twelve national championships are the most of any program. They last prevailed in the WCWS in 2019, beating Oklahoma in the championship series. The old rivals meet again in the winner's bracket at the 2024 WCWS. The game turns into an old-fashioned pitcher's duel between Maxwell and UCLA's Kaitlyn Terry. After her see-saw outing against Duke, Maxwell's confidence is low; she's on the receiving end of a Gasso pep talk, which proves the boost the pitcher needs. Maxwell does something rare, lasting for the entire game; she only gives up two hits. No Bruin rounds the bases to score, and Maxwell strikes out eleven batters, an astounding number. Tiare Jennings's solo home run in the third inning is enough for a 1–0 victory.

The Sooners move on to face Florida in the national semifinal. The Gators enter the matchup at a disadvantage. Because they lost their first game in the winner's bracket, a 10–0 thumping by Texas, the Gators must beat the Sooners twice to advance to the championship series.

Henderson feels confident, though there's a nagging worry in the back of her mind about the lack of scoring in the UCLA game. On the other hand, there's the beating Florida suffered at the hands of Texas to consider; Henderson, forever anti-Texas, believes that anything the Longhorns can do the Sooners can do better.

With storms and lightning in Oklahoma City, the game is delayed several hours. The Gators take a 1–0 lead in the first inning with Nicole May pitching for the Sooners. Some stellar defense keeps Oklahoma from responding with runs of their own. In the bottom half of the second, with two outs, left fielder Rylie Boone leaps to try and catch a ball that loops into her area; in a rare miscue, she can't get there, and the ball bounces in front of her and then beyond, dribbling into the left-field corner. The Gator batter, Kendra Falby, speeds around the bases for an astonishing inside-the-park home run. A series of hits in the third makes it 4–0, and Gasso pulls May for Kierston Deal. Kinzie Hansen's RBI single in the fourth puts Oklahoma on the scoreboard only for Florida to score three more runs. In the fifth inning, with the score 7–1, Jennings' two-run homer gives the Sooners hope. But another home run from the Gators, their fourth of the day, stretches the lead to 9–3. The Sooners can't mount a comeback; suddenly, a favorable draw has turned into a must-win situation.

Originally, a second and deciding game (if needed) was meant to be played on the same day, but the weather has messed up the schedule. The Sooners get time to regroup.

Henderson's confidence has evaporated. She feels both resigned and grateful. She thinks: "The four-peat may be out of reach, but we had a great three-year run." By the next day, back at Devon Park, a part of her has accepted that the Sooners won't be moving on to the championship series. She thinks: "I'd rather lose to Florida twice in the WCWS than lose to Texas once; it would haunt me forever."

Kelly Maxwell's tendency to struggle early strikes again in the elimination game. She gives up a two-run homer in the first inning. Freshman Ella Parker, however, ties the game with a home run of her own, with a runner on base. Florida repeats its first-inning success with another two-run homer in the second, and half an inning later Keagan Rothrock, pitching consecutive games for the Gators, gets out of trouble with runners on first and third. Florida homers again to make it 5–2.

Any sports fan can tell you about games or series that started to feel predetermined, as if one team was always going to win. Florida looks like that team of destiny. But then, in the bottom of the fourth inning, Cyd Sanders adds to the tidal wave of home runs, blasting a two-run shot and cutting Florida's lead to one.

Maxwell and her defense stop the bleeding in innings four, five, and six. In the bottom of the sixth, Avery Hodge hits a line drive into the right field corner, reaching second base. Two batters later, and with two outs, Parker is the hero again, singling into center field to score Hodge and tie the game. Neither team can score in the seventh; extra innings will decide the game. At the top of the eighth, the Sooners get a 1-2-3 inning from Maxwell, who's still in the circle. Rothrock is still pitching too.

Jayda Coleman, at the top of the Sooner batting order, is up. She's a graduating senior, a vital piece of the teams that won three straight national championships. But this could literally be her last at-bat for the Sooners. She's one for three on the day. Her previous duel with Rothrock did not go in her favor. Her teammates recognize that this is a big moment, a big opportunity. The bat is in the hands of the right person. Rylie Boone jokes around with Coleman. Then, in a moment of solemnity, Alyssa Brito approaches her and together they pray. For a few seconds, they're a world away from Devon Park, in a bubble of their own making, and what's on the line appears to be more than a softball game. Then it's time to play.

Coleman takes a ball. When she gets caught looking at a strike, she makes an audible sound of frustration. The next pitch is down the middle but high; Coleman is right not to swing. The fourth pitch is down the middle and at a good height for the batter. Coleman is all over it; her timing is perfect, the moment of contact producing a loud and promising crack. The ball sails to opposite field where the outfielder makes a valiant effort, leaping high, but she's just out of reach. It's a home run, and Coleman rounds the bases, jubilant, her arms uplifted. She looks to the sky. Her teammates are waiting at home plate to swarm her: a circle of celebration. The Florida players huddle to console their freshman pitcher who's in tears.

Coleman is asked about her triumphant moment, which sends Oklahoma to the championship series, in a postgame interview. She goes straight to her spirituality, revealing what happened with her teammate before she stepped to the plate. "Brito prayed over me before that at-bat, and I swear God just took over me," she says. "And I trusted it, I surrendered all of my control to him."

In the aftermath of all that joy, Henderson thinks: Sooner Magic. It's a real thing and affects other teams. They know that a Sooner comeback is always in the cards. They know Jayda Coleman with her glove can reach over the wall to steal a home run or, with her bat, put one out to win the game, as she just did with Florida.

▪ ▪ ▪

Henderson is in two minds ahead of game one with Texas. On the one hand, she feels confident. The Sooners, after struggles in the regular season, are a rejuvenated team; the swagger has returned. Moreover, when Henderson looks at Texas, she doesn't see the same senior leadership; OU's seniors, with all their experience, should make a difference. Can Texas handle all the pressure that comes with facing a three-peat champion with the national title on the line? Henderson doesn't think so.

On the other hand, knowing the unpredictability of sports, she feels very nervous about the series. A pitcher can have an off night. Players make errors in the infield and outfield. Conversely, someone on the other side can have the game of her life. Whatever happens, Henderson acknowledges that watching the championship series, against OU's bitter rival no less, is going to be many things rolled into one: stressful, nail-biting, and breathtaking.

▪ ▪ ▪

Oklahoma's seniors get the team off to an electric start. After Coleman reaches first base, Tiare Jennings sends a pitch to the outfield bleachers. Right away it's 2–0. Texas gets one back in the bottom of the first, blasting a solo home run off pitcher Kelly Maxwell. Freshman Ella Parker is timing her swing just right. She singles in the third inning after doubling in the first. Then, Kinzie Hansen homers to put two more runs on the board for Oklahoma. Freshman Kasidi Pickering rides the wave of Sooner momentum; she's next at-bat and smashes a solo homer, stretching the lead to 5–1. Longhorns reach first and second in the next half inning, but Maxwell doesn't give up any runs. Neither Maxwell nor the Longhorns' second pitcher of the day, Mac Morgan, struggles in the fourth. In the fifth, Hansen slaps the ball to left center, rounds first, and slides into second. An error from the Texas second baseman, with two outs, gives Hansen the chance to score. Another Longhorn error, in the sixth, allows an alert Hodge to advance from second to third base; the catcher, after a strikeout, thought the inning was over and flipped the ball to her pitcher. Jennings' looping single to shallow left scores Hodge.

At 7–1, Henderson's prediction is coming true. OU's seniors are producing; Texas is failing to rise to the occasion.

Texas manages a mini rally in the bottom of the sixth, scoring two. Things look sketchy for Maxwell for the first time. However, with runners on first and second, Maxwell fans a Texas batter to end the inning. In the seventh, Sooner batters aren't resting on what they've already done; with a full count, Alyssa Brito doubles into the right center gap. The Longhorn catcher makes a second error, trying to catch Brito at third; the loose ball rolls down the third-base line into left field and Brito walks in to make the score 8–3. Pickering almost makes it nine, but the Longhorn outfielder, Ashton Maloney, robs her of a home run. Maxwell strikes out two in a routine seventh to close out the game; though her catcher, Kinzie Hansen, exults, Maxwell walks away from the circle showing no emotion, with a slight grin on her face, as if she's finished off a non-ranked team in the preseason and not a top-ranked team in the finals of the WCWS.

Henderson and her tailgating friends are thrilled with the win, but they end the evening with a "loss." A security guard confiscates the popular poster of Texas head coach Mike White. Henderson figures that some Texas fan, unable to take a joke, tattled.

■ ■ ■

Maxwell is the star, but she's only human and needs a rest. Graduate pitcher Karlie Keeney starts game two for the Sooners. The Longhorns refuse to bend the knee; they're not here to lose gracefully, and they take a second-inning lead. Oklahoma responds immediately; in the next half inning, Brito nearly homers. The ball bounces off the outfield wall and Brito gets to second. Then Pickering homers for the second consecutive game; she grins as she rounds the bases, points at the sky. With the score 2–1, in the third inning, the Longhorns load the bases with two outs. A single up the middle scores a runner to tie the game. Coach Gasso brings on a new pitcher, sophomore Paytn Monticelli, who gets the next batter to ground out, ending the Longhorn threat. In the fourth, Gasso keeps rotating pitchers, with Kierston Deal in the circle. Avery Hodge, playing second base, fails to field a ground ball—in fairness, the ball takes a nasty hop in the dirt—and a Longhorn scores. They've taken the lead. Pickering gets another hit in the bottom of the fourth, sending Hansen to second base. Rylie Boone then loads the bases, doing what she often does: making contact with the ball and then sprinting up the first-base line to beat the throw. She performs her signature move once she reaches safely, throwing her hands up in the air to petition the crowd: Are you not entertained? Cyd Sanders then takes advantage of the situation, sending the ball through the right field gap and scoring all those on base. The Sooners have flipped the momentum of the game; it's now 5–3. The Longhorns escape the inning without suffering any further damage. Senior Nicole May, the Sooners' "matriarch," enters the game in the fifth, delivering a 1-2-3 inning, with two strikeouts. Gutierrez, the Longhorn pitcher, is just as good, and it's a scoreless inning for both teams. The sixth inning proves decisive. After Texas gets a run off May, Maxwell leaves the bullpen to jog onto the field; Sooner fans cheer. She inherits a tough moment: runners on second and third, with the go-ahead run at the plate. The Texas batter, Mia Scott, hits a pitch into the dirt and the ball loops in the infield; it's another tough play for Hodge as the ball bounces in front of her outstretched glove. Hodge can't field it properly; a runner scores and Scott reaches first safely. But

Hodge then shows championship concentration; she's alert to the fact that Scott has rounded first base. Hodge spins and tosses the ball to first baseman Sanders who tags out Scott. The Sooners have given up a run, but it could have been worse. It's 5–4.

In the bottom half of the sixth, Boone singles to right outfield. Sanders walks to put runners on first and second. Then Hodge is hit by an errant pitch, and the bases are loaded. Coleman, up next, proves clutch; her single scores Boone and keeps the bases loaded. Then, with two outs, Ella Parker demonstrates again the value of the two Sooner freshmen in this postseason; the duel between her and Gutierrez is well-fought, but the pitcher leaves one high and in the strike zone. Parker slaps the ball to center field, and two runs score. The crowd noise is deafening; Sooner fans sense a championship. Their team has a four-run cushion going into the final inning.

Maxwell has been close to unhittable late in games all season. With only three batters between her and her first national championship, she gets the first Texas batter to pop out. Then she strikes out the Big 12 Player of Year, Reese Atwood. After delivering the strikeout, Maxwell turns around in the circle, looking poised and calm. Her stoicism must be, to some extent, a smokescreen. There must be a swirl of thoughts and emotions inside her brain. The fact that she can stay so composed is a testament to her character and competitiveness.

The Longhorns' freshman star, Katie Stewart, is their last hope. It's a huge moment, and you almost feel sorry for the player. It feels like the weight of history is against her; this moment, with only one out remaining, suddenly feels inevitable. The whole shape of the season, with its ups and downs for the Sooners, materializes in a way that feels right and symmetrical and even poetic. Of course, it ended up this way, with Maxwell, the controversial transfer from Oklahoma State, in charge of the final inning and out. Of course, it ended up this way, with OU's decorated senior class—Boone, Coleman, Jennings, May, and Hansen—all contributing in this final game.

Maxwell gets ahead early in the count: 0–2. Then she grounds a pitch in the dirt for ball one. Stewart makes good contact with the next pitch, which is hit hard toward Brito at third base. Brito, the senior, backhands the bouncing ball and then fires it to Sanders at first base, an assured defensive play that exemplifies the greatness of the past four seasons. The four-peat has been achieved.

The players rush the pitching circle; Hansen, the catcher, gets there first, and hugs Maxwell with all her considerable might. The group of players falls to ground. It becomes a mound of celebration. Yards away, Gasso and her coaches engage in their own group hug. There are tears of joy and maybe even relief; it's been the most challenging of seasons. Gasso's women, in the end, have proven their mettle. The vast majority of the twelve thousand fans at Devon Park produce a loud and constant thrum of delight. Texas fans are silent.

Henderson is not silent. From her vantage point, she has a close-up view of the celebrations on the field. She's jumping up and down and hugging her friend. The Washington fan, an irritation for the past week, is not around; sensing a Sooner victory, she left before the final out.

Friends from the tailgate have seats on the upper deck, and Henderson heads there to celebrate with them. They hug and take group pictures with the field and team in the background. Blue and white confetti falls on the players holding aloft the national championship trophy, with cameramen on the periphery filming the scene.

Henderson and friends stay in the stands until the team leaves the field. When it's time to go, they walk back to the parking lot where the tailgate needs to be taken down. Dutifully, they go to work. Everyone is suddenly exhausted. They've tailgated hard for a whole week; the comforts of home beckon.

■ ■ ■

Months after the Sooners' fourth national championship in a row, Henderson thinks about the University of Oklahoma and the passage of years. In 1982, when she arrived at OU, she was just a seventeen-year-old kid "with no real goals other than playing the game I loved." During her freshman year, the outer boundaries of her new life included Reaves Park and Campus Corner; she didn't go beyond those places. Inevitably, she thinks about her coach Marita Hynes, who took her outside the state for the first time. Hynes was a second mother as well as a confidant; Henderson was honest with her and got honesty in return. After Henderson graduated, Hynes became a family friend; once, while traveling for a golf tournament, the Sooner softball coach was invited to stay in the lake home owned by Henderson's parents. As a gesture of appreciation, Hynes bought them a brand-new grilling set, leaving it at the lake home for them to find.

After Henderson gave birth to the twins, she sent pictures of the boys every Christmas to Hynes, who put them on display on her microwave. Over the years, reunions took place in Norman where Henderson and Hynes would attend Sooner softball games. In the fall of 2023, they changed things up. Henderson flew with friends, including former teammate and pitcher Blenda Selvey, to New Mexico to visit Hynes. They played golf, and Hynes gave them a tour of Ruidoso: a resort town of seven thousand residents in the Sierra Blanca mountains and her home since her retirement in 2003.

More recently, Hynes had been a shoulder to lean on during a family crisis.

Henderson can't imagine her life without Hynes in it.

Another thing she can't imagine: allowing her twin boys, now grown men and Sooner alumni, to wear anything orange. The Henderson family is loyal to the University of Oklahoma. Win or lose, the teams from Norman, outfitted in crimson and cream, get Henderson's unconditional support—because that's what Sooners do.

Part V

STRUGGLE AND BELONGING

▪ 14 ▪

HEROIC ACTORS

WHILE RESEARCHING MEX, OU's first mascot, I read a couple of articles that gave me pause. They served as a stark reminder of a historical reality.

Both articles came from *The Oklahoma Daily* in the early 1920s. The first recounted a time when Mex, on a road trip with the football team, wasn't allowed on a streetcar because of his canine status. The team, in protest, left the streetcar and walked the mile or so to the football field for the game. The story was supposed to convey a sense of solidarity: all for one and one for all. But when the writer made mention of the players' objections to the streetcar conductor, I winced. The players noticed that "negroes" were allowed to ride in the streetcar next to whites. If "negroes" were allowed, then why not Mex?

The second article reported on Mex's poisoning in late September 1921. Of the three dogs poisoned, the one that died was a "brindle bulldog" owned by football team captain "Snorter" Dewey Luster from Chickasha. Luster's team was exceptional, having recently gone undefeated to win the 1920 Missouri Valley title. The bulldog's name was given, along with some facts about his short life that were laced with pathos. The dog was "but a youth but he was receiving valuable instructions from the older houn' [*sic*] Mex. . . . [The bulldog] was pledged Acacia last week during the big rushing season and he was buried in his colors." The bulldog's name didn't register at first, but then it did, and I couldn't believe my eyes. His name was composed of the first three letters of the "N" word.

Did it mean what I thought it meant? The Merriam-Webster online dictionary defined the term as an intransitive verb synonymous to revoke or renege. There was a transitive form too, which meant to "dress (stone) with a sharp-pointed hammer."

Neither connotation made sense within the context of naming a dog. Other sources, though less reliable, made more sense. Urban Dictionary defined it as "an awesomely derogative word toward [B]lack people." Wikipedia, though no source was given, described it as a nickname bestowed on white professional baseball players from the late nineteenth and early twentieth centuries whose skin was judged to be darker than normal: "Before the integration of baseball, a number of baseball players were known by the nickname, often adjudged to be a reference to someone's dark complexion."

I found on Amazon a listing for a book that was originally published as an "autobiographical narrative" in the mid-nineteenth century. The book was titled *Our Nig: or, Sketches from the Life of a Free Black* and was about "a spirited black girl who is abused and overworked as the indentured servant to a New England family."

For me, this stood as final proof that the term was used as a racist nickname.

The unflinching use of Luster's bulldog's name in the student newspaper spoke to the university's racist past. David Levy, in his official history of the university, tells the story of Monroe Work, who in 1892 traveled to Norman from Arkansas City, Kansas, looking for President David Ross Boyd. The university's first president, a progressive Presbyterian who believed in integration, had loaned the young African American man a hundred dollars to help him finish high school, and Work was in town to pay him back. On his arrival, a rumor spread that a Black man was matriculating to the university. An angry group of Normanites assembled to look for Boyd, intending to share their thoughts on an integrated university and town.

Frustrated that they could not find him, a few burned Boyd in effigy that night. The president was in Guthrie on business but later heard the story and got the message. (Incidentally, the talented Work continued his education, earning a PhD and becoming one of the leading Black scholars of the era.)

The Oklahoma Territorial legislature had already enacted the first segregation laws, in the late 1890s, when in 1907, after statehood, the legislature further codified racism with a series of Jim Crow statutes. Segregation in the schools was one result. White students attended either Oklahoma or Oklahoma A&M (now Oklahoma State). Black students were steered toward the Oklahoma Colored Agricultural and Normal University (now Langston University).

It wasn't until 1948, fifty-five years after the university first enrolled students, that Oklahoma admitted its first African American. Lengthy court battles forced the issue. Historian John T. Hubbell provides a detailed narrative of how the legal drama unfolded in his article "The Desegregation of the University of Oklahoma, 1946–1950." In January 1946, twenty-two-year-old Ada Lois Sipuel Fisher applied for admission to OU's College of Law but was rejected. With the help of the NAACP, she sought a court order to compel the university, her argument relying on a legal precedent established through two Missouri cases from the 1930s. Essentially, the Supreme Court had ruled that states must provide equal educational opportunities to citizens, a decision that nevertheless left the "separate but equal" doctrine of *Plessy v. Ferguson* intact. Since Langston University, from which she was already an honors graduate, did not have a law program, the University of Oklahoma was her only option; therefore, the institution was obligated to admit her. She'd been rejected due to her race. The district court in Norman was not swayed by this argument; a procedural aspect was invoked. In one of the Missouri cases, it had been established that the petitioner must try to find accommodation through administrative channels before seeking relief through the courts. In other words, Fisher had skipped a step; her appeal needed to go to the State Regents for Higher Education first.

Thurgood Marshall, later the first African American Supreme Court justice, joined Fisher's legal team in 1947 as they tried a different legal strategy. This time, they targeted state laws on segregation, describing them as unconstitutional: a violation of the "equal protection" clause of the Fourteenth Amendment. In Hubbell's words, "The result was predictable. Because she had made no demands on administrative officials, the court could only rule that Miss Sipuel [Fisher] had no real interest in instruction in a separate school but rather wished to break down the segregation statutes in Oklahoma."

Marshall and the NAACP appealed to the Supreme Court, which ruled in January 1948 that Fisher was legally entitled to a legal education at a state institution in Oklahoma. State officials responded by creating a separate law school, affiliated with Langston University, to be housed in the state capitol building in Oklahoma City. Marshall poured scorn on the facility, calling it a "Jim Crow law school," and Fisher refused to enroll, instead applying to OU's College of Law, which refused her again. The legal battle continued, with the NAACP contending sensibly but unsuccessfully in district court that the separate law school could not compare to OU and therefore was not an equal facility, contravening the law.

Fisher's pressure, along with an increase in graduate school applications at OU from Black applicants, led the state of Oklahoma to study the cost of creating graduate programs for African American students that were separate but comparable to those at Oklahoma and Oklahoma State. They discovered a litany of problems and challenges; implementation would cost the state tens of millions of dollars. In the end, money was the deciding factor in convincing the study's authors to recommend admitting Black students to all graduate and specialized programs offered by the state.

Meanwhile, others had joined Fisher in seeking legal remedy. In January 1948, George McLaurin, the holder of a master's degree from the University of Kansas, was retired from teaching at Langston, where he'd been for thirty-three years, when he applied to the doctoral program in OU's College of Education. He was denied admission. McLaurin tried again in June, to no avail, after which he petitioned the federal district court. In September, the court ruled that since the state hadn't provided McLaurin with an alternative graduate program it was obligated to admit him to the University of Oklahoma. Walking a tightrope, the Board of Regents sought to appease both the court and the state legislature. Consequently, when McLaurin, at fifty-four years old, began attending classes in October 1948 as OU's first African American student, he was forced to deal with an absurd learning environment. All his classes were in the same classroom—room 104 of the Carnegie Building—to which was attached an alcove where his desk was located. A wall kept him out of the sight line of his thirty fellow students who were seated in traditional rows. Reporters were present during McLaurin's first class, and photographers maneuvered about the room snapping pictures. According to *The Oklahoma Daily*, McLaurin "remained silent" as the professor and several students discussed the topic of the day: "racial differences between European and Indian Americans."

To this indignity was added others: a special desk for McLaurin in Bizzell library and a designated table in the cafeteria at the student union. Understandably, McLaurin and his legal team found these conditions unacceptable. They returned to federal court, but at the November hearing the court ruled against them; the judges said that McLaurin, in spite of segregated facilities, was receiving a quality graduate education. McLaurin's team appealed to the Supreme Court.

As McLaurin's case sat with the justices, other African Americans, including an indefatigable Ada Lois Sipuel Fisher, joined the student body. By summer 1949, twenty-six African Americans had enrolled in graduate study at OU. Their presence compelled the university to think about extracurricular activities, namely spectatorship at football games. Before 1949, Memorial Stadium was a whites-only space. The Board of Regents realized that this would have to change since all students, according to policy, were considered eligible to attend home football games. At a July 1949 Board of Regents meeting, President Cross proposed the allocation of a "row or rows beginning at the top of the stadium in section 30, the student 50 yard line section" for use by African American graduate students. Though the meeting minutes are terse and dispassionate, one can sense an underlying anxiety about the whole issue. The regents were well aware of the fact that people were "in much closer proximity to each other in the stadium than in the classrooms." Therefore, in their estimation, it wouldn't be enough to separate the races with a railing.

Two different plans, including sketches, were presented to the regents. The simpler one involved blocking off a row between the Black and white students. The other suggested "erecting a temporary solid 'wall' behind the first top row of white students; such wall to be as high as a person's head when seated on the row in front of the 'wall.'"

It says something about the regents' views on human nature and segregation that they unanimously went with option two. In addition to a physical barrier, the proposal included separate bathrooms for African American fans as well as the creation of signs "with adhesive backs" to be put up the morning of game day and taken down once the game was over. On a practical level, these signs guided African American fans to their separate facilities. On a public relations level, the signs posed a potential headache for the university given the presence of reporters and photographers at games; it was important to get the signs out of sight as soon as possible.

Special game tickets, with a "simple rubber stamp overprint," went to African American fans, along with private instructions to arrive early to games to "avoid the surging crowds" (again, one sees in the language a quiet anxiety about the potential for violence or other ugliness).

In practice, the "wooden, plywood" barrier was less than sturdy, and, according to historian Hubbell, it got "pushed back because white students were using it as a back rest." It was recommended to President Cross that the "barrier be strengthened, or, a rope or chain be substituted for it." Another option was to remove the plywood and mark a row of empty seats as "reserved for Negro students," but in the end, since the barrier was ordered by the Board of Regents, it stayed until season's end. Ultimately, despite the regents' worst fears, Black and white fans coexisted in the stadium without significant problems during the football season of 1949.

In June 1950, the Supreme Court delivered its verdict on the McLaurin case. Chief Justice Fred M. Vinson spoke for a unanimous court. The state's separate facilities had "handicapped" McLaurin and should be abolished: "Such restrictions impair and inhibit his ability to study, to engage in discussions and exchange views with other students, and, in general to learn his profession."

This led President Cross to declare that official segregation had ended at the university. The passage of time would expose his statement as naive and wishful. Exclusion and alienation, felt deeply and painfully by OU's African American students, would continue on campus for decades.

▪ ▪ ▪

In fall 1955, Prentice Gautt was a star running back for Oklahoma City's Douglass High, an all–African American school. In November, he and the team made history when they played in the state's first integrated high school football game. Gautt then distinguished himself further with his selection to the All-Star game, full of Oklahoma's best high school football players, during which he ran for a touchdown and returned a kickoff ninety yards for a touchdown. Gautt was named MVP.

Gautt was no doubt on Bud Wilkinson's radar as a recruit. The Sooner football coach, thirty-nine, was educated and progressive, the holder of a master's degree in English education. Integration was already a fact of life in the Big 10 conference—the first Black players had appeared on the field in the early 1890s—where Wilkinson played college football for the University of Minnesota in the 1930s; he starred on a team that won three national titles. According to his biographer John Scott, Wilkinson was determined to integrate OU athletics. Unlike some of his coaching peers, he wasn't entirely focused on winning; he saw beyond football. In a hundred years, Wilkinson thought, no one would care about his football record, but they would remember that he facilitated integration.

Gautt wasn't the first African American player to try and integrate the football team. Andy Dement, a talented quarterback and honors student at Douglass High School, met with Wilkinson in 1954 about playing for the Sooners. One account of the meeting says that Dement was told the program was out of scholarship money. Another account, from Dement's nephew many decades later, says that Wilkinson, though "open to the idea," told Dement that the university wasn't yet ready for Black players. In any event, Dement ended up playing football at Maryland State University, where he led the team to a 52–1 record in four seasons.

In 1955, other intrepid Black players embraced the challenge: George Farmer Jr., Sylvester Norwood, Charles Parker, and Frank Wilson Jr. They made it onto the practice field for the freshman team, according to historian Andrew McGregor, but a combination of injury and harassment—Farmer's car was vandalized with racist language—led to all four leaving the team.

Scott, Wilkinson's biographer, describes the coach as calculated in his approach to integration. In an echo of the logic that attended Jackie Robinson's introduction to Major League Baseball, the "right" person with the appropriate disposition and character would have to be found to break the color barrier at OU.

Wilkinson believed that Gautt's outstanding track record as a scholar, athlete, and leader made him the ideal candidate. President of his senior class at Douglass High and a member of the National Honor Society, Gautt was dignified and soft-spoken, studious and self-aware. He understood the stakes involved if he were to play football for OU.

Wilkinson came up with a plan, according to his biographer. Before Gautt's freshman year at Oklahoma, the coach contacted an association of Black doctors and dentists in Oklahoma City, sharing his wish for Gautt to star at the University of Oklahoma but explaining the bind he was in. If he offered Gautt a football scholarship, it would cause an uproar among donors, politicians, and fans. It would be better to get the young man enrolled as a student and then have him walk on as a player. His obvious talent would convince the naysayers; even the racists, motivated by their love of Big Red, would get behind this act of integration. Wilkinson asked that the association pay for Gautt's first year of college, and the doctors and dentists came through, raising four thousand dollars.

Wilkinson's plan succeeded in part. Gautt quickly proved that he belonged on the team, and a scholarship came his way. But the skeptics and naysayers didn't exit the scene. Many weren't happy about Gautt's presence, including some of his teammates.

Adversity showed up early and often in Gautt's time at OU. During that first year, he was with the freshman team on a road trip to Tulsa when segregation reared its head at a restaurant. The game had been played, and on the way home the team stopped for dinner. According to a 2019 *OU Daily* article celebrating Gautt's life and legacy, the restaurant's owner told Gautt that he would have to dine in the basement. Gautt nodded and left the restaurant, not wanting to make a scene. He planned to sit on the bus and wait for his teammates. When he got outside, though, he turned around and saw that the entire team had followed him out of the restaurant in solidarity.

It was an encouraging moment but hardly the end of Gautt's troubles. The Oklahoma Historical Society documents an incident in Gautt's sophomore year, after his promotion to varsity, when disgruntled teammates delivered gratuitous hits in practice, sending a message: Know your place.

Even into his senior year, when he was an established star for the Sooners, some of his teammates continued to oppose Gautt, voicing their bigotry behind his back. One afternoon, the players were gathered beneath a tree on the practice field, waiting for their calisthenics session to start, when Coach Wilkinson came over to tell them to return to the locker room; there would be no practice today. Once inside the locker room, the coach said that he'd heard that certain players were talking behind Gautt's back, using racial slurs. If they had a problem with Gautt, Wilkinson said, they should talk to him man-to-man. Then the coach left the room. Players took turns standing up to apologize. Gautt was not one to call attention to himself. After the sixth player apologized, Gautt stood up, his face covered in tears. "I can't take any more of this," he said. "This is too much for me." Then he left the locker room. The players remained to talk. Just days after the emotional meeting, the Sooners defeated Army 28–20.

Decades later, Gautt spoke to a group of OU students about the experience: "It probably melded us as a team."

His life as a student offered no escape from the pressures of the gridiron. Gautt felt watched and monitored on campus. This was particularly true when it came to socializing with the opposite sex. For most male students, dating was a rite of passage and normal enough; in any case, it wasn't a minefield in which one's personal safety was at risk. Young African Americans knew a different reality, and Gautt was well-aware of the dangers. In an in-depth profile written by Carol J. Burr for *Sooner Magazine* in 1987,

Gautt spoke of the anxiety he felt just talking to a young white woman. He recalled a situation in his sophomore year when he'd developed a friendship with a white female student in art class. At the end of class one day, they left the building together, walking side by side; she was headed to her dorm room with Gautt headed to the practice field. The stares they received from other students, including some of his teammates, sent an indelible message. For the rest of the semester, Gautt made sure that he and his female friend never left class together. He told *Sooner Magazine*, "I can remember slowly putting up my brushes one at a time . . . washing them and washing them and thinking 'Holy cow, we have to do all this.'"

Plenty of people at the university—professors, students, teammates, and administrators—admired Gautt for his even-keeled approach to such indignities, which occurred often, but Gautt was hard on himself. He was blessed (and cursed) with self-awareness, understanding that by nature he was a nonconfrontational person who just wanted to get along with others. At the same time, he was deeply conscious of the racial injustice that shaped not only his life but the lives of his fellow African Americans. Even in his later years, Gautt wished he'd done more to push back against the racism he faced. "To this day, whenever I talk about those experiences, I think that I really should have said something when this thing happened or that thing happened," he told *Sooner Magazine*. "But what would it have served? The only thing it would have served would be for me to vent my frustration, and more than likely I would have lost the opportunity to play at the University."

Fortunately, there was light to balance the darkness. Gautt exceled in his studies; he'd grown up in an environment—at home and in school—that prioritized education. At OU, he finished with a bachelor's degree in education and earned Academic All-American honors his senior season.

He made his breakthrough on the football field in the first game of his junior year. Playing at fullback against West Virginia, he burst through the defense with the ball tucked beneath his arm; three different tacklers bounced off him, failing to bring him down. Twenty-seven yards later, Gautt stood in the end zone. On the ensuing play, the Sooner offense went for two points, and Gautt made the key block that allowed quarterback

David Baker to waltz into the endzone. These two plays, along with a stellar performance at linebacker (in those days, talented athletes played both offense and defense), endeared him to the Oklahoma faithful.

The accolades came his way. Twice, Gautt was an All-Big 8 selection. In 1959, his senior year, he was named Orange Bowl MVP as OU defeated Syracuse 21–6. (Despite his MVP status, Gautt was the only member of the Sooner team not invited to the lavish afterparty at a Miami country club.) Though the team didn't win a national title during his tenure, it had 10–1 seasons in 1957 and 1958, finishing fourth and fifth respectively in the national polls.

After leaving OU, Gautt enjoyed success in the NFL. He was a second-round draft pick of the Cleveland Browns and played eight years total: one for the Browns and seven for the St. Louis Cardinals.

Once his pro career was over, he coached at the University of Missouri, where he earned first a master's then a doctorate in psychology. College athletics remained a passion, and Gautt worked in different capacities for the Big Eight and Big Twelve Conferences as well as for the NCAA.

When Gautt died in 2005 at the age of sixty-seven, friends and former teammates spoke about his life and the people he inspired. George Henderson, Gautt's friend, broke barriers himself, becoming the third African American professor at OU in 1967 and founding the university's human relations program. He and his wife were the first African Americans to purchase a home in Norman. He said of Gautt in the *OU Daily*: "If you think of Prentice as the first [B]lack scholarship football player at OU, also think of him as one of the first to leave football, become very successful in his occupation, continuing his education by getting the highest degree and being humble through it all."

Jimmy Harris, OU's quarterback during the back-to-back title seasons in 1955 and 1956, viewed Gautt as a man of the world. Harris told *The Oklahoman* in 2005: "If you had a team of Prentice Gautts, you'd have a winner all the way. . . . He was just extraordinary. He was like a sponge, absorbing not just football but culture and living in this world."

Gautt led the way for thousands of Black student-athletes in Norman. His presence can be felt today. Located in offices at the north end of

Memorial Stadium, the Prentice Gautt Academic Center opened in September 1999, a tribute to the man who dedicated himself to scholarship and athletics with grace and dignity. The center offers academic support to OU's hundreds of student-athletes.

In October 2022, against Kansas, the football team wore its alternate "Unity" uniform for the first time. Designed by student-athletes to represent togetherness and societal change, the uniform is the color of polished steel, with "TOGETHER" sewn on the collar and "UNITY" on the jersey nameplate. The uniform celebrated Gautt as a pioneer.

Caleb Kelly, a former OU linebacker who helped design the uniform, said about the project to *OU Daily*, "We wanted to honor Prentice for being the first African American scholarship football player here. He stood for unity, he stood for doing things the right way. He stood for making sure that you handled academics and football. He was one of the founding fathers who made Oklahoma football what it is and gave all the African American players who have come through OU that opportunity."

Dr. Martin Luther King Jr. said that "the arc of the moral universe is long but it bends toward justice." One sees this arc in the history of the University of Oklahoma. Once an institution that excluded African Americans, it has become one that venerates them. In recent years, incidents on campus have been a reminder that racism is still with us. Members of Sigma Alpha Epsilon were caught on video in 2015 using the "N" word liberally as they chanted that no Black man would ever be allowed to join the fraternity. The incident made headlines around the world. White supremacist posters were found hanging in campus buildings in 2016 and 2018. Clearly, the work of King and generations of activists continues. While these shameful episodes should temper any sense of triumph, we should not be reluctant to acknowledge and appreciate the progress made. A hundred years ago, Norman was a "sundown" town with an unwritten rule about African Americans leaving by nightfall. In 1920, a page of the Sooner yearbook was devoted to a student branch of the KKK. Twenty-eight years later, in October 1948, George McLaurin stepped on campus as the first African American student. A year later, Ada Lois Sipuel Fisher became OU's first Black law student. Prentice Gautt followed them nearly a decade later as the first Black scholarship athlete. In 1976, Thomas Lott became OU's first Black starting quarterback in an era starring Black football players like Joe Washington and the Selmon brothers: Lee Roy, Lucious, and Dewey. Also in 1976, Dunn Cumby became the first Black graduate of the OU College of Dentistry. His career included private practice as well as teaching duties at his alma mater.

Moments of struggle deserve to be mentioned in the same breath as moments of accomplishment. In 1968, OU's Black student-athletes banded together to petition the athletic department, outlining adverse conditions that they collectively faced. According to *Sooner Magazine*, they took issue with the coaches' antagonism toward interracial dating, which had resulted in the unfair punishment of some Black athletes. They also called attention to a perceived favoritism toward white athletes when it came to summer employment. Furthermore, they objected to decisions, made by coaches, which kept Blacks and whites apart in the dorms and on road trips with their teams. The group's statement read, in part: "It is true that we are caught up in the struggle of [B]lack Americans for racial equality. This, however, cannot be equated with [B]lack separatist movements. The fact that we are seeking to become *fully* integrated on and off athletic fields should be adequate testimony to our concerns for and commitment to a democratic society."

As first a student at OU in the late 1950s and then a professor in the following decades, Henderson experienced the campus as a hostile place for African Americans. In an interview with *The Oklahoman* in 2003, he said that Black students and staff were routinely harassed and even "physically accosted." Most student groups and activities did not include ethnic minorities at the time.

C. Don Bradley, a national diversity admissions counselor in OU's Office of Admissions and Recruitment, came to Norman in 1985 as a freshman. He told *The Oklahoman* in 2003 that even into the eighties a kind of de facto segregation operated at OU: "In 1985, it was a very segregated campus. We went to OU but we weren't a part of the total university experience. The invitations were not available."

In 1994, David Boren took over as president of the university, and thereafter, according to Henderson, substantive change happened, with Boren doing much to bring Black students into the OU "family."

"I don't believe it would have happened without him," Henderson said.

The above facts tell an edifying story of progress and integration, with all its messiness and labors. Another fact reveals that these changes at the University of Oklahoma, regarding racial equality, are far from cosmetic. Of the eight statues built for football legends, which stand along Jenkins to the east of Memorial Stadium, three were built for African Americans. Running back Billy Sims and quarterback Kyler Murray earned their statues by winning the Heisman Trophy in 1978 and 2018 respectively. The Selmon brothers did not win a Heisman, but so great were their contributions to Barry Switzer's championship teams in the 1970s that a statue of the trio was unveiled in September 2022. The brothers embodied an ethos that Oklahomans could appreciate. Raised on a Eufaula farm, they were hardworking and humble. Like Prentice Gautt, they exceled in the classroom and on the football field.

It cannot be overstated what these statues represent. The work of cultural anthropologist Ernest Becker is useful here. Becker saw human beings as an imaginative species that needed life to mean something in order to combat the fear of death. Life was full of symbolic action, which could be characterized as good or bad. Heroism represented the greatest of symbolic action. And those who behaved heroically occupied places of honor and privilege in our society. They became our heroes. For most of OU's history, the heroes were the pioneering educators, like President Boyd, who established the university and moved it forward as well as the athletes who dazzled on the field and won championships. Most, if not all, were white men. Prentice Gautt was the first of a lineage of Black football players who performed valiantly on a stage built for heroic action: Memorial Stadium. Consequently, African Americans began to enter the Sooner imagination as heroes.

The bronze statue of Heisman winner Billy Sims, unveiled in September 2007, signaled a new phase of representation. A blend of metals, often copper and tin, bronze was first used thousands of years ago for tools and weapons because of its durability. The Greeks and Romans of classical antiquity discovered bronze's suppleness, its ability to capture the finest of details: the curls in a beard or the striations of muscle. They sculpted life-sized, bronze statues of their gods, leaders, and heroes. Bronze is built to last. It has a polished gold sheen that darkens to brown over time and when exposed to weather. The oxidation process, eventually, can produce an attractive green patina. Though few of the thousands of bronze statues from antiquity remain—they were melted down and the metal repurposed—a few dozen survive, a testament to both the material and the craftsmanship of their makers. All of this is to say that bronze speaks of permanence. Like the other "forever" structures associated with the university (Memorial Stadium and Bizzell library, for instance), the statues of Sims, Murray, and the Selmon Brothers are tangible fixtures upon which Sooner fans, present and future, project their hopes, dreams, and desires. The Black experience and the Sooner experience, finally interwoven, endure together.

▪ 15 ▪

PUTTING DOWN FIRE

A 1991 ARTICLE in *The Oklahoman* describes how in 1939 OU band director William R. Wehrend, inspired by the fact that his young trombonist Jack Redbird was a member of the Kiowa tribe, imagined a baton-twirling drum major, in full Native American dress, marching in front of the Pride on Owen Field. The idea appealed to Redbird, and at home football games for the next three seasons, before he left to serve in World War II with the US Army, he wore Native regalia consisting of "buckskin leggings, a long-sleeved shirt, beadwork, and a feathered war bonnet" as he twirled a baton during the band's halftime show. Once the Pride was done performing, Redbird joined his bandmates in the stands. He swapped the baton for his trombone.

More than a decade later, another OU student, freshman Mike Dymond, appeared at Owen Field while dressed in Native American attire. According to a 1953 article in *The Oklahoma Daily*, which called Dymond the "OU Spirit Man," the Seminole tribe member wore "the full regalia of an Indian warrior," and at decisive moments of home football games, while the Pride pounded out rhythms on tom-tom drums, Dymond performed a "stomping war dance" to support Big Red.

An issue of *The Oklahoma Daily* in October 1955 featured a photograph of OU student Jim Gabbard, of Anadarko, wearing a resplendent warbonnet on his head. The photo's caption said that Gabbard's warbonnet was paid for through the fundraising efforts of sorority Alpha Delta Pi. Included in the caption, whose title read "LITTLE RED NOW BIG CHIEF," was the fact that Gabbard served as a "University of Oklahoma mascot" and that his duties included performing a "wardance" at Owen Field after Sooner touchdowns.

Like Gabbard, OU student Phil Waller was from Anadarko, Oklahoma. When he enrolled in classes his freshman year, Waller was told he was too small for the football team but to report to George Churchill, the university's director of public relations. According to an article in an April 1961 issue of *The Oklahoma Daily*, Churchill asked Waller, who was half Cherokee and half Ojibway, if "he would like to become an Indian mascot for the football team and do an occasional war dance." Waller said that he would.

In his four years as Little Red, Waller's experiences ran the gamut. Dressed in a war bonnet and pants with no shirt, he said that the only time he got cold was at the OU–Army game in Norman in November 1959. The high temperature on that chilly day was thirty degrees, with a low of fifteen. Before an OU–Texas game, Waller walked the streets of Dallas barefoot, trying to avoid the shards of broken glass that were everywhere: a gift to the city from drunken football fans. Unfortunately, Waller cut his foot badly. At home games, Little Red found himself in high demand. Fans got close to him, pulling on the feathers of his warbonnet and touching his face to see if he was wearing makeup. Often, some of the young and elderly looked at him with trepidation. Was this Indian warrior dangerous?

With his tenure as Little Red ending, Waller reflected on the travel he'd done—two trips to the Orange Bowl in Miami where his hotel room was next to OU president Cross's—and the people he had met. He was especially fond of the "wide-eyed" children who alternated between getting close to him and scrambling away. With all the Sooner fans who wanted a piece of him, the job as mascot had taught him poise and composure, which should no doubt help him—as a graduate in business management—in the professional world. Waller felt proud to know that fans considered him the personification of Sooner spirit. The article in *The Oklahoma Daily* took note of the fact that he was recently married, with a four-month-old daughter. Waller said that Indian children were taught to dance soon after they were born; in a few months' time, the lessons for his daughter would begin.

▪ ▪ ▪

In OU's early days, the Native Americans of Indian Territory occupied a conspicuous place in the university's imagination. A vignette from the November 1897 issue of *The University Umpire* depicts a fictional Osage chief named "Pretty Hair." A writer is not attached to the untitled piece about "Pretty Hair," and one is tempted to ascribe the work, which is written elegantly, to Professor Vernon Parrington who chaired the English department, coached the Varsity football team, and wrote for and edited *The Umpire*. The portrait of this old Osage chief is full of surfaces. Husband to two wives, he lives "in comfort and contentment" in a cabin north of the Arkansas River "at the foot of a sloping, wooded hill, and looks down across as beautiful a field as ever was plowed and planted." A wigwam next to the cabin keeps him and his family cool during the summer months; this is where the chief spends the bulk of his day, sitting in contemplation with a "long-stemmed pipe" at his lips. Instead of talking, he grunts from time to time. He may look passive, even indolent, but the writer assures us that the chief's mind is a place of fervent activity.

The narrative switches from the landscape to "Pretty Hair's" appearance. He is tall with good posture. His "copper-colored" face is solemn, with small, black eyes protected by a pair of "scowling brows." His long, black hair is braided through with eagle feathers and flows down his back. He wears a red blanket like a cape that he cinches at the waist; his buckskin pants are decorated with red and white beads. He wears "soft moccasins" on his feet.

The chief's inscrutability is epitomized in the way he sits before the fire, like the North American version of Rodin's sculpture *The Thinker*, with chin in hand, elbow on knee, watching the smoke from his pipe curl toward the wigwam's ceiling. The writer struggles to imagine the man's inner world: "Evidently no thoughts of the exciting chase flit through his mind; or if they do they fail to find expression in his stolid countenance."

This speculative and fictional portrait of an Osage chief reads like a tribute as well as an acknowledgement of the Native American's rightful place in a territory where encroachment by whites is an ongoing process. From one angle the vignette is a commendable, if romantic, effort. From another angle, however, it traffics in cliches that don't tell us anything of substance about the Native experience.

The literary efforts of Oklushe Degataga, an early Native American student organization at OU, provide us with a more credible look at the hearts and minds of Native people. The first Native American students enrolled at the university in the 1898–99 academic year, encouraged by the Board of Regents' offer of a tuition-free education to inhabitants of Indian Territory. According to historian David Levy, the number of Native students that first year was six. The increases thereafter were steady, with twenty students in the second year. By the spring semester of 1904, 56 students of Native heritage were studying at the university. To put this in context, the size of the student body was 506 in 1903–1904; 11 percent came from Indian Territory.

To go along with this growing demographic, several student organizations were created to serve their interests including the American Indian Student Association (AISA), the Sequoya Club, Med-e-win, and the aforementioned Oklushe Degataga.

The Native students from Oklushe Degataga, which translates to "Tribes Standing Together," were given the reins of *The University of Oklahoma Magazine* for one issue in February/March 1915. They filled this edition with tales, legends, and poems that reflected the Native imagination. Old warriors are everywhere. Lyrical poems extol nature. Origin stories explain age-old customs like the naming of children in Cherokee society and the birth of their written language. A Comanche parable about two gung-ho warriors turns fatal for both, gleaming like a riddle as it delivers truths about bravery and fairness. There's a feeling of belatedness, the early twentieth century a kind of limbo for the Indians who find themselves stuck in the white man's world. As a result, they look backward and gaze at a glorious past, lament its passing. Women are almost entirely absent except for in one tale, which portrays the feminine in a treacherous light.

In this special issue of the magazine, the reader finds political commentary about the present and future; the students of Oklushe Degataga are eager to engage with the world. Medicine Arrow, the pseudonym of the essayist who pens "Wherefore White Man," blasts the leaders of white civilization for counseling Native peoples to give up war ("All that you told us to do, we have done. Our lances are broken. Our bows are burned and our arrows are lost.") only to perpetuate the practice themselves. With the First World War raging in Europe, the essayist urges the "White Man" to listen to his "Red Brother who is humble and weak" and swear off war for good: "Learn for yourself the lesson you once taught to him. Turn your ways of war into the paths of peace."

▪ ▪ ▪

The 1960s saw Little Red become OU's official mascot. After Phil Waller's four years in the role, the cheerleaders held tryouts in fall 1961; Little Red was considered part of the spirit squad. Candidates had to be at least one-quarter Native, unmarried, and in good standing with the university. Art major Danny Timmons, from Norman, was selected as Waller's replacement. For two years, Timmons served as Little Red, dancing at Owen Field and traveling with the football team. When he transferred to a drafting school in Oklahoma City in 1963, he necessarily vacated the role.

Kirke Kickingbird, a history major from El Reno and member of the Kiowa tribe, heard about the open position through an article in the student newspaper. Kickingbird dismissed the opportunity outright; he had neither a costume nor the ability to dance. But that weekend, when Kickingbird went home, his father read his copy of *The Oklahoma Daily*, spotting the article about Little Red. On Saturday, Kickingbird and his father drove to Anadarko to borrow a Native outfit from a relative. Then they drove to Indian City to see a family friend who knew about native dancing. Kickingbird learned a routine and spent the rest of the weekend practicing.

On Monday, Kickingbird auditioned in front of the OU cheerleaders while wearing his borrowed Native regalia. He won the job.

During the 1963 football season, Kickingbird took to Owen Field as Little Red. The regalia lent by the family member was replaced with ceremonial attire that Kickingbird assembled himself, consisting of a red and white warbonnet, a breastplate made of animal bones, a bustle of feathers, beaded moccasins made by his grandmother, and rims of Angora goat fur that went around his ankles. After Sooner touchdowns, he danced to the beat of a tom-tom. When the Pride of Oklahoma played "Boomer Sooner," he danced again, lifting a fist toward the sky before opening his hand and flashing the victory sign. Away from the field, Kickingbird signed autographs for fans and gave feathers to children. The day before the homecoming game, the Sequoyah Club held its annual powwow, beating a ceremonial drum from dusk till dawn; Kickingbird was there, performing. He danced and rested. Then he danced again.

Kickingbird was the direct descendant of a famous Kiowa chief who made peace with the United States through the Medicine Lodge Treaty, signed in 1867, which moved several tribes to reservations in western Indian Territory, according to the Oklahoma Historical Society. Considered by his tribal enemies a collaborationist with the white man, Kickingbird's great-great grandfather was later assassinated.

During his time at OU, Kickingbird was active as a member of the Student Senate, the Sequoyah Club, and Delta Upsilon fraternity. One summer, a scholarship enabled him to study international relations at the University of Hawaii. The following summer, in 1965, Kickingbird was one of a handful of "Sooner guides" at the World's Fair in New York City, where he and his colleagues supervised an Oklahoma exhibit. As far as his academic and professional ambitions, he told *The Oklahoma Daily* in 1964 that he sought to develop a "mature political philosophy" while pursuing a master's in government or a JD in law. A teaching or government job might be in his future.

Kickingbird's term as Little Red stretched across most of the decade as he remained an OU student, moving on to the law school after graduating with his bachelor's in 1966. In self-deprecating fashion, he acknowledged that he'd been the mascot for a long time in a *Daily* article he penned in November 1968, drawing the reader's attention to his "receding hairline and lined face." His long tenure at OU was a prelude to professional success; Kickingbird prospered as an attorney, serving in various capacities, his career spanning the decades. He also authored books and taught law at Oklahoma City University.

Returning to November 1968, Kickingbird's lighthearted essay in the student newspaper was printed on the same page as an article that, in retrospect, speaks to the activist spirit of the sixties. It was also a portent of Little Red's future.

The article's subject was the Indian Community Task Group, composed of thirty OU students, whose purpose was the pursuit of human rights for Native people. Already the group had worked on a voter registration drive and transported Native voters to the polls on election day. They'd also hosted an "Indian weekend program" for "Indian youth" during OU's homecoming. In the future, they wanted to focus on young people "by arranging field trips, guest speakers, demonstrations, movies and most important—offering one-on-one counseling to the youth." They decried systemic injustices aimed at Native Americans including racial discrimination from police, teachers, and employers.

A November 1969 meeting of Native OU students gave voice to a movement to abolish Little Red as university mascot. *The Oklahoma Daily* recorded the arguments for and against the mascot's existence. Some viewed Little Red as no more than a "clown," whose presence at Owen Field was degrading to Native Americans. Junior Melvin Coffey from Oklahoma City said, "Other colleges and universities have animals as mascots, but OU has an Indian. Are Indians in the same classification as animals?" Not everyone at the meeting agreed that the mascot was dehumanizing. Ron Benally, Kickingbird's successor as Little Red, argued that the mascot was an expression of "ethnic pride": "Little Red is a symbol of the Indian culture. I want to show my pride in being an Indian by dancing out there on the field." Other students were on the fence. Senior Lana Sue Grant said, "Although I don't like the image it presents, I am not convinced as yet."

Before the month of November was over, OU's chapter of the National Indian Youth Council (NIYC) had delivered a petition to OU president J. Herbert Hollomon Jr. seeking the abolition of Little Red as university mascot. *Sooner Magazine* in October 1970 offered a timeline of events. President Hollomon sent the petition to the Human Resources Committee, which had been created in 1969 to deal with charges of discrimination at the university. The committee's investigation lasted two months; its report, released in February 1970, recommended two things that, taken together, represented a kind of compromise. First, Little Red should be abolished as official mascot. Second, OU cheerleaders of Native descent should not be barred from dance and dress "that reflect their unique heritage." In other words, in their official capacity as OU cheerleaders, Native students could choose, of their own volition, to dress in regalia and dance in celebration of their heritage. President Hollomon gave his blessing to the committee's recommendations in April. His statement read, "We are removing only the official recognition of Little Red as the OU mascot."

The university's decision did not go over well with everybody. Republican governor Dewey F. Bartlett said in a speech that he hoped that Little Red would return. Newspaper editorials, letters to the editor, and cartoons expressed the same sentiment. On the eve of the 1970 football season, OU freshman Randy Palmer gave hope to those firmly in Little Red's camp when he declared publicly that he would appear at the home opener with Wisconsin dressed in Native costume. In response, OU's student court issued a restraining order against him. Palmer never materialized as the long-time Sooner mascot; however, at the September 26 game with Oregon State, someone else did: Phil Waller, who served as Little Red from 1957 to 1961. Waller was told that he was in violation of the restraining order.

A legal tit for tat commenced, with first Floyd Harjo, assistant chief of the Seminole Indian tribe, filing suit with Cleveland County District Court and then Palmer filing suit with the Oklahoma State Supreme Court. Both men objected to the Little Red ban.

Various circumstances—some procedural, some to do with the effect this drama was having on student mental health, especially Palmer's—led to OU's student court dropping the restraining order. As a result, Harjo and Palmer withdrew their legal petitions. The matter seemed resolved in mid-October when Palmer was elected a yell leader by the Sooner Rally Council, which managed all spirit groups and activities. At the tryout, Palmer had worn Native regalia.

Dave Poolaw, sophomore president of OU's chapter of NIYC, regretted that so much emphasis had been placed on Little Red. To his mind, bigger issues remained. He said at a press conference: "Little Red is a minor and somewhat questionable part of the Indian heritage. We say now to the white people, you can have your mascot. All we want is an Indian studies program, our cultural lounge, scholarships and encouragement and help for Indian students. . . . Little Red will never feed hungry Indian children; Little Red will never help more Indian students come to OU."

The loophole allowing Native cheerleaders to wear regalia didn't last for long. In 1973, OU augmented its policy, banning performers in "Indian costume" at all Sooner games, regardless of the sport. This was challenged later that year when Ruf Nek Bill Lamebull, a Cheyenne tribe member, took the field as Little Red before a football game. According to a 1991 article in *The Oklahoman*, Native American students, perturbed by Little Red's shock appearance, chased Lamebull down the length of Owen Field, with police officers in pursuit of both parties. In 1984, Waller reappeared as Little Red in Dallas at the Red River Rivalry matchup; he said he was inspired by alumni and Native Americans who wanted to see him as mascot again. Fourteen years after dressing as Little Red in defiance of a restraining order, he and his nine-year-old daughter Chelsea led the football team onto the field in the second half. In rainy weather and in Native costume, they waved to Sooner fans. When OU scored a touchdown, the Ruf Neks brought the father and daughter back onto the field. The fallout was inevitable. In the pages of *The Oklahoma Daily*, Stephanie Wickliffe of AISA reminded the university that a ban was in place and must be enforced. AISA wanted an apology from Waller and the OU alumni who encouraged his return. Waller and his supporters questioned whether AISA spoke for all Native students at OU. They entertained a vision of funding Little Red through a scholarship. "But it would be a great honor if, partly through what I did, an Indian student was offered a scholarship and could represent the pride of Indians in the state," he told the student newspaper.

But there was no going back. "Little Red is dead," declared Glenn Solomon, faculty adviser to AISA, and so it came to pass. The divisive mascot disappeared.

■ ■ ■

On an afternoon in May 1976, Donald Fixico held three paper copies of his thesis under an arm as he walked from the Memorial Union with his head down, deep in thought, toward Bizzell library. The work was close to done—he'd be graduating soon with a master's in history—though a rigorous review by his thesis committee lay ahead. To say that one of his committee members, H. Wayne Morgan, gave him anxiety (due to the man's towering intellect and demand for academic rigor) would have been the understatement of the year.

Fixico's journey began six years earlier, in 1970, when he transferred to OU after studying at Bacone junior college in Muscogee. But the university had been on his radar long before that. Fixico was born in Shawnee, Oklahoma, to Native American parents whose bloodline connected to several tribes: Sac and Fox, Shawnee, Seminole, and Muscogee Creek. The family of five—Fixico had a younger sister and younger brother—moved every few years because of his father's work in construction. Over time, they would live in Midwest City, Oklahoma City, and Tulsa.

This hardscrabble life made a permanent impression on Fixico. His grandmother, who lived in a house with no running water, was a huge influence too, and she taught him four important values: respect for other people, hard work, family, and cleanliness. The owner of two ironing boards, she made sure that everyone in the family had perfect creases in their blue jeans.

Sports were important. Fixico's father had been an amateur boxer, and almost every night, as a fan of the New York Yankees, he sat in the living room reading the box scores in the newspaper. As a boy, Fixico was a Chicago White Sox fan and played baseball along with football and basketball. While his brother had inherited their father's broad shoulders and was destined to play linebacker in high school, Fixico was smaller in stature with fewer physical gifts, though he also embraced the "bone and blood" of contact sports, especially football.

Fixico started following OU football in the late 1950s. As he grew up, he continued to root for the team, and his fandom, along with the university's strong reputation for engineering, attracted him to Norman after junior college. That said, matriculating to the University of Oklahoma terrified him. Fixico was a first-generation college student; neither of his parents had finished high school.

His story at OU was classic fish-out-of-water. In the beginning, what caused his alienation had more to do with class than race. Fixico came from a family of modest means. In contrast, his roommate in Walker Tower came from a well-to-do family in Midland, Texas; the boy's father was a surgeon. Across the hallway, his neighbors were from the East Coast: New York and New Jersey. On the weekends, as their hobby, they flew airplanes out of Norman's Westheimer Airport.

In the classroom, Fixico struggled. Chemical engineering was his declared major, but the classes were fast paced; he couldn't keep up. In the end, he scrapped chemical engineering and "fell into history through the back door," inspired largely by classes taken with Arrell Gibson, a renowned scholar of Oklahoma and the American West, who taught at OU from 1957 into the 1980s.

Though he'd switched to history, Fixico didn't exactly thrive. What he had going for him was a desire to learn. "I always admired learning," he says to me in an interview, "and I always felt like walking out of Bizzell library you get to that last step and there's an indentation. So many people have stepped there and I thought: What can I learn from the library through reading?"

Still, the feeling of not measuring up shadowed him as an undergraduate and even into graduate school. OU football games in the fall were one of his only comforts. "I lived and died for those games," he says.

Adding to his stress was the specter of the Vietnam War, which was still being fought in Southeast Asia. During the war, 42,000 Native Americans served in the US armed forces and 248 were killed. Though in college, Fixico was still eligible for the draft. College students, if drafted, could apply for a deferment, but there was no guarantee it would be granted. It depended on the discretion of your draft board.

Each week, with dread, Fixico would call home and ask his mother if they'd gotten a letter from the government for him. Fixico had heard that soldiers of color often walked point in Vietnam; in other words, they were on the front lines and at the greatest risk, trudging through jungles and rice paddies.

Fixico had a bad feeling about the war. "If I go to Vietnam," he thought, "I'm not coming back."

Ultimately, he escaped the draft, which came to an end in 1973 with the signing of the Paris Peace Accords.

After two years as an undergraduate, Fixico graduated with his bachelor's and then won a place in the master's program. However, he found himself in a financial bind; he wasn't offered a coveted spot as a teaching assistant, which would have covered tuition and paid him a stipend.

It seemed like the equivalent of a Hail Mary pass when he applied for a prestigious Ford Foundation fellowship, which provided financial support to select graduate students. Annually, dozens of applicants from around the country applied to become a Ford fellow, with the success rate hovering around 4 to 5 percent. Fixico made it to the interview stage, and the foundation flew him out to San Francisco. It was his first time on an airplane. As Fixico describes it, he was "part of the last group to be interviewed and I was the last one interviewed."

A Cherokee scholar from UCLA was on the three-person committee and told him that if he were selected for the fellowship, down the line, it would pay his tuition even if he chose to do a PhD at Harvard or one of the other Ivy League schools. The thought that he could end up studying at an elite university had never crossed Fixico's mind; it sounded like a fantasy.

To his relief and delight, Fixico won the fellowship. His colleagues in graduate school at OU came from far and wide, attracted by the history program's reputation, especially its faculty's expertise on the American

West. Everyone in his hours-long seminars seemed to know so much already. The program itself was grueling, the professors demanding.

One faculty member loomed large in his life and imagination: Professor Morgan, who would end up on his thesis committee. The man was an expert on late nineteenth century American history, especially the Gilded Age: a period of economic boom after the Civil War that ended in economic tailspin. In 1963, Morgan's book *William McKinley and His America* had been published to acclaim; it was the first biography of the assassinated president to appear in decades.

"Dr. Morgan was brilliant and he knew it," Fixico says. "If he saw any kind of potential in you he prodded you. And he wanted you to do more, even though he didn't want you to know he might be a supporter."

Fixico's education at OU stretched across the 1970s. Morgan seemed to be there at every turn.

"It was like he was meant to intersect with my life," Fixico says. "He would remind me of who I am and my lowly status and [ask] if I was going to do anything about it."

Fixico would look up from his study spot in the library and see his professor. Driving down Boyd one day he noticed that the owner of the black Lincoln ahead of him was none other than Professor Morgan. Sometime later, after an evening seminar with Morgan in Dale Hall, Fixico discovered to his dismay that they had parked next to each other in the parking lot. Awkwardly, they made it to their respective cars at the same time. Night had fallen and it was raining.

A characteristic hand on hip, Morgan said enigmatically, "Mr. Fixico, you just need to get out and see the world."

Then the man was in his car, leaving Fixico to wonder at his words.

It was no surprise then that Morgan showed up as Fixico was walking toward Bizzell that May afternoon in 1976, with his master's thesis tucked under an arm. There was a hedge next to the sidewalk leading to the library. Lost in thought, Fixico looked up and saw Morgan walking toward him.

"He was so intimidating I felt like jumping over the hedge," Fixico says.

The professor put a hand on his hip before addressing his student.

"Mr. Fixico, when is that master's thesis going to be done?" he asked.

"Dr. Morgan, I have a copy of it right here."

"Well, well, well. Put a copy in my mailbox."

Later, after he had dropped off his thesis in the history department, Fixico was in his apartment when the phone rang. To his surprise, it was Morgan. Had he done something wrong?

"I'd like for you to be in my office at nine o'clock in the morning," the professor said. "I want to talk to you."

The phone clicked. The man had hung up without saying goodbye.

Riddled with anxiety, Fixico was twenty minutes early to their appointment. When he knocked on his professor's door, a voice told him to come inside. Morgan was sitting at his desk, with Fixico's thesis in front of him.

"Pull that chair over here," the professor said.

Fixico sat beside him and for the next couple hours they went over his thesis page by page. Morgan had marked up his copy with a red pen.

"Red ink was spilled all over it," Fixico says.

This one-on-one experience between a distinguished professor and his nervous but eager pupil emblazoned itself on Fixico's brain.

"The things he taught me [that day] I still teach," he says.

Fixico went on to the PhD program where the challenges continued. Since he wasn't granted a teaching assistantship by the history department, he sought experience elsewhere. One semester, he graded papers for the Anthropology Department for free.

"Every graduate student gets kicked at least twice by the department," Fixico says. "If someone says they loved their graduate program, then it probably wasn't a real demanding program."

In the late seventies, as Fixico worked toward his PhD, he was hired to teach Native American history at Rose State College in nearby Midwest City. During his first class of the semester, it finally dawned on him what Morgan had meant when he urged Fixico to go out and see the world.

"During that first lecture, I taught them everything I knew," he says with a laugh. "I realized how much I didn't know and how I needed to experience more."

At times in graduate school, Fixico felt he was treated unfairly. Outside of the classroom, racism aimed in his direction brought anger and frustration. But he noticed something as he got closer to finishing the PhD.

"What I realized was that some people [in the history department] had become very supportive of my work. I always thought it was like climbing Mount Everest, but some people began to pull me up and say, 'Apply for this, apply for that scholarship. Apply for this post-doc.'"

Their efforts motivated him and eventually bore fruit. Fixico won postdoctoral fellowships at UCLA and the Newberry Library in Chicago. He responded to Morgan's exhortation; across four decades, he's taught all over the country and the world: University of Kansas, University of California at Berkeley, UCLA, San Diego State, and University of Michigan. He's lectured at universities in China, Japan, and New Zealand. Since 2004, he's been at Arizona State University where he is Regents and Distinguished Foundation Professor of History. Fixico has published seventeen books on topics related to Native American history. He's also worked on twenty-five documentary films. In 2000, President Bill Clinton appointed him to the Advisory Council of the National Endowment for the Humanities.

Reflecting on his career, he sees his own story as part of a larger story about marginalized groups—Native Americans, Chicanos, African Americans, and women, to name a few—and the fight for social justice. Fixico believes he was a beneficiary of those movements and takes a long view of history, which he sees as cyclical. Periods of decline alternate with periods of renewal. He introduces me to a term that Native people use to describe this process of renewal and rebuilding: "putting down fire."

He cites a recent visit to Oklahoma. At dinner with a cousin, he heard something that amazed him: The country club where they presently dined was owned by the tribe.

Fixico says, "Who would have thought [this would happen when] in the twentieth century the entire Indian population dropped below 238,000 and [there were] all these floating rumors of a vanishing race? And look at the twenty-first century now. What change. What progress. What resilience and rebuilding."

Through it all, Fixico has remained a lifelong fan of OU sports. The football teams of the 1980s, with their wishbone formation on offense, stand out. Fixico compares the wishbone to a “shell game”; the defense didn’t know where the ball was or where it was going. The confusion led to long runs for the offense and blowout score lines, especially given the strength of OU’s defense.

I ask him if he sees any connection between football and Native traditions. Fixico is quick to answer. The same “spiritual energy” he sees in a Native sport like stickball (a relative to lacrosse) he sees in an OU football game. The Native emphasis on community and togetherness is replicated at Owen Field.

“When I see the players on the football field, when I see that sense of loyalty, especially when you see one player coming up and helping another player, pulling him up, it’s a togetherness that carries over from what I remember [of stickball],” he says.

I feel compelled to ask him about the Sooner Schooner and the iconography of the Land Run. In 2015, a student group called Indigenize OU successfully petitioned the university to recognize Indigenous Peoples’ Day instead of Columbus Day. The group was less successful with a petition to do away with OU mascots Boomer and Sooner, which they associated with the displacement of Native people.

Responding to Indigenize OU, then university president David Boren argued that time and the winds of progressivism had shifted the meaning of Boomer and Sooner. These words no longer gestured toward those land stealers of yesteryear. He said in a 2015 statement, “The term today stands for a spirit which is very inclusive, sets high standards of excellence and represents a strong sense of a common family.”

Indigenize OU’s Sydne Gray found Boren’s logic convenient. She told *OU Daily*, “I don’t think it’s that easy to just redefine ‘boomer sooner’ whenever it carries such a heavy, historical background. . . . I wish he would understand . . . how this impacts a much greater community outside of OU.”

Fixico sympathizes with the aims and vision of Indigenize OU. The iconography is a painful reminder to Native people of all that they’ve lost.

"It stings because of the greed for the land," he says. "That's what the Sooner Schooner represents: disregarding Native people's rights."

A troubling dilemma exists for anyone who supports the university and its sports teams but understands OU's history of racism and sexism. How does one reconcile the tension between two emotions: love for OU sports and revulsion for some aspects of OU's past? A rudimentary knowledge of psychology tells us that humans excel at rationalization. We compartmentalize. We avoid discomfort, taking the easy way out instead. Sometimes this translates into a long detour to dodge our unpleasant past.

Fixico offers a proposal, centering around education, that would tackle this dilemma head-on. He believes that OU students and football fans should learn the history of Indian Territory and about the promises that were made to the Five Tribes—Cherokee, Choctaw, Chickasaw, Creek, and Seminole—before their forced emigration in the 1830s: the infamous Trail of Tears. Indian Territory should have belonged to Native people in perpetuity because of a series of treaties that were eventually undermined by the same US government which created them.

To this end, Fixico proposes a required course for all OU students on Oklahoma and the Native American experience; therein, this history can be taught. For those fans who aren't in school, a short documentary could be shown on the video boards before every home game.

"We should face up to [our dark history]," Fixico says. "Acknowledge it. Say we're sorry. We respect what Native people have done."

Fixico's relationship to the University of Oklahoma is as complicated and nuanced as the state's history. He's not afraid to criticize the university, but he's also a big supporter, especially when it comes to sports. In the fall, Fixico cheers for the football team. In the spring, he's a passionate fan of OU softball.

His daily routine speaks to his feelings about his alma mater. Every morning, he jogs in the desert splendor of Arizona. He's out of the house while it's still dark, and as the sun rises in the east he thinks of the Muscogee maxim: At dawn, it's like the sun is "on fire, with a sacred glow around it."

Every morning, without fail, Fixico wears a University of Oklahoma T-shirt.

Part VI

▪ ▪ ▪

SEC

▪ 16 ▪

A SEASON OF TURBULENCE

THE SOUTH OVAL is already packed with students—maybe a couple hundred—when I arrive at 3:30 in the morning. It's September 21, 2024. *College Game Day* has been on campus since Wednesday, its semitrucks parked down one side of the oval. In the darkness I can see the main stage; it faces south so that the regal exterior of Bizzell library will show in the television background. The barricades have been set up that establish the perimeter of the "Pit," the mecca for disciples of this popular and long-running show. The Pit is where students hold up their playful signs and mug for the camera. Once inside, they'll be part of the background as the pundits of *College Game Day*—Kirk Herbstreit, Lee Corso, Desmond Howard, Pat McAfee, and Nick Saban—make their predictions on Saturday's biggest football games.

I'm supposed to meet a group of college guys I know from Koda CrossFit Norman, the gym where we all work out. The guys are upperclassmen at OU; outside of the gym, where admittedly we spend a lot of time, they'll come to John Hurd's tailgate on game day, but they've also got the restless energy of youth. As a result, they're never in one place for long. One of them, Colin, always carries a twenty-four pack of Coors Light on his shoulder like a boombox. Whenever the guys make a stop at someone's tailgate, they shotgun a beer.

I don't know if they're here yet and walk north alongside the semitrucks, cutting across the grass to the rear of the massive statue of President William Bennett Bizzell, dressed somberly in his academic robe, that stands watch over the library. It's here that I see what students have left behind. There's a circle of folding chairs with no one sitting in them, as if their owners were suddenly raptured. Plastic bottles and bags litter the ground. A half-eaten slice of pizza rests on a paper plate, abandoned in the grass. Someone has left a temporary bed: a small sheet of foam covered by a blanket. A trash can nearby is piled high with garbage.

South of Bizzell's statue is a mass of hopeful students gathered behind the entrance to the Pit and restrained by metal barriers. Music is playing from a speaker somewhere.

My phone rings; it's Colin, a senior accounting major, who tells me that they are on the east side of the oval, just outside the metal barriers and to the left of the stage. I start walking in that direction. On the way, I walk around a huge pool of vomit on the concrete.

Six guys are in the group. They're all in OU gear except for EJ, a senior mechanical engineering major, who's wearing a blue Indianapolis Colts' jersey with "McAfee" on the back. (McAfee, a former YouTube star and NFL punter, is a recent addition to the *Game Day* crew.) They are standing just off the sidewalk in the grass. Currently, they're trash talking a guy in red and white overalls. What's more, they're not happy with a group of young women dressed as trolls: red wigs, glitter on faces, and red and white overalls. Everyone is jockeying for position and getting annoyed.

From the mass outside the Pit someone shouts "Boomer!" The crowd is supposed to call back "Sooner!" but it's four o'clock in the morning and most are not in the spirit.

There's a tree directly to our right with sturdy, accessible branches. A couple guys in our group discuss climbing the tree for a better view. Large video boards are stationed to the left and right of the stage; in a few hours, they will broadcast the show. Now the boards send a message about *College Game Day* etiquette. No political or religious signs will be allowed. No vulgar or ".com" signs either. Untoward behavior will result in removal. The powers that be will start letting people into the Pit at 5:30 A.M.

Until then we stand around and wait. The prospect of being on my feet for the next six to seven hours (*College Game Day* runs from 8 to 11 A.M.) fills me with dread, though it must be said that I don't feel too bad. This shocks me since I slept for maybe four hours.

Music continues to play through ESPN's sound system: Phil Collins's "In the Air Tonight," which carries a foreboding note. I keep glancing at the ever-growing mass of students waiting to fill the Pit, and I wonder how things will work at 5:30. For a second, I imagine a free-for-all, with students sprinting and falling. Some get trampled. It's like a scene of medieval battle.

As time crawls along, people appear behind us, the space filling in. The September weather is beyond pleasant, in the seventies, but our new neighbors bring body heat. I start to feel claustrophobic.

A young woman to my left is already holding up her sign, which is a good one. She's blown up a picture of conservative YouTuber Steven Crowder, who became a meme through a video segment in which he set up a table, with a provocative sign, and invited strangers to debate him. In the photo on this student's sign, Crowder holds a cup of coffee with an impish grin on his face. The message attached to his table reads: "It took an OU coach to rebuild Tennessee's football program. CHANGE MY MIND."

The Volunteers' head coach Josh Heupel is an OU legend; as quarterback, he led the Sooners to their last national championship in 2000. As an assistant coach at his alma mater, he served from 2004 to 2014.

Tennessee fans, wearing the colors of their university, walk down the oval, and when they're spotted a chorus of boos erupts. The guys in my group, not fond of any shade of orange, shout, "Looks like baby shit!"

My phone finally tells me it's 5:30. The stampede fails to materialize. Instead, over the next half hour, students trickle into the Pit, setting up against the barriers closest to the stage. Two of my friends, Edgar and Kruz, climb into the neighboring tree, looking pleased with themselves as they sit with their clear view.

Expectation tips over into jubilation at 6 A.M. when the DJ arrives, suitably wearing sunglasses in the darkness. He starts "spinning records" on his laptop computer. Early on in his set, he gets the crowd going with a knock-knock joke.

"Knock, knock," he says into his microphone.

"Who's there?" the crowd calls back.

"Norman."

"Norman who?"

"Norman coming for that SEC ass!"

Everyone cheers. Then a chant of "SEC! SEC!" starts.

ESPN employees begin to hand out gear from Home Depot, primary sponsor of *College Game Day*: orange gloves and hard hats. OU students suddenly adore the color orange; they clamber for gear, their arms outstretched. Decked out, they look less like construction workers than supremely happy kids on Christmas morning.

Party standards like Bon Jovi's "Livin' on a Prayer" and Darius Rucker's "Wagon Wheel" enliven the crowd, but one song sends them into raptures: Sheck Wes's 2018 hip-hop anthem "Mo Bamba." When it starts, there's a roar, and then everyone around me is bouncing up and down and knocking shoulders as if they're in a mosh pit. I fear for my safety.

Heisman Trophy winner Desmond Howard, at around seven o'clock, is the first pundit to arrive. He's on his own at the *Game Day* table when he brings up, in the first live broadcast segment, the matchup between Oklahoma and Tennessee. At the mention of the Sooners, the crowd cheers. When the footage on the broadcast shows Tennessee beating up on Kent State the week before, everyone boos.

Something similar happens when Lee Corso arrives for work. Day is beginning to break, light bleeding into the sky. As Corso faces the Pit, he holds up a Tennessee helmet, and the students shower the eighty-nine-year-old, a constant presence at *College Game Day* since 1987, with boos. Then he puts the helmet down and picks up an Oklahoma helmet; the cheers are deafening. Corso goes back and forth in this pantomime until he pitches the Tennessee helmet to the floor; he holds aloft the Oklahoma helmet, and it reminds me of that iconic scene from *The Lion King*: young Simba presented as the next ruler. Will OU be the new king of the SEC?

■ ■ ■

That question circles around in my mind as I lounge at John Hurd's tailgate several hours later, looking at the balcony of the Porch, the Campus Corner bar, where Tennessee fans lean on the guardrail, drinking cocktails and getting assaulted by the Oklahoma sun. It's going to be a late September scorcher today, with the temperature in the mid-nineties. It's also about eleven hours since I dragged myself out of bed to join my college friends on the South Oval. I left campus at 9:30 A.M., only ninety minutes into the *College Gameday* broadcast, my feet aching from hours of standing. I was dehydrated and hungry. I could endure no longer.

Breakfast at home made me feel better. Then, at 12:30, I walked back to campus with Jenn. Tennessee fans strolled across the lawn in front of Carpenter Hall, visiting tailgates. Right now, we've got six or seven at Hurd's: grown men in middle age, dressed in Tennessee orange. They are wonderfully agreeable, the soft lilt of their southern accent pleasing to the ear. Some of the chatter for months has been about the chemistry involved when OU and Texas fans, newcomers to the conference, finally meet with SEC fans. Will the mixture be combustible? The answer seems obvious now. The atmosphere of kumbaya is palpable. Hurd's visitors are complimentary about Norman and our campus. The football helmet beer dispenser, of course, is a popular attraction, eliciting nods of approval. They envy our Campus Corner, just across the street, with its bars and restaurants. The only thing they don't like is the heat.

The DJ's bravado from this morning comes back to me: "Norman coming for that SEC ass!" Will we, in fact, prosper in our new conference?

The SEC's motto is "It Just Means More," referring to the fact that its teams are generally considered the elite of college football; SEC conference games are consequential. Six of the past ten national champions have come from the conference, which is also elite in terms of riches. The SEC's reported revenue for 2022–2023 was $741 million, with $51 million delivered to each of the fourteen member schools. With OU and Texas joining the conference, revenue is expected to top $1 billion in 2024. (In fact, revenue did not surpass this whopping number in 2023-2024, with the SEC taking in $808 million. Fourteen schools received $52.5 million apiece. Oklahoma and Texas, which joined the conference late in the fiscal year, each got $27.5 million.)

So much is on the line as we kick off our tenure in the SEC. Today, we're all about the game against Tennessee, but we shouldn't forget that every OU athletic program is entering uncharted waters. The competition should prove stiff, even for those programs used to winning, like women's gymnastics and softball. What if we don't win? What if we turn into a mid-tier school in the SEC? What effect would this have on our identity? (From the administrator's perspective, what effect would this have on enrollment?) We're used to being the big dog; we ruled the Big 12. What if the SEC turns us into a Pomeranian or Chihuahua?

These questions strike me as premature and paranoid. But they must exist somewhere in OU's collective psyche. I decide to go to this dark place. If the worst-case scenario happens and Oklahoma athletics, on the whole, ends up a mediocrity in the SEC, I worry that the consequences will be dire. I see Memorial Stadium half-filled, the student section virtually empty. On campus, I see fewer canopy tents on game day than ever before. Lloyd Noble becomes a library, Love's Field a ghost town. In my mind, I watch demoralized fans shrug their shoulders with apathy or indifference: "We suck." Soonerland, a once proud nation, has been humbled by defeat in war; we are Germany or Japan following World War II. It took those nations many years to recover.

▪ ▪ ▪

This fallen image of OU sports gives me heartburn (or it could just be the margarita I drank). The acidic lump in my throat is still there at five o'clock when Jenn and I join the human traffic for the stadium. To my surprise, it doesn't take long to get to our seats. We are in section two, on the west side and closer to the south end zone than the fifty-yard line. Our seats are in a unique position: beneath the overhang of the upper level, so that we are entirely in shade. We can't see the video boards at all; instead, flat screen TVs fixed to the overhang show the field. I feel a bit removed from our fellow fans.

Orange is sprinkled all around the stadium, with most of Tennessee's fans concentrated on the north end. According to SEC rules, the home team must supply five thousand tickets for visiting fans; half that number is required in the Big 12, a huge difference that should have an impact on the game's atmosphere.

It's hard to quibble with the conference motto as the Pride of Oklahoma performs its traditional pregame routine. While the state flag is unfurled on the north side of Owen Field and the band plays "Fanfare and Oklahoma," I can't help the emotion that swells inside me. It reaches a crescendo when the team locks arms and advances toward the south end zone like an army on the move. This indeed feels like a special day: Sooner football's debut in the SEC.

Everyone else feels it too. There's an electricity in the air. As the game starts, the decibel level is the highest I've ever experienced at Memorial Stadium. On each seat was placed a crimson pom-pom, a fan feature borrowed from the SEC, and tens of thousands of Sooners shake their souvenir as Tennessee starts on offense. OU's defense swarms, forcing a three and out.

The intensity of the atmosphere is sustained, even after Jackson Arnold throws an interception on the Sooners' second possession. To say the least, our five-star quarterback, the heir apparent to Dillon Gabriel, has underwhelmed this season; the whole offense, decimated by injuries and a lack of identity, has struggled.

The score is 3–3, with less than ten seconds left in the first quarter, when Tennessee's wide receiver runs a post route, receives the pass, and then sprints sixty-six yards for a touchdown. The big-time play takes the air out of the stadium. OU fans go quiet for the first time.

There's hope when the Sooner defense strip-sacks Tennessee's quarterback, recovering the ball on the five-yard line. But on the very next play, Arnold tries to bulldoze his way through the defensive line and . . . fumbles. No one seems to notice: too many bodies in the way. But suddenly the referee is signaling a change in possession.

It doesn't get any better for Arnold. The offense gives up a safety. Then, with five minutes left in the first half, the defense forces another turnover, in Tennessee territory. We feel hope again but not for long: Arnold's errant backward pass is collected by the Tennessee defense. The Vols turn the takeaway into a touchdown. It's 19–3.

Everyone around us is calling for Jackson to be benched. They get their wish just before halftime. Michael Hawkins Jr., a true freshman whose father played linebacker for OU in the early 2000s, steps into the fray at quarterback. His first play from scrimmage is hardly auspicious. From shotgun, the snap from center is poor, and Hawkins dives onto the ball: a wasted down.

The freshman continues to lead the offense in the second half, but the third quarter looks like the first half minus the turnovers, with the offense struggling to move the ball. In the fourth quarter, however, Hawkins engineers two touchdown drives. The final scoreline is respectable but deceptive: 25–15. In truth, we never looked like winning the game.

The chatter, after the loss, is all about the quarterback position, with YouTube pundits—an impressive number of online shows exist, hosted by Sooner enthusiasts—mostly declaring that Hawkins should be our QB1. Early in the week, with Auburn up next, Coach Venables makes the decision: Hawkins will start.

There's reason for optimism the following Saturday. On the road, Hawkins plays well enough, in spurts, and a pick-six by OU's defense improbably turns the game in our favor. Sooner Magic is in the air as Oklahoma overcomes an eleven-point deficit in the fourth quarter to win 27–21, its first victory in the SEC.

Still, no Sooner fan is exactly confident for the Red River Rivalry. The renaissance under Longhorn coach Steve Sarkisian is disconcerting. Texas is ranked number one in the country, and the team made the playoff the season before. We draw some comfort from the fact that the rivalry game is almost universally close—seven of the past ten have been decided by a touchdown or less—and the first quarter of the 2024 edition bears this out: The Sooners play the better ball and lead 3–0. But after that it's not competitive. OU's offense goes nowhere, and the defense looks oddly apathetic. As I watch from home, the heartburn last felt at the Tennessee game returns; in fact, it's worse. The 34–3 scoreline is an embarrassment to rival the 49–0 drubbing in 2022.

■ ■ ■

The University of Oklahoma's social media posts provide teasers in the run-up to homecoming 2024. When I see the first post, I'm giddy with excitement. The caption reads "The return of something Big," and the music belongs to a Hollywood trailer: a beast or monster is about to appear onscreen. We see a car's red hood, shiny with fresh paint, with the words "BIG RED ROCKET" stenciled in white. Then we see, up close and reborn, other features of the iconic Ford Model T: the years of our seven national titles in football, a squeeze bulb horn, and an old, cracked license plate with "BIG RED" on it. At the end, we learn that the Model T will make its public return during homecoming weekend.

Cecil Samara's Rocket has been resurrected.

At the homecoming parade on Friday night in mid-October, the car is part of the procession. Then, on Saturday before the game with South Carolina, it's one of the attractions at the Party at the Palace, just north of the stadium. I don't get to see the Rocket. Jenn and I are out of town for a wedding. The game itself is one of quarterback miscues, with Hawkins Jr. turning over the ball three times in the first quarter, gifting the Gamecocks twenty-one points. Arnold replaces him, but three touchdowns, for this OU offense, might as well be ten. There's no coming back.

Football aside, I suffer from FOMO while Jenn and I watch this depressing game from our Airbnb in Florida. The Big Red Rocket swims in my imagination. It feels like I've missed an opportunity to reconnect with an old friend.

■ ■ ■

The morning after the emphatic loss to South Carolina, offensive coordinator Seth Littrell is finally held responsible for an ineffectual offense. He's fired, with co-offensive coordinator Joe Jon Finley promoted to play-caller. Less than a week later, on the road against Ole Miss, miscues and mishaps abound, but Arnold and the offense enjoy some bright moments too: The Sooners lead at halftime 14–10. The second half, however, is shambolic, a dreaded return to form. Ole Miss cruises to a 26–14 win.

Things feel so hopeless that many Sooner fans think we'll lose to incoming visitors Maine. The Black Bears' record is 4–4, and they play in the unheralded Coastal Athletic Association. This doomsday thinking turns out to be unfounded. On a cloudy day, Oklahoma beats Maine 59–14. It's noteworthy that the student section is nearly empty.

OU then travels to Columbia to take on Missouri, ranked twenty-fourth in the nation. Across the decades, the two schools have built a rivalry. Now, in the SEC, the rivalry can be resumed. OU leads until the five-minute mark of the third quarter when Missouri scores its first touchdown to make it 10–9. Missouri then extends the lead to make it 16–9 (the Tigers fail on the two-point conversion) with under nine minutes left. A trick play sees Arnold score an unlikely receiving touchdown to tie the game. Three minutes are on the clock: time for either team to make the decisive score. The air feels dusted with Sooner Magic when the Tigers' running back fumbles, with Billy Bowman Jr. scooping up the ball and racing into the end zone. There are just two minutes left. But the Tigers engineer a drive, capped off by a touchdown pass to former Sooner receiver Theo Wease Jr. It's tied at 16. We look headed to overtime when a catastrophic play, with Arnold at the helm, decides the game; it's a symbol for the entire season. Ball protection should be the number one priority, but Arnold is hit on a pass play and coughs up the ball. The Missouri defense, in an echo of Bowman's touchdown, collects the ball and scores.

■ ■ ■

The home finale at Memorial Stadium takes place two weeks later. Everyone has been looking forward to the visit of Alabama on November 23 since the SEC schedule was released. It's a cool Saturday morning—hoodie weather—when Jenn and I arrive on campus at 9 A.M. to help with the tailgate. Earlier in the season, Hurd replaced the old inflatable tents with new ones. The two tents are massive: bright red and taller than their predecessors. The interlocking OU, in white, sits atop the curved opening of each tent. Expecting a huge turnout, the biggest of the season, John texted us earlier in the week to let us know that he had purchased a *third* tent.

The setup takes a couple of hours thanks to the new tent. Layers of clothing come off as the sun announces itself. Before noon, it's clear that the weather is going to be perfect: mid-seventies in late November. I'm skeptical, however, about Hurd's claim of needing a third tent. There's just a handful of tailgaters when Jenn and I leave to eat lunch at Fuzzy's.

An hour later, the scene has changed. More people have showed up. Over the next couple hours Hurd's prediction comes true. The three tents are full of people. Kids are on the lawn chasing each other around. A group of Alabama fans, four young men in their twenties, are hanging out, sipping their beverages. Every so often Hurd blasts "Boomer Sooner" through the sound system. A couple of my friends (Tony and Bobby), whom I haven't seen in a while, show up, and we talk for a long time, catching up. At one point, I scan the scene, taking it all in, and appreciate what Hurd has built: a home away from home for friends and family who call the Sooners their team. With the sun shining down on us, short-sleeve weather, I can't think of a more perfect ending to the tailgating season.

This isn't quite true. The perfect ending involves an Oklahoma win, but given where the two teams stand, in terms of record and prospects, a win seems impossible. Alabama is ranked seventh in the country, with its eyes on the SEC championship game and the twelve-team playoff. OU is 5–5 overall, and 1–5 in the SEC: a season that recalls the woeful John Blake era of the nineties. To be honest, I can't even imagine a Sooner win today.

As a result, I feel loose, no trace of the usual tension before a big game. It's dark outside, the temperature dropping, when Jenn and I leave Hurd's tailgate for the stadium. Brooks Pedestrian Mall is full of human traffic, moving in all directions. The scene is chaotic, everyone trying to get somewhere. I've got a purpose too. The Big Red Rocket is supposed to be part of the festivities at the Party at the Palace. I worry that we've missed it, the Model T led away like a senior citizen as soon as night falls. But then I see the Rocket, parked on the grass beside Jenkins.

The car blinks because of the red light bulbs that have been affixed to each fender. The Rocket's refurbishment looks total and complete. The carriage has been repainted a deep maroon. The stenciled messages on the body of the car feature fresh paint ("National Record 47 WINS IN A ROW"). The interior is beautiful, with a dashboard of coated aluminum: the embedded gauges feature a deep red background with white arrows that measure gas and speed. The seats have been upholstered in red and white leather. The tires are new with red and white rims and new wooden spokes. It's safe to say that this Ford Model T, born in 1923, never looked as nice as it does now.

As I walk around the car, I'm taken aback by its smallness; the interior is tiny. Two adults, larger than average, would look comical squeezed into the Rocket. Though I don't look up at the sky, I imagine Cecil Samara's face up there, looking down with approval: He's bespectacled and wearing his cowboy hat, with a perpetual grin showing off his specially made dentures that spell out "BIG RED."

▪ ▪ ▪

Our seats, purchased from StubHub, were put on sale by an Alabama fan. As a result, we're sitting on the upper level on the stadium's east side, with a great view but surrounded by opposing fans. I'd rather be sitting with my tribe, but soon enough the whole experience turns interesting.

At kickoff, I discover that Alabama fans have their own ritual. While Oklahoma fans hold up an index finger and say, "O-O-O-U!," their crimson counterparts say, "Roll Tide Roll!" In fact, "Roll Tide" is used in nearly all interactions between Alabama fans. They pass each other on the concourse and say it. When one Bama fan pauses at the top of the stadium stairs to allow another Bama fan to climb up, a gesture of courtesy, the beneficiary calls out "Roll Tide" like a thank you.

In the first quarter, Oklahoma's offensive line plays its best football of the season, opening holes for Arnold and the running backs. However, a fumble deep in Alabama territory ends the first drive, and the Crimson Tide respond with a long drive of their own, finishing with a field goal. Oklahoma's offense continues to move the ball well, eliciting cries of frustration from the Alabama fans all around us. They've been vocal so far, especially one that's directly behind us. The voice must belong to a middle-aged guy, his Alabama accent unmistakable. "Bring some heat D!" he yells. Then, a second later: "They're kicking our butts!"

He and the others sound alarmed. They sound close to hysterical. Can't they see the score? Though just by three points, Alabama is winning the game. OU is playing well but has zero points; surely, it's a matter of time before the better team takes over.

Oklahoma kicks a field goal to tie the score. The Alabama offense can't get going, with star quarterback Jalen Milroe missing throws. A lot of it has to do with Oklahoma's pass rush. "We gotta run the damn ball!" says the Bama fan behind us, unhappy with the play selection.

Arnold is proving a master of the run-pass option tonight. Often, he keeps the ball and, using his speed, darts around the edge or up the middle for significant yardage. Passing the ball is almost entirely off the menu. To be fair, why should Arnold throw when the Tide can't stop the run? With under a minute to play in the first half, Arnold hands the ball off to Xavier Robinson, inactive for most of the season, and the freshman outruns several defenders on the right edge, diving for the pylon and a touchdown. Unbelievably, the Sooners have taken the lead. Jenn and I, like spies in hostile territory, have been quiet during the first half. Now we are on our feet, cheering Robinson and the offense.

At the halftime signal, the crowd roars in approval and the Pride plays "Boomer Sooner" as our players jog off the field toward the locker room with vigor and belief. The Bama players walk, looking dejected.

Predictably, the Bama fan behind us spews a litany of criticism. "We can't tackle! We can't diagnose a play! We haven't stopped them all night!"

I know this lament: the disbelief and frustration of a fan astonished by his team, the underperforming favorite.

The temperature is in the low sixties, which doesn't sound cold, but the swirling wind has an effect. Jenn and I get up to move around. We hang out on the concourse with its long lines for the bathroom. We eavesdrop on Bama fans standing around who don't seem panicked; after all, it's only a seven-point lead. Eventually, I join the bathroom line, which means we miss the start of the third quarter. I'm at a urinal when I hear a groundswell: thousands of voices rising as one. Something has happened. I rush out of the bathroom; Jenn is staring at a TV hanging above concessions. An interception from freshman Eli Bowen has put us in scoring position. Maybe, it's our night . . .

A pitch from Arnold to Robinson finishes the drive; the freshman running back, a star of the game, crashes into the end zone. We celebrate with Oklahoma fans on the concourse. It's 17–3.

Back in our seats, we hear the neighbors' lament, which has picked up pace and volume. They're not happy with their quarterback. Then Milroe does something to increase their misery: With eight minutes left in the quarter, he takes the snap from shotgun and tries a quick throw to the sideline only for OU linebacker Kip Lewis to read the play and step in front. With the ball in his hands, he races down the sideline, evading Milroe, and crosses the goal line: a pick six. I can't control my reaction. I'm out of my seat and punching the air with my fist.

After the extra point, a group of Bama fans descends the stairs in front of us. Are they leaving for good?

I sensed it in the first half, a special feeling in the air, but wasn't ready to believe in it. After a dominant third quarter, with a twenty-one-point lead, that special feeling can't be denied anymore. The atmosphere at Owen Field feels unique and electric tonight, with Sooner fans on the same wavelength. From the beginning, this has felt like a celebration of who we are: a carnival for Sooner Nation. Never mind that we're playing Alabama; the opponent tonight is irrelevant. We have gathered here, in this stadium that turned one hundred years old in October, in the final home game of a disappointing season, to support our team and celebrate our university. What happens between the third and fourth quarters is simply another expression of this togetherness, arguably the most poignant one. It's happened all season: The lights go out and fans turn on their phone's flashlight. Then we hear Toby Keith, a Sooner till the day he died from cancer in February, start singing "Courtesy of the Red, White and Blue (The Angry American)." When it was released, the song was a patriotic response to the terror attacks of 9–11. Now it's a tribute to Toby as well as an expression of patriotism. Even some of the Bama fans sing along. On the video board, students sing and sway to the music, arms draped around each other.

In the fourth quarter, when the referees rob Alabama of a touchdown with a dubious flag, I know it to be true: Whatever divine force governs college football has decided emphatically in our favor. It's our night.

The wheels come off for Bama fans. They start to leave their seats in droves. One drunk Bama fan, a young woman, loses control of herself and hurdles toward the railing; by some miracle, her hand grabs a rail, saving her from a tumble down the stairs.

The fan with the huge mouth, his own team's biggest critic, indulges in profanity for the first time. This causes the Bama fans around him to self-police. One man reminds him pointedly that children are around. Another says, "Alright, that's enough! Calm down! You don't need to be doing all that!"

Our area isn't exclusively a haven for the visitors; there are some Oklahoma fans too. A man in Sooner gear, in his twenties, ascends the stairs, returning from the bathroom or concessions, and calls out, "Roll Tide!" A beat later, he adds sardonically, "Psych!"

With a couple minutes left, I turn and survey the rows behind us. They're almost emptied out of Bama fans. The Bama critic, however, remains. He speaks to me, and I recognize his voice. He's got a gray beard and is in his fifties or early sixties; he's bundled up for the game with a thick coat and crimson ski cap.

"Ya'll played a helluva game," he says, a different person now, mellow and resigned.

I shrug. "It was just our night," I reply.

We shake hands.

I'm shocked by what happens with twenty-eight seconds to play. Fans leap onto the field from the stands behind both end zones. Quickly they cover the field. What's more, they pull both goal posts to the ground, without snapping the center post, which is anchored in the grass. The crossbar and uprights look like they've done a face-plant.

Storming the field is a rare occurrence in Norman. The last time it happened was when Oklahoma beat top-ranked Nebraska in 2000.

The refs, following the rules, insist on one more play to run out the clock. The fans on the field are pushed to the back of the end zones.

When Arnold takes a knee with the ball, ending the game, the fans rush back, joined by Sooner players. The Pride of Oklahoma plays "Boomer Sooner" as more people enter the field from the stands. After a few minutes, Owen Field is no longer green; it's red and white from all the fans. It's an astonishing scene. The university, to its credit, doesn't spoil the fun right away. The White Stripes' "Seven Nation Army" and House of Pain's "Jump Around" are pumped through the sound system, and fans hop in place to the music, shoulder to shoulder.

Jenn and I stay and watch, soaking it all in, certain that we're witnessing a piece of Sooner history.

Back at Hurd's tailgate, the tents have already been taken down and stored in large plastic bins; they'll be in hibernation for the next nine months. Helpers are moving the myriad pieces of the tailgate to Hurd's trailer, parked a short distance away on Asp. I've been dreading this part; packing the trailer in the dark when you're tired is never fun, especially after a loss. But we haven't lost. In beating Alabama, we've shocked the college football world. Though the season overall has been a bust (and next week, in our last conference game, Oklahoma will lose convincingly to LSU in Baton Rouge), this unexpected win over the most storied college football program in recent memory is a tonic for the soul. It might be enough to tide us over (pun intended) until next season when hopefully Venables and a new offensive coordinator can get us back on track.

I'm in the best mood and feel none of the long day's effects as I push a cart full of folding chairs down the sidewalk to Asp. I turn up the road toward Hurd's trailer, and it feels fated when I see a group of RUF/NEKS walking in my direction, perhaps headed to Campus Corner to celebrate. Their maroon shirts and white jeans seem to glow in the dark. I can't help myself. I shout, "RUF/NEKS!," and hold out my hand for high-fives. Bless them, these five young men eye me with caution, but all of them slap my hand.

EPILOGUE

BY 1976, Dallas police had learned enough about the annual matchup between OU and Texas that they came prepared. According to the *New York Times*, four hundred officers patrolled downtown's Commerce Street on Friday evening, with two hundred more officers on standby. Barricades and ambulances were in place, with the deputy police chief leading the whole operation from a command post nearby.

For all their preparation, law enforcement officers were unable to stop the chaos that ensued. Overnight, twenty thousand people filled the streets, committed to revelry. Brawls between drunken fans were rampant, and 119 arrests were made. With dawn about to break, "a water truck gently hosed down" the bedraggled survivors, including OU's number one fan, Cecil "Big Red" Samara.

And this was a relatively tame year. In 1967, police arrested more than a thousand people during OU–Texas weekend. The Friday before the game was dubbed "The Night It Rained Furniture." Journalist Gary Cartwright wrote about the insanity of that night—along with a history of the Red River Rivalry—for a 1981 issue of *Inside Sports* magazine:

> The bonfire on the street between the Baker and Adolphus [hotels] flickered as high as the second floor, illuminating the glazed faces

> that danced around it or hung from windows. We were standing near the fire, talking to a man in a chiffon dress, when something crashed and splintered on the street, barely missing some people.

The "something" was a desk chair, which was swiftly followed by a desk, with hotel stationery fluttering to the ground as an encore. Drunken guests of the Adolphus Hotel, like out-of-control rock stars, were tossing furniture out the windows.

The mayhem of 1967—a bonfire in downtown Dallas!—included the arrest of a man and woman joined in amorous embrace beneath a painting of the Last Supper in the Adolphus lobby. Empty bottles of booze and human bodies were used as projectiles to shatter the windows of downtown businesses. The injuries suffered by combatants included broken jaws and arms as well as dislocated shoulders.

Every year the calls to end the madness—to erase the OU–Texas game from the calendar—came from politicians, journalists, and local residents. It all fell on deaf ears. Too much money was being made by the two universities and the city of Dallas.

More than fifty years later, in October 2023, I experienced for myself the rush of blood that comes with the annual rivalry game. With Jenn, I migrated to Dallas and felt the emotions while on downtown streets, in our hotel, and at the Texas State Fair and in the Cotton Bowl. Along with the players, I was a warrior on Saturday; the universe, for reasons beyond me, placed in my vicinity a teenage Texas fan, dressed in all black and armed with a Longhorn rally towel (perhaps the reader remembers him from the very beginning of this book). Across four quarters, we competed in our fandom on every play. He was foul-mouthed; I kept the profanity to a minimum, though I was no less vociferous when I shouted or pumped a fist. The kid was tall, and after every good play from the Longhorns I felt his rally towel circling close to my head like a buzzing fly. I thought that if it smacked me in the face I would lose control of my body. I'd be grabbing and shaking this kid, my destiny a Dallas drunk tank and charges from the city DA.

All around us were allies since this was the Oklahoma side of the stadium. There was an inebriated good ol' boy, middle-aged and funny, who took off his crimson windbreaker as the day warmed and tied the arms around his neck. Late in this nail-biting game, he chewed nervously on one of the jacket arms. Behind us were two thirty-something men both dressed in red and white overalls. One was obsessed with the speed of play from our offense; throughout the game, he shouted and clapped, "Tempo! Tempo! Tempo!"

In the fourth quarter, a Texas touchdown, after a missed Oklahoma field goal, brought parity between the two teams. The momentum was in Texas's favor, and the game seemed theirs to lose after the Longhorns kicked a go-ahead field goal with less than ninety seconds to play.

My neighbor the teenage fan jumped up and down and, sensing victory, dared to put his prediction out into the world. "We got this!" he yelled. "We got this!"

The ballgame was in Dillon Gabriel's hands. He'd been very good today, brave and aggressive as he scampered downfield for first downs; he'd thrown the ball accurately too. Quickly, he drove the OU offense to a spot inside the Longhorns' ten-yard line.

The teenager to my left went quiet. I was quiet too, my body vibrating with tension. Everyone in the stadium was standing. On first and goal, Gabriel clapped, received the ball in shotgun, and darted forward for two yards. The clock ticked, falling below thirty seconds as the offense, slowly it seemed, settled into formation for second and goal. Wide receiver Nic Anderson ran in motion and then sprinted up field at the snap of the ball. Gabriel, in shotgun, looked in peril right away. The pocket collapsed, the Texas defenders swarming. Gabriel stepped forward but there was nowhere to go; then, in a split second, the next move became clear to him. He hopped to elevate himself then threw the ball to Anderson in a pocket of space at the back of the endzone. Touchdown. The Sooner fans around us churned in ecstasy. After high-fiving Jenn, I twisted around and high-fived the two guys in overalls.

With fifteen seconds left, Texas needed a miracle: God's intervention. But God was an Oklahoman today, an agent of Sooner Magic. We watched the football on the final play, a Hail Mary, as it arced toward the end zone; our defenders batted the ball to earth.

I thought my teenage neighbor might slink away, pissed off and maybe a little embarrassed; after all, he'd prematurely called the game for his Longhorns. But he didn't make that choice. To his credit, he extended an olive branch before leaving.

"Good game," he said.

I was holding my index finger aloft—there's only one Oklahoma—when I heard his voice. I turned and saw the teenager's right hand: open and offered for a handshake.

"Good game," I replied, shaking his hand. We nodded at each other. Then, past jubilant Oklahoma fans, the young man and his quiet buddy sidestepped down the row.

■ ■ ■

Fandom at Oklahoma wouldn't be possible without the student-athletes who lead a kind of double life. As students, they're ordinary, just like the rest of us. They struggle to wake up and get to class. They have their friends, their routines. They have good and bad days. As athletes, however, they leave the ordinary behind to don the uniform of the University of Oklahoma. When they step on the field or court, they become symbols of everything the university stands for. What does our university stand for?

To answer this question, let us return to Cailey England, my former student and captain of the OU women's soccer team.

With her senior season ending, England had a decision to make. Because of the disruptions of COVID, England was offered another year of eligibility, which she opted to take.

The 2024 season was like the others, with ups and downs and a unique set of challenges. Jenn and I were there again, for many of the home games at John Crain Field. England, as captain, was ever present on the field. She played through injuries—a strained hamstring and knee tendonitis—and once collided violently with a teammate: the result, a bloody gash on her forehead from her teammate's tooth that required stitches. (England showed me a picture of the damage; in it, she's grinning.) The Sooners were electric on offense and broke the program record for goals scored in a season. The soccer team was also involved in the first SEC game in OU's history, a 2–0 loss to Mississippi State in mid-September. In conference play, against very strong teams, the Sooners were competitive but lost more games than they won. In the end, the Sooners finished the season (conference and nonconference) with a winning record.

From an individual standpoint, it was a historic season for England. In early October, she started her eighty-fifth game for the Sooners, a program record. Then, a couple weeks later, she broke the soccer program's record for time played in an OU shirt: more than seven thousand minutes. For the volunteer work Cailey performed (among other things, she helped lead a donation drive for a Norman homeless shelter, packed meals to send to Haiti, and taught math at local elementary schools), she was named to the SEC Soccer Community Service Team.

A look at her entire collegiate career, with its many accolades, told a story of excellence on the field and in the classroom. She was named to the Academic All-Big 12 First Team for four of her five seasons. In 2022, she was Big 12 Co-Scholar-Athlete of the Year. She graduated Phi Beta Kappa with a perfect 4.0 grade point average. She was a finalist for the Dodge College of Arts & Sciences Outstanding Senior Award. Twice, Cailey won the Dan Gibbons Outstanding Scholar-Athlete of the Year Award, which goes to one student across all Sooner sports.

I was reminded of an OU student-athlete from more than a hundred years ago. I came across Ed Meacham in my research. He played guard on the football team for Bennie Owen for three seasons while pursuing a bachelor's degree in mathematics. As a student, Meacham busied himself with campus activities. He was editor of the 1913 Sooner yearbook, president of Sigma Delta Chi, and a member of the track team. After graduation, he earned an MA from Harvard and a PhD from the University of Chicago. He returned to his alma mater, where he served in a variety of roles but firstly as Owen's assistant football coach. He climbed the academic ladder, starting as an assistant professor of mathematics and working his way up to full professor. In 1926, Meacham was appointed assistant dean of the College of Arts and Sciences. In 1940, he was made dean. This farmer's son enjoyed turns as sportsman, student, coach, professor, and administrator. Meacham Auditorium, inside of Oklahoma Memorial Union, is named for him. Owen and others at the university must have seen Meacham in the best of lights: He was cultured and well-rounded, exactly what they wanted for their students.

This is the Sooner standard: what the university stands for. Sports and academics present opportunities to excel in life; in fact, they can catapult students to greatness.

As a faculty member on the front lines, so to speak, I'm not naive. I understand that great swaths of the student body—"regular" students and student-athletes alike—fail to meet this high standard, but I would argue it's enough that the standard exists, as a beacon, and that occasionally someone like Cailey England meets it.

I talked to England after her final season. She felt both proud and "hurt." The team had put together one of its best seasons in recent memory. By hurt, she meant that they were only one point away from qualifying for the SEC tournament; the "what ifs" still played through her mind. At the end of the day, though, she felt so much gratitude; she wasn't burned out on the sport. There wasn't a bitter taste in her mouth that it was all over. Individually, she'd been able to contribute so much across five seasons. "I touched the field more than any other [soccer] player in Oklahoma history," she said. Legacy was a word that resonated with her. England believed that the soccer program was in a much better place than it was five years ago.

Away from the soccer field, there was much to look forward to. Recently, she'd gotten engaged to her long-time boyfriend, Josh. She'd applied to fifteen medical schools and interviewed already with three: OU, Texas Tech, and Arkansas. Soon she would interview with UT Southwestern Medical School in Dallas, a highly ranked program where only 20 percent of applicants made the interview stage.

There was also the possibility that she might get to play soccer professionally in Europe. (I'm happy to report that for a season, in spring 2025, she did experience life as a pro athlete, with a soccer club in the Czech Republic.)

I told her about Carrie Henderson, who played for Marita Hynes's softball team in the eighties, and her journey from OU student-athlete to OU parent to dedicated OU fan.

Henderson's story got England talking about her own journey to come. She'd met Sooner alumni who gave back to the institution, and she wanted to follow in their footsteps. The soccer program lacked an alumni club to keep former players connected to their alma mater. England and her teammates had already talked about starting one. Such was her attachment to OU that OU's College of Medicine ranked number one on her list of schools; she was eager to hear back from them.

Beyond medical school, England wanted to stay in Oklahoma for her residency. She could see herself and Josh making a life here. In fact, she imagined their children going to school at the University of Oklahoma.

This vision of her future kickstarted a movie in my mind. I could see England and her husband returning to campus with two small children by their side. It's a game day weekend in the fall. Everyone is wearing crimson. Dr. England and her family are standing on the expanse of lawn in front of Carpenter Hall. Tailgates are everywhere, with the smell of barbecue in the air from a nearby smoker. Music suddenly can be heard; the Pride of Oklahoma is marching east down Boyd. Dr. England points, and as soon as her children see the band one is pulling her father toward the sound and spectacle; the other is pulling his mother in the same direction. They want to get close to the action.

The family stands on the curb alongside other families as the Pride advances, and for a moment Dr. England thinks she recognizes one of the musicians: a young woman playing trumpet resembles a Sooner teammate from years ago. Of course, it's just a trick of the mind, but it starts a series of remembrances. Images from the past come flooding back. She sees the bleachers at John Crain Field packed with Sooner fans and feels again the rush of joy; they've just beaten Texas. She's walking up to Bizzell library, with its red Gothic columns, a ring of gargoyles perched at the top. Then she's sitting in her favorite study spot on an upper level; through a window the South Oval appears, dotted with students. In her student days, Dr. England always took notice of the trees (more than a hundred years ago, President Boyd was dedicated to beautifying campus with trees), loving the color changes in the fall and then the return of leaves in the spring. A favorite memory then splashes across her mind;

to be fair, it's never very far away, despite the years gone by. She's sitting in her biology professor's office, her heart thumping, about to find out her MCAT score. Katie Willis, her favorite professor, has baked a pan of brownies for the occasion. England remembers leaving the testing center, a month prior, feeling like she had bombed the MCAT, the standardized test for medical school; many students take it two or three times to get the score they want. It's a bad sign when she has trouble accessing the score on her laptop, which only increases her anxiety. Then she finds another way to get into the system. As she looks at the screen, taking in her score, pride and relief surge through her body. She's done well.

Her professor decorated the brownie for two different scenarios: one side says "yay" (for a good score) while the other says "nay" (for a bad score). England and her professor, both grinning, start to eat the "yay" side.

This memory of Willis burns bright for a moment and then dissolves. Dr. England is back in the present, feeling her son's hand in her own; the Pride of Oklahoma is past them and turning south on Asp: a vibrant column of young people in their red and white uniforms. It's time to follow the musicians to Owen Field. The game starts soon.

▪ ▪ ▪

At exactly eight o'clock on a cool evening in late October 2023, the homecoming parade began with gunshots from the RUF/NEKS. The procession of floats lumbered north on Elm Avenue before turning east on Boyd. The president's house entered my line of sight; it sat across the street from campus, originally built in 1906 by President Boyd. The house, stately and two stories, had been decorated for homecoming; ribbons of red and white balloons twisted around the two columns in front.

We heard the parade first: percussionists from the Pride of Oklahoma, the crack and roll of snare drums, the hiss of cymbals. An emcee announced the marchers in the parade as they came down Boyd. The ROTC groups were first—army, navy, and air force—in their uniforms. Members of the band waved to the crowd as they took a right onto Parrington Oval. The tuba players, in sync, dipped the large bell of their instruments, like a dancing partner, and then were upright again. The trombonists leaned back and waved their trombones from side to side. Next were the white ponies and the Sooner Schooner, escorted by members of the RUF/NEKS and Lil' Sis. One RUF/NEK carried an oversized paddle the length of a rifle on his shoulder. Cheerleaders, wearing neon sunglasses that glowed in the dark, smiled and shook their pom-poms while their male counterparts shouted "Boomer!" through white megaphones. The crowd called back "Sooner!" There was a contingent of international students, carrying the flags of their home nations. Greek life students walked behind their floats. One such float had a Mario Brothers theme. Another featured a huge chess set with brown and white pieces. Impressively, one float hosted a boxing ring, with a young man and woman inside dressed like boxers, their hands encased in gloves. Convertible sports cars carried members of the homecoming royalty court who sat on the rear seats, wearing a sash and tiara.

I was surprised at the brevity of the parade route. I thought it would travel east on Boyd in front of campus, but it only curved around Parrington Oval before coming to a stop. The crowd moved from the street to the lawn north of Jacobson Hall where a stage, which looked like a blue playing field with hash marks, had been set up. The stage was not elevated. It was illuminated by lights with a video screen on one end. People gathered around the stage; the Rah! Rally was about to start.

The band was off to the side of the stage, and it kicked off the pep rally at 9 P.M. with "Fanfare and Oklahoma." The stage was full with a chorus line of cheerleaders and members of the OU Pom Squad, their movements in sync and aligned with the music. A series of songs and chants followed, with a couple hundred Sooner fans watching.

All of this seemed routine and ordinary for a pep rally. As I looked around me, I realized I was in the middle of the crowd. Some people were standing while others sat on the grass because the emcee, concerned about everyone's ability to see, had instructed us to do so.

The competition started. I'd read about it on the OU homecoming website; sororities and fraternities would show their spirit by performing for the crowd as well as for judges. For whatever reason, I'd imagined comedy skits. What I saw onstage was something else.

Everyone on TikTok was dancing, and so it was at the Rah! Rally. The theme of the competition was "games," which explained the float decorations I'd seen earlier. The two boxers were onstage, amid a dance team whose members were not dressed alike. Some of the women wore tennis dresses or unbuttoned baseball jerseys with black shorts. The men wore bowling-style jerseys with shorts. They went through a complex routine that included cheerleading stunts, a woman held in the air by a base of three people.

Brothers Mario and Luigi, the former in red overalls and the latter in green, had their own cohort of dancers; they lacked any aerial movements in their routine. Drake was part of their background music as well as sounds presumably taken from the Mario Brothers game. One group had the old board game Candy Land as its theme. My favorite was inspired by Guitar Hero. The students onstage banged their heads and played air guitar to Black Sabbath and AC/DC.

Quickly I got bored. If you've seen one dancing troupe of students you've seen them all. If I hadn't felt so boxed in by the crowd I would have stood up and left.

But then, at the risk of sounding ridiculous, I had a revelation. It wasn't the type of revelation that strikes you suddenly. It was more like the tide coming in. I could see the truth at a distance and gradually it got closer until it covered me. This mundane spectacle of dancers became charged with meaning.

It felt as if I had traveled to the past. The students onstage, in all their youthful glory, reminded me that Greek life had been a part of university life since 1905. Off to the side, the Pride of Oklahoma was born the year before, in 1904. The RUF/NEKS were formed in 1915, with Lil' Sis following in 1973. Football became central to campus life in the late 1890s. I remembered a 1912 article from *The Umpire* student newspaper expressing its disappointment at the lack of spirit at a recent game versus Kingfisher. The writer urgently called for a corrective: "In order to arouse this enthusiasm we should have a rousing football rally at once, elect a yell leader, teach the 'Varsity songs and yell to new students, and show that we still have the much vaunted Sooner spirit of which we boast."

The Rah! Rally was not new but the continuation of practices that started more than a hundred years ago. OU's first homecoming took place in 1915, with more than five hundred alumni returning for a halftime snake dance on Boyd Field and refreshments with President Stratton Brooks before and after the game with Kansas; the night before, at a pep rally, students shocked Norman residents by wearing "the flowing robes of Grecian dancers" while the Ruf Neks wore "gaudy silk pajamas." Some freshmen wore only their white cotton briefs. Many things had changed at OU, but certain student groups remained as the foundation of campus life. More than that, these groups had transcended their original status. For a long time now, they were symbols of the University of Oklahoma, so that when you saw the band, the RUF/NEKS, cheerleaders, and even members of Greek life you thought of the university. They were one and the same.

I thought of Nathan McKibbon, whom I met tailgating: an attorney and OU alumnus. His father, brother, aunt, and uncle were all OU graduates, and he was dead set on his young daughter, Emily Grace, graduating a Sooner too. I was sure that if it were up to him the family lineage at OU would go on forever.

Forever was an important word. When alumni and fans returned to campus for homecoming and football games, they expected to see these student groups. To see the football team, cheerleaders, RUF/NEKS and Lil' Sis, on game day, was to bear witness to forever. To watch the Pride of Oklahoma march east on Boyd in front of campus and then turn south on Asp, the band's destination its rightful place in Memorial Stadium, was to bear witness to forever. These rituals had been happening for decades, and though the names and faces of the young people in these roles constantly changed, the groups did not. They lived on, unchanged in what they did and what they represented. They were symbols of forever providing comfort to all those who felt close to the university. I am destined to die, but the university lives on. (The last line of the "OU Chant" provides an echo of this sentiment: "Live on, University!") A hundred years from now, when I'm long gone, the university in Norman will still be here. The football team will take to Owen Field. The Pride of Oklahoma will play "Boomer Sooner." The Sooner Schooner will race onto the field after each touchdown. These student groups are symbols of immortality, and homecoming itself is an immortality ritual: a demonstration of the continuity of the university.

A demonstration of the continuity of life.

These truths washed over me until this vision of the past and present finally came to an end. I blinked and, in a sense, woke up. Sitting in the grass, I stood up and found a winding path through the crowd. I did my best not to step on anybody. Jacobson Hall was brightly lit in the darkness.

ACKNOWLEDGMENTS

This book wouldn't have been possible without access to the student newspapers that chronicled life in the early days of the University of Oklahoma. Thanks to the work of the Oklahoma Digital Newspaper Program (sponsored by the Oklahoma Historical Society), which digitized these student newspapers, I was able to spend countless hours at home on the computer combing through issues of *The Umpire*, *The University Oklahoman*, and *The Oklahoma Daily*. I can't thank the program enough.

I am also grateful to the University of Oklahoma Foundation for digitizing its publication, *Sooner Magazine*, where I found a wealth of material, much of which is in this book.

So many people were generous with their time and trusted me with their stories. Antonio Record, aka Mr. OU, sat for interviews and showed me what it was like to be an OU superfan. Laurisa and Aron England saved seats for Jenn and me at John Crain Field, so that we could watch their daughter Cailey break Sooner records on the soccer field. The England family answered all my questions and treated me with warmth and kindness. Donald Fixico was the first person I interviewed; his compelling journey as a student, full of trials and triumphs, spoke volumes about the Native American experience at OU. It also said plenty about the bond that can grow between students and their university. Marcus Macktima was the second person I interviewed, and though he doesn't appear in the book his story provided invaluable context. John Hurd and Mike Vickrey welcomed me to their respective tailgates and entrusted me with their stories. John Carter, RUF/NEK alumnus, delivered insights about the current makeup of the celebrated spirit group.

Brian Britt has unrivaled knowledge about the Pride of Oklahoma and the University of Oklahoma. He's seen and experienced just about everything in his different roles at OU: student, band member, and band director. I was thrilled to get to speak with him.

Carrie Henderson is one of the unsung pioneers of women's sports at OU. I got to know her first as an interview subject. Then she invited me to the ballpark where we enjoyed each other's company while watching the softball team continue the great legacy that Carrie helped to start. To my mind, Carrie embodies the Oklahoma spirit; she's kind, generous, and feisty.

I'd like to thank Marita Hynes for recommending that I talk to Carrie. In my interview with Marita, I felt that I'd gained access to a person from OU's history on par with other great figures from the past. One can make the argument that she deserves her own statue for her contributions to the university.

David W. Levy's *The University of Oklahoma: A History*, the university's official history, was indispensable as I sought to understand and write about the early years on campus. Moreover, Professor Levy offered words of encouragement and advice at the early stages of this book. Sadly, the eminent historian passed away in summer 2025. I met with him in person a month before his death, an experience for which I'll always be grateful. I'd like to think he'd be pleased with the final version of this book that his own work—so full of vivid storytelling—helped to inspire.

I was starstruck at the discovery that Sooner softball player Kasidi Pickering was enrolled in one of my classes in spring 2024. A few months prior, I watched her hit home runs in the Women's College World Series. When I had questions about softball culture, Kasidi was kind enough to indulge me; her answers were clear and colorful.

Jacquelyn Reese in OU's Western History Collections responded promptly to my queries and often sent emails when she came across material that might be useful to me. When I visited the collections to do research, she was always an enthusiastic and gracious host.

My editor at OU Press, Andrew Berzanskis, guided this project with authority and grace, providing the right balance of creative freedom and constructive criticism that all writers crave. Riley Hines, also at OU Press, was another valued shepherd of this project; her patience and attention to detail helped immensely.

Financial support for publication was provided from the University Libraries, the Office of the Vice President for Research and Partnerships, and the Office of the Provost, University of Oklahoma.

My colleague Rilla Askew, the renowned Oklahoma author, provided a veteran's advice at different stages of this book. My friend and fellow CrossFitter Rosa Guardiola used her considerable talents as a photographer to capture life at Sooner tailgates. Likewise, Ladonna Shaffer photographed Mr. OU in all his glory, and Chad Hamilton took many striking photographs of the OU softball team in their four-peat season, with one featuring in this book. I'm grateful to Lisa Hall, photographer for OU Athletics for close to thirty years, for giving me permission to use her wonderful photographs. The McKibbon family—Nathan, Erika, and Emily Grace—shared their story and taught me about continuity: a core theme of this book. My friends Steve Morrow and Shalaine Foreman introduced me to Rex Craig, a member of the Pride of Oklahoma in the 1950s, who put me in touch with David Miller, the "enthusiastic" bass drummer who caught everyone's attention at the tail end of Oklahoma football's forty-seven-game win streak. It was a joy to talk to Mr. Miller about his memories of the band.

I'd like to apologize to Captain Brian Trabun of the US Army. An account of his singing, from his seat in Memorial Stadium, of "The Army Goes Rolling Along" (played brilliantly by the Pride of Oklahoma on Armed Forces Appreciation Day at Owen Field in November 2023) appeared in an early draft of the book. Alas, his full-throated rendition became a casualty of the revision process.

Thank you to the scores of fans and tailgaters who poured me drinks, fed me food, and shared their love for the Sooners (the Turnt Up tailgate comes immediately to mind). Sooner Nation, you love your teams and university. I hope I captured that love in this book.

Finally, I can't say enough about Jenn Peek's contributions. She accompanied me to games and tailgates, saw things that I failed to see, helped with the photography, read my rough drafts, and urged me to keep going. (Moreover, on a daily basis, she put up with my nonsense.) Jenn was this book's biggest fan; it couldn't have been written without her. She has both my love and gratitude.

BIBLIOGRAPHY

Aber, Ryan, et al. *Crimson Empire: How Patty Gasso Built the Sooners into a College Softball Dynasty.* Pediment Publishing, 2023.

Allain, Rhett. "Why Did Oklahoma's Sooner Schooner Tip Over?" *Wired*, October 23, 2019. https://www.wired.com/story/why-did-oklahomas-sooner-schooner-tip-over/.

Becker, Ernest. *The Denial of Death.* Free Press, 1997.

Cartwright, Gary. "The Crude Feud." *Inside Sports*, October 31, 1981, pp. 104–12.

Clark, J. Brent. *Sooner Century: 100 Glorious Years of Oklahoma Football.* Quality Sports Publications, 1995.

Cooter, Terri, et al. "100 Years of Pride 1904–2004: A Documented History of the Pride of Oklahoma Marching Band," 2004. Western History Collections, University of Oklahoma.

Cross, George Lynn. *Presidents Can't Punt: The OU Football Tradition.* University of Oklahoma Press, 1977.

Debo, Angie. *Oklahoma: Foot-Loose and Fancy-Free.* University of Oklahoma Press, 1949.

"Education: Floggers." *Time*, January 2, 1933. https://time.com/archive/6891017/education-floggers/.

"40 year [*sic*] later, former OU band members remember 'the day The Pride won Bedlam.'" KOCO 5 News, November 4, 2023 (video). https://www.youtube.com/watch?v=shQWWrOTkdo.

Gibson, Heather, et al. "'We're Gators . . . Not Just Gator Fans': Serious Leisure and University of Florida Football." *Journal of Leisure Research* 34, no. 4 (2002): 397–425. https://doi.org/10.1080/00222216.2002.11949979.

Harjo, Chinubbie, et al. "Indian Number." *The University of Oklahoma Magazine* 4, no. 5–6 (February/March 1915).

Hubbell, John T. "The Desegregation of the University of Oklahoma, 1946–1950." *The Journal of Negro History* 57, no. 4 (October 1972). https://doi.org/10.2307/2716982.

Ingrassia, Brian M. *The Rise of Gridiron University: Higher Education's Uneasy Alliance with Big-Time Football.* University Press of Kansas, 2012.

"Interview with Cecil Samara." Oklahoma Historical Society, July 18, 2019 (audio). https://www.youtube.com/watch?v=RYsDl4I-6S4.

Jones, Mark. "Crimson and Cream Memories." *Killer Nashville* website. https://www.killernashville.com/creative-nonfiction/crimson-and-cream-memories.

Keith, Harold. *Oklahoma Kickoff: An Informal History of the First Twenty-Five Years of Football at the University of Oklahoma, and of the Amusing Hardships That Attended Its Pioneering.* University of Oklahoma Press, 1948.

Kelso, John. "Me, Be Nice to Oklahoma? That's Baloney." *Austin American-Statesman*, September 1, 2012. https://www.statesman.com/story/news/local/2012/09/01/me-be-nice-to-oklahoma-thats-baloney/9833653007/?itm_campaign=confirmation&itm_content=news&itm_medium=onsite&itm_source=onsite.

King, Gary. *An Autumn Remembered: Bud Wilkinson's Legendary '56 Sooners.* University of Oklahoma Press, 2006.

Levy, David W. *The University of Oklahoma: A History; Volume I, 1890–1917.* University of Oklahoma Press, 2005.

———. *The University of Oklahoma: A History; Volume II, 1917–1950.* University of Oklahoma Press, 2015.

Linn, Stephen. *The Ultimate Tailgater's Handbook.* Thomas Nelson, 2005.

McGregor, Andrew. "Becoming a Sooner: Prentice Gautt and the Integration of Oklahoma Football." *Sport in American History* (blog), April 7, 2016. https://ussporthistory.com/2016/04/07/becoming-a-sooner-prentice-gautt-and-the-integration-of-oklahoma-football/.

Minutes of a Regular Meeting, the University of Oklahoma Board of Regents, July 1949. "Regents' Minutes," The University of Oklahoma Board of Regents. https://www.ou.edu/regents/minutes.

Morrison, Jim. "The Early History of Football's Forward Pass." *Smithsonian*, December 28, 2010. https://www.smithsonianmag.com/history/the-early-history-of-footballs-forward-pass-78015237/.

"Patty Gasso: How to Coach the Female Athlete." Championship Productions, 2008 (video). https://www.youtube.com/watch?v=k4ktCcUoYqk.

"Patty Gasso Wraps Up OU Softball's Fall Slate after final Battle Series Scrimmage." *Tulsa World*, November 10, 2023 (video). https://www.youtube.com/watch?v=4Fs7dzvhOIo.

"Prentice Gautt Talks about a Team Meeting." *OU Daily*, February 10, 2019 (video). https://www.youtube.com/watch?v=8qID2SBiFHI&t=167s.

Robbins, Alexandra. *Fraternity: An Inside Look at a Year of College Boys Becoming Men*. Dutton, 2019.

Romano, Jason. "Loyalty and Leadership with Oklahoma Softball Coach Patty Gasso." *Sports Spectrum* (podcast), March 1, 2023. https://www.youtube.com/watch?v=weEW2fzT4hk.

Scobey, Derrick. "My Grandfather Andy Dement Sr., More than a Clean Up Man." *derrickscobey* (blog), June 9, 2015. https://derrickscobey.wordpress.com/2015/06/09/my-grandfather-andy-dement-sr-more-than-a-clean-up-man/.

Scott, John. "KGOU Readers Club: *Bud Wilkinson and the Rise of Oklahoma Football*." Interview by Logan Layden. KGOU, November 29, 2022. https://www.kgou.org/show/kgou-readers-club/2022-11-29/kgou-readers-club-bud-wilkinson-and-the-rise-of-oklahoma-football.

Smith, Loran. "A History of One of College Football's Rich Traditions: Tailgating." *Athens Banner Herald*, August 17, 2023. https://www.onlineathens.com/story/sports/college/bulldogs-extra/2023/08/17college-football-tailgating-uga-bulldogs-loran-smith/70609526007/.

"Tailgate." Oxford English Dictionary. Oxford University Press, 1986. https://www.oed.com/dictionary/tailgate_n?tl=true.

Williams Bradford, Tonya, and John F. Sherry Jr. "Domesticating Public Space through Ritual: Tailgating as Vestaval." *Journal of Consumer Research* 42, no. 1 (June 2015): 130–51. https://doi.org/10.1093/jcr/ucv001.

Yost, Fielding H., and Wayne DeNeff. *Football for Player and Spectator*. The Sarah Jennings Press, 1992.

INDEX